THE RHETORIC OF SOBRIETY

The Rhetoric of Sobriety

Wine in Early Islam

Kathryn Kueny

State University of New York Press

Published by
State University of New York Press, Albany

Printed in the United States of America

For information, address the State University of New York Press,
90 State Street, Suite 700, Albany, NY 12207

Production by Laurie Searl
Marketing by Michael Campochiaro

Library of Congress Cataloging-in-Publication Data

Keuny, Kathryn, 1963–
The rhetoric of sobriety : wine in early Islam / Kathryn Keuny.
p. cm.
Includes bibliographical references and indexes.
ISBN 0-7914-5053-8 (alk. paper). — ISBN 0-7914-5054-6 (pbk. : alk. paper)
1. Temperance and Islam. 2. Alcoholism—Religious aspects—Islam. I. Title.

HV5197.5.K84 2001
297.2'6—dc21

00-054911

10 9 8 7 6 5 4 3 2 1

For Andrew

Contents

Acknowledgments

Filled with bits and pieces of facts, padded with vagrant twists of the imagination, and then drawn-out over long stretches of time, a work such as this is eminently multifaceted. In spite of the inescapable variegations that come from composing anything over an extended period of time, there have been many who have helped ground, focus, and direct this production in a number of ways. To those colleagues, friends, and family members who supported me through this taxing but rewarding process, I am grateful.

First of all, I would like to thank Lawrence University for a Faculty Research Grant that allowed me to travel to the Regenstein Library at the University of Chicago over the course of two summers (1996, 1997) to complete my research. In addition, the grant also provided for two undergraduate student researchers: Andrew Emley, who contributed to the editing of the manuscript, and Lauren Osborne, who assisted with the index. The late Dean of Faculty, Richard A. Harrison, should strongly be commended for his commitment to supporting junior faculty research. Special thanks also goes to Gerri Moeller, the Lawrence University interlibrary loan assistant, who tracked down many difficult references with great skill and timeliness.

Second, I extend my deepest appreciation to those fellow colleagues who offered many comments on and criticisms of this work throughout its various stages of development. Frank E. Reynolds (University of Chicago) forced me to explore, expand, and hone the boundaries of my argument in ways I hadn't imagined were possible. Fred M. Donner (University of Chicago), Gordon D. Newby (Emory University), McGuire Gibson (University of Chicago), and Daniel Martin Varisco (Hofstra University) have also given me much encouragement, confidence as well as many critical suggestions while I worked to turn what was a dissertation into a book. All four of these scholars have guided me in some significant way through the difficult transition from consumer (student) to producer (scholar). By welcoming me into the folds of the academy, they represent models of true collegiality I aspire to emulate. I am especially indebted to Jonathan Z. Smith (University of Chicago), whose discerning thoughts on things human and religious have shaped my overall orientation over and above what could be captured in a single footnote. His words have forever altered my vision of the world; it is now difficult to view the mundane, familiar, gritty, peculiar, and disturbing events, artifacts, and behaviors of the world without somehow encountering the "sacred."

Let me conclude with a few words to those who freely lent humor, warmth, wisdom, and focus to one in need. Much gratitude goes to my parents, Robert and June Kueny, for their unyielding support and love through some of the most difficult phases of this project. My beautiful son, Josiah Foster, should also be commended for his patience with a mother who often had to "go to work" rather than play with him. His empathy, wisdom, and generous nature go well beyond his three years. This work would never have been completed, however, without the help and support of my husband, J. Andrew Foster. Andrew's critical mind and suspicious eye improved the quality of the argument and prose considerably. Reading the manuscript again and again, and cheerfully offering much editorial suggestion and biting commentary, he unselfishly supported me through the final but most difficult phase of completing this work. His encouragement, help, and calming demeanor were much welcomed as I struggled against time: to complete the book before the much-anticipated birth of our second child, Iris. It is to Andrew, for all his wit, intelligence, courage, energy, devotion, and love, that I dedicate this work.

Introduction

> There is a curious sentimental illusion, fostered by liberals, that though the minds of men may differ, the heart is the same everywhere; the curious history of the association between men and the grape-vines is part of the evidence that the converse may be true.
>
> —Edward Hyams, *Dionysus: A Social History of the Wine Vine*

Throughout human history the grape-vine has long been associated with religious practice and belief. In a variety of religious contexts, wine plays or has played a rather ambiguous role on several fronts. Consumed as a symbol of blood, the sweet yet pungent liquids sucked from the grape-vine represent the forces of life that ultimately determine both the limits and potentials of human existence. And, contrary to these material associations, wine quaffed in a state of religious frenzy frees the mind from its biological constraints and allows it to sample the soaring heights and plunging depths of sacred expression. Because of this strange yet exhilarating, fearful yet coveted, sensual yet non-sensual power of wine and intoxication, it is no wonder why many belief systems consider the fruit of the vine to be a necessary and vital part of religious expression.

Some religious traditions, like certain forms of Christianity and the Bacchanalia, have been eager to capitalize on the power and danger that stem from wine's inherent ambiguity to harness, channel, or capture sacred experience. However, other traditions, like Islam, saw anarchy lurking within wine's liberating potential, and took drastic steps to contain the chaos that would inevitably erupt from its consumption or even its very presence in this world. In the Islamic context, the potency derived from wine's polyvalent nature did not serve to bond humans more closely with one another or with their God, but rather threatened to undermine those very relationships. Ultimately wine could well corrupt both the sacred and profane realms. Wine and other intoxicating liquids do not create the potential for the devotee's union with God; on the contrary, they prevent the true believer from cultivating a right relationship with God.

Curiously, with this interest in maintaining a proper relationship with one's God, a call for abstinence in Islam can hardly be linked to ascetic sentiments. Asceticism can be defined as a "voluntary, sustained, and at least partially systematic program of self-discipline and self-denial in which immediate sensual, or profane gratifications are renounced in order to attain a higher spiritual state or a more thorough absorption in the sacred."[1] Abstaining from wine for ascetic purposes may have played a vital role in many monotheistic traditions, including Christianity and Judaism, but the emphasis on altering one's mind as a way to seek a personal union with one's deity has no place in the Islamic context. Rather, abstinence served more as an internal and external expression of one's unwavering dedication and clear devotion to God. Here, one's status in relation to God is based on correct and proper belief as opposed to spiritual condition or ecstatic sensation.

Abstinence as merely a sign of commitment to one's deity is not confined to the Islamic context alone; clear parallels exist in other traditions. The Torah discusses how the Nazirites had to abstain from wine in order to devote themselves completely to God in Numbers 6:3–4; in Leviticus 10:9 the priests stopped from drinking alcoholic beverages before administering their sacred rites in the Temple. Likewise the Nabataens also abstained from wine; one of their gods was even called "the good god who drinks no wine."[2] In addition, the Rechabites refrained from the consumption of wine in order to make a proper petition to their Lord:

> And we threw off our clothing from our body; and we did not eat bread from fire, and did not drink a carafe of wine, neither honey nor liquor, and we lamented a great lament and petitioned the Lord. And he heard our prayer, and turned his anger from the city of Jerusalem.[3]

Abstinence played a similar role in the maintenance of a proper relationship between man and God after the second destruction of the Temple. People refrained from activities that took place during a time when the Temple stood and all was right with the world; the cosmos properly ordered:

> R. Joshua engaged with them saying to them, "My children, how come you are not eating meat or drinking wine?" They said to him, "Should we eat meat, from which offerings were made on the altar, and now the rite is no more, and should we drink wine, which they would pour out in libations on the altar, and which now is no more?"[4]

Like their Jewish brothers, Christian monks did not drink wine for a designated period of time so that they could avoid any form of blasphemous behavior.[5]

Islam also links abstinence with the establishment and maintenance of a proper relationship with God. However, rather than being the anomalous or exceptional practice of the ascetic, abstinence becomes a part of one's normal course of life. By refraining from alcoholic beverages, Muslims demonstrate their willingness to submit to a God who mandates his creatures to follow his laws. As opposed to setting things right once the world (or one's individual actions) has gone astray, abstinence becomes a part of one's daily regime to ensure that the individual, communal, and cosmic realms are in perfect harmony with the divine will.

During Islam's early history, however, sobriety was neither as practically normal as espoused, nor was abstinence so clearly linked with the divine will. Much debate over what could or could not be consumed by whom plagued the early tradition, as evidenced in the often ambivalent discussions over wine and alcohol that appear in early Islamic texts. While most of these works accept the general prohibition of wine, there was no obvious consensus as to *why* wine or other alcoholic beverages should be permitted or prohibited, what happens to those who consume such drinks, or whether intoxicating drinks other than wine could be quaffed without consequence (to mention a few). The struggle to resolve such issues lends rare insight into the formation of the early tradition; that is, what strategies and patterns of thought believers used to articulate what would constitute a proper relationship with the divine.

Since drinking for pleasure or otherwise is—at least in theory—condemned by Islamic legalists, the production, sale, and (sometimes over) consumption of wine and other alcoholic beverages in the early Islamic tradition are topics not often embraced by Western or non-Western scholars. However, as suggested above, the study of how the early Islamic tradition identified, labeled, and classified wine as a marginal/prohibited substance is really a study of how believers sought to resolve issues of conflict, structure their world, and govern human behavior, which in turn shaped their understandings of the divine message. The types of language employed to work out points of contention that arose concurrently with questions of ambiguity—such as those surrounding the use and abuse of wine—were intricately tied to issues having to do with how the early tradition defined itself, ordered its world, honed its interpretive boundaries, and ultimately distinguished itself from other traditions.

Wine, as an *ambiguous substance*, called for some of the most extreme and creative of all exegetical strategies that would not only level the equivocal nature of this beverage, but would also generate the fluidity necessary for present and future (re)interpretations regarding its prohibited status. Just as wine itself was considered to be ambiguous by nature, so, too, were the modes of discourse employed in the vast discussions surrounding this marginalized drink. By using prophetic, analytic, narrative, poetic, and mystical language, early Islamic authors found suitable rhetorical solutions that were conservative enough to erase all traces of ambiguity while still operating within the fixed framework of religious ideas and rules of logic, but flexible enough to allow for the generation of new ideas, beliefs, and practices as the tradition began to expand and develop.

To say in a straightforward fashion that "wine is prohibited" is to state that wine is not acceptable in Islam, and Muslims should never drink wine. But to surround this statement with didactic examples of how the Prophet refused to drink wine, to lay detailed circumstances in which this statement was uttered, or to put it in a context that suggests that all other like substances must also be prohibited suggests a deeper interest in issues concerning how the world is constructed, and how the divine is to be understood within that world. A study of how wine was portrayed across a given set of contemporaneous texts and literary genres allows access into the characteristic strategies of thought involved in the ongoing process of defining, negotiating, and resolving these fundamental religious concerns.

WINE AS ANOMALY, WINE AS AMBIGUITY

As stated above, the primary focus of this project is to examine the diverse ways in which wine's ambiguity is defined, described, extended, or resolved through strategic choices in language put forth in early Islamic texts, and to demonstrate how these choices were informed by particular understandings of the fragile relationship between the human and divine. One of the primary themes that permeates the discussion of ambiguity in these early Islamic texts is the notion that the human realm was, and had to remain, necessarily distinct from the divine. Any threat or danger to that order had to be harnassed, controlled, or somehow absorbed into a system that maintained strict separations between the human and divine. Wine represented just such a threat.

The ambiguous nature of wine, and the ways that ambiguity was resolved, ties in closely with Mary Douglas' discussion of "dirt." For Douglas,

> dirt is essentially disorder. There is no such thing as absolute dirt: it exists in the eye of the beholder. . . . Eliminating it is not a negative movement, but a positive effort to organise the environment.[6]

Wine in many ways can be viewed as "dirt," for reflection upon it "involves reflection on the relation of order to disorder, being to non-being, form to formlessness, life to death."[7]

While wine was not always viewed as an impurity within the early Islamic context, it was understood as something that presented a threat or danger to the fundamental classifications privileged by the tradition and in fact, contributed to the articulation and solidification of those classifications. As such, it has been viewed as both an anomaly (an element that does not fit a given set or series),[8] and an ambiguity (a character of statements capable of two interpretations)[9] within the tradition. Anomalies pose certain challenges to any culture or society in that they require groups of individuals to define what they feel is ordered, and thus acceptable, or disordered, and therefore unacceptable. Ambiguities, on the other hand, can enrich meanings, or draw one's attention to other levels of existence.[10] Wine as both anomaly and ambiguity resided on the margins of the society, and therefore threatened the order of that society by challenging and altering the shape of fundamental human experience within that society.[11] Wine, like "dirt" or other forms of impurities, required some sort of resolution, and further strengthened and defined the culture's boundaries as it attempted to formulate the very processes of such resolution.

In the Islamic context, wine both threatens yet transcends the established boundaries of the tradition. Conquering such powers that threatened to destroy the established order represents the triumph of the good, ordered world over and against the forces of chaos.[12] However, a completely ordered world presented its problems as well, for life and experience cannot be contained and defined so completely that change can never be accommodated. So while the ultimate condemnation of wine in the Islamic tradition is achieved on one level, the tradition still allows for some interpretive "play" within such a prohibition. As Douglas states:

> It is part of our human condition to long for hard lines and clear concepts. When we have them we have to either face the fact that some realities elude them, or else blind ourselves to the inadequacy of the concepts.[13]

In the ambiguous and diverse and often contradictory treatment of wine preserved in the variety of literary genres noted above, the early Islamic tradition was able to harness the threat of wine on its margins and assert order, but still allow for the flexibility and pliability necessary in maintaining the validity and integrity of the divine law over against the threat of chaos or change.

A WORD ON METHOD

This study is very much indebted to two previous works on the subject of wine. Two scholars have already raised vital questions concerning wine in Islam, including Ignaz Goldziher[14] and A. J. Wensinck.[15] Goldziher's contribution to the study of wine was to point out major incongruities between doctrinal laws and the evidence provided by actual practices.[16] For Goldziher, these incongruities revealed much about the range and scope of the legal debates, as well as public resistance to, or ignorance of, the laws that existed within the early Islamic community.[17] The example of wine offers an illustrative case in point.

Goldziher first points out that the Qur'an treats wine as an abomination.[18] Accepting that this view must have been considered to be a divine precept by the Islamic community, he looked to see if patterns in social conduct were more or less in line with this strict standard. Rather than finding a consonant set of behaviors, Goldziher discovered that individual Muslims—including caliphs and other prominent members of society—were actively and regularly involved in transgressing the law, often indulging freely in the consumption of wine.[19] For example, even though he took strict measures against wine drinkers, singers, and singing girls, the caliph al-Qahir, the executor of divine law, "was hardly ever found sober."[20]

Given what he believed to be the rigid nature of the Qur'anic position against wine, Goldziher looked to the traditions (*Hadith*)[21] and other chronicles to show how, through "the growth of legal ingenuity in the interpretation of religious law, various means were contrived to mitigate the literal rigor of the text."[22] In other words, through various processes of exegesis, legal scholars strove to align law with practice. Goldziher rightly noted that many interpretive steps were taken in these exegetical texts to palliate the law and to accommodate some of the wide range of conflicting opinions and practices concerning wine. This need to soften, clarify, or legitimate the basic prohibition explains the vast number of Hadith involved with either the definition of wine, the description of what drinks fell under that heading, or the discussion of whether the substance or the effect of drinking was the source of the problem. The contours of these debates are all captured in the works by traditional commentators, who demonstrate how a slight variation in the definition of "wine" can completely transform one's understanding of the Qur'anic prohibition.[23]

Goldziher's work on wine as presented in the Hadith, chronicles, and pre-Islamic (*Jahiliya*) poetry[24] was continued by Wensinck, who expanded upon some of these same themes. Wensinck created an extensive typology that highlights some of the debates over wine in the generations following the death of the Prophet.[25] As a result of his exhaustive cataloging of these varying statements on wine, Wensinck held the view that the Hadith were generated to justify the prevailing opinions of the legal schools.[26] In order to gain some appreciation for these opinions, as well as how they were locked in debate, Wensinck called for a close analysis of the historical formation of these Hadith. Unfortunately, he did not follow up on his own suggestion to conduct such an exhaustive, interpretive study. No wonder as the shreds of a historical record are probably the most one can ever hope to attain. Certainly an anthropologist's "thick description" is out of the question and in all likelihood the kind of close historical analysis Wensinck proposes.

The work of Goldziher and Wensinck did much to expose the incongruities between law and practice, as well as to establish some of the debates over the status of wine. While this work maintains that the Hadith and other exegetical texts underscore the wide-ranging concerns over wine and its prohibition, it will shift the focus away from legal debate to the exegetical processes of limiting and negotiating an ambiguous, or marginal substance. Through these processes of negotiation, one can see how issues of ambiguity were resolved through the formation of interpretive strategies, which in turn shaped and were shaped by perceptions of how the world was to be ordered, and how the divine was to be understood. This approach, which highlights interpretive, rather than social, political, historical, or theological concerns, is not meant to replace these more traditional studies, but to complement them.

ISSUES OF TEXT AND CONTEXT

Like the works of Goldziher and Wensinck, this discussion of wine mainly focuses on the Qur'an and canonical collections of Hadith. However, it also includes information gleaned from several noncanonical collections of Sunni Hadith, the Biography (*Sira*) of the Prophet, al-Tabari's monumental history (*Ta'rikh*), several commentaries on the Qur'an (*Tafsir*), three collections of authoritative Shi'ite Hadith, and selected poetry from the Jahiliya and the Sufi mystics. Mainly grounded in the sixth to twelfth centuries, these texts represent distinct genres of literature that were highly visible and significant in the development of the early Islamic tradition. The genres represented are: prophetic,[27] analytic,[28] narrative,[29] poetic, and mystical.[30] The attitudes toward wine displayed in these works reflect different yet *privileged and accepted* ways of describing and defining this ambiguous substance.

Taken separately, each genre of literature pulls the discussion of wine in a particular direction through a given mode of thought, pattern of language, or religious understanding that makes sense of the world through different sets of assumptions and distinctions. Taken as a whole, the dialectical relationships that occur among genres create a more comprehensive portrait of the tradition's portrayal of wine in this early period, as well as the variety of interpretive solutions developed in light of wine's ambiguous nature. These solutions ultimately keep the debate over resolving wine's ambiguity open, flexible, but highly controlled through diverse structures of interpretation that all adhere to a limited set of ideological or religious suppositions gradually privileged by the tradition in its formative years.

A focus on genre moves this study away from the complex issues surrounding the chronological development of certain legal opinions towards wine. Therefore, this work will not attempt to date any of the texts under consideration, nor will it draw any conclusions, other than the most general, as to what the presence of these different types of genres suggest about the overall historical or geographical contexts in which they flourished. Given the inherent problems involved in the traditional versus nontraditional dating of the Qur'an,[31] individual Hadith, and Jahiliya poetry, it is in many ways more productive to focus on what these texts reveal about language and interpretation.

At the time the texts under consideration were "canonized" within the Islamic tradition, a choice had been made in favor of a type of legitimacy and authority that lifted abstract law, Muhammad's exemplary behavior, and Qur'anic revelations over and above personal biography, inspiration, and the popular traditions inspired by Jewish and Christian biblical models (*Isra'iliyat*). The tradition came to prefer law and exempla due in part to the internal and external conflicts and pressures confronting the 'Abbasid regime, including the increasing internal divisions within what was then the Muslim minority, the rise of anti-Muslim revolts, and, most importantly, the growing theological conflicts between the new believers and their fellow competitors for truth: the Jews and the Christians. Given this combative and often hostile environment; an environment that underwent radical social change as a political, religious minority (the Muslims, who comprised only eight percent of the total population by the middle of the second Islamic century)[32] vied for legitimacy and power, it is not surprising that the authorititative theological opinions of those in the religious majority (the Jews and Christians) would have been rejected.[33] The presence, then, of these different types of genres in the discussion of wine is evidence for the debate over what was to be considered proper sources or models for authority: poetry versus prophecy; Abrahamic versus Arabian history; teleological versus didactic model; propositional argument versus narrative story; ecstatic experience versus sobriety.

The fact that all these different possibilities of interpretation were preserved within the tradition in hierarchical fashion, that is, that some texts and genres were ranked above others in terms of their perceived legitimacy (the key being that they were *preserved* in a particular order rather than purged), is one interpretive solution developed within the tradition to deal with rival claims to authority. It is the contours of the conflicts created among these competing or alternative claims to authority, as well as the ways in which these tensions were resolved and dispersed, that will be examined in this work.

THE KEY TO TRANSLITERATION, TRANSLATION, AND NOTATION

A simple system of transliteration removes most diacritical marks from the body of the text. Only the glottal stop (*hamza*) and voiced pharyngeal fricative (*'ayn*) will be marked by the symbol ('). Frequently used foreign vocabulary will be introduced in italics within the body of the text, and from then on written in normal print. Some less-common Arabic terms will be provided sparingly in parentheses or italics when vital for purposes of clarification. The footnotes will present all foreign vocabulary, including personal names, with full diacritical marks.

Given the various editions of Arabic texts, I have opted to present all primary references in generic fashion (specific works will be noted in full in the Bibliography). Whenever possible, rather than noting volume and page number, I cite the chapter name and number (of a tradition, for example) for a particular reference. This simplified system of notation will allow the reader to locate a single reference in a variety of Arabic editions.

In the following chapters, all Arabic translations, except where noted, are my own.

1

Qur'anic Vignettes of the Vine

Prophetic Discourse and the Signs for Those Who Know

> And in the fruits of the date-palm and the grape-vine you obtain an intoxicant and good food. In this are signs for those who understand.
>
> —Sura 16:67 (al-Nahl)

Given the current prohibition of wine in the Islamic tradition, one would expect to find the Qur'an forcefully condemning the consumption of wine and other intoxicants. However, a careful and critical analysis of all references reveals that the Qur'an treats wine with a great ambivalence; the potent liquid that constitutes an abomination in one verse becomes a source of "good food" in another.[1] A close scrutiny of all the varied contexts in which wine or intoxication are mentioned shows that the Qur'an condemns wine only when consumption takes place in contexts deemed unsuitable or inappropriate; the prohibition is hardly unconditional or absolute. As we shall see, when wine and intoxication surface in the right place under the proper conditions, they become a glorious sign from the divine. But first, what constitutes an "inappropriate" or for that matter a "proper" condition in the Qur'anic context? And how is one to know? The canon itself does not provide clear answers to these basic questions.

In order to understand the Qur'an's ambiguous treatment of wine, we must first examine its self-proclaimed, revelatory agenda.[2] The Qur'an states and restates, in a variety of ways, who God is and what he demands from his subjects. By continuously signifying the nature of the deity as well as exhibiting the proper human response to his nature, the Qur'an's revelatory language, or perhaps what may be better described as prophetic discourse, defines and redefines a *cosmic* and *world* order. Cosmic order refers to issues of ontology, while world order is concerned with social norms and ethical behavior.

The Qur'an evokes a sense of cosmic order through its many depictions of a Paradise that stands more as a projected image of an ideal Earth than one that is godly or heavenly. Those who have heeded God's word will recline on soft couches near flowing fountains of luscious drink, but those who have turned away from his message will find themselves washing down sharp thorns with boiling water.[3] Cosmic order is also asserted through the various proclamations about God's awe-inspiring activities, such as his folding up of night over day,[4] his creation of men and jinn,[5] and his roasting of Abu-Lahab, a man who strayed from his word.[6] Both the repetitive descriptions of Paradise and numerous listings of God's daunting deeds (past, present, and future) reveal certain fundamental truths about the nature and structure of the cosmos.

Given what is ontologically true, humans must act in the world according to what this truth demands. By laying out a tentative social order, and by establishing ethical norms, the Qur'an attempts to locate a world order that at least mirrors the cosmic one. For example, the Qur'an states very clearly how those communities that turn away from God's word will be destroyed.[7] In addition, believers as a whole are instructed not to hold unbelievers as friends in preference to the faithful.[8] In these two examples, the world is divided into those who embrace or conform to what is of God, and those who do not. In terms of situating ethical norms, the Qur'an offers some general (but certainly not exhaustive) guidelines for human behavior by recommending the giving of alms,[9] the restricting of inheritance,[10] the need for ritual purification,[11] and the shunning of adultery.[12] Again, all of these worldly concerns and activities are manifestations of divine truths evoked through statements about the order of the cosmos.

At times, the Qur'an employs items and objects of the everyday in order to elicit certain truths about God. What often appears to be a statement or mandate about a particular behavior or object is just as likely a display or evocation of some dimension of the divine. So intertwined are these modes of thought that it is not even clear what frame of reference—ethical (world) or ontological (cosmic)—is in play. In some instances, the categories do not appear mutually exclusive. An object or an event can be meaningful on both a cosmic and mundane level; an ethical exemplar and a cosmological truth. Note the following example:

> Those who believe—Jews, Sabians and Christians—
> whoever believes in God and the Last Day and does good deeds
> will have nothing to fear or regret.[13]

On a worldly level the Qur'an appears to be making some ethical statements about what one must do in order to be included among the community of believers. On the cosmic, the text clearly denies what Jews, Christians, and Sabians say is fundamentally true about the universe, and asserts its own version of the truth that must be realized by the faithful. How can the two interpretations be reconciled?

Given that these two levels of understanding overlap, a certain ambiguity arises when what is perceived from an earthly perspective conflicts with what is viewed from the cosmic. For example, Christians may believe in God and the Last Day, and do good works, but they also believe that God had a son who should be worshipped and glorified. Should these individuals be embraced by the community or condemned?[14] Since the Qur'an does not always clearly demarcate or indicate its cosmic or worldly referential frames or offer any solutions to the ambiguity that results when both are taken into consideration, the revelatory, prophetic discourse that appears unyielding in its relentless presentation of divine truths in reality allows for much fluidity of interpretation.

Wine in particular reveals the categorical ambiguities or incongruities inherent in these conceptual models. Wine is a beverage that is both shunned and glorified, or praised and condemned; its meaning shifting according to what frame of reference is being employed. From a cosmic perspective, the Qur'an glorifies wine as a positive feature of its pastoral, agrarian, *ideal* image of Paradise; wine is praised as one of the rewards God has given to the righteous.[15] When its cosmic frame of reference shifts to a worldly one, wine becomes a beverage that is ethically corrosive. For example, when the text lays out the tenets of proper prayer, intoxication is listed as one of the behaviors that diverts men from God.[16] Depending on the context and the frame of reference, wine can take on very different meanings.[17]

The Qur'an is not concerned with resolving such incongruities. Rather, the text actually exploits both frames of reference to evoke that which is of God and that which is not. Wine, itself an object of profound ambiguity, is pliable enough to accommodate and facilitate the necessary manifestations of the divine will, as well as the proper responses to them. Qur'anic utterances on wine, therefore, have little to do with the status or legality of the beverage—as a *substance*—since their role is solely to elicit divine truth, as well as a variety of human understandings and responses to that truth.

To summarize, the differing and often contradictory statements about wine, as well as those surrounding a broad range of other topics,[18] all serve to repeat, evoke, or reinforce some fundamental, revelatory points by supplying a constant flow of examples from the everyday that instruct humans on what they need to know about God, and how they should respond to God based upon what has been revealed to them. In order to illustrate, present, and underscore these general points, wine can be counted among the signs for those who understand,[19] the rewards of a heavenly Paradise,[20] and the works of Satan.[21] Depending on the frame of reference that is privileged at any given point, each revelation on wine provides an essential clue or insight into the many ways in which believers can determine, as well as adhere to, the true path of the one God.

LOW HANG THE GRAPES: A SUMMARY AND ANALYSIS OF QUR'ANIC WINE REFERENCES

The most common word for wine in the Qur'an is *khamr*. Although *khamr* often surfaces in early Arabic poetry, some scholars have suggested it is most likely a loan-word from Aramaic.[22] In the Qur'anic context, the feminine noun for wine (*khamr*) appears on six separate occasions: Suras 2:219 (al-Baqara); 5:90 (al-Ma'ida); 5:91 (al-Ma'ida); 12:36 (Yusuf); 12:41 (Yusuf); and 47:15 (Muhammad). While the first five examples refer to an earthly wine, the sixth points to the paradisical brand. The root *kh-m-r* does appear in the masculine form in Sura 24:31 (al-Nur), when believing women are advised to "cast their veils (*khumur*) over their bosoms" so as not to display their finery to strange men who stand outside the protective family circle. In a context that has nothing to do with wine or intoxication but with the proper behavior of believing women, the root in this form denotes a sense of concealment, of covering, of hiding. Interestingly enough, this meaning is nowhere linked with wine in the Qur'an but is inextricably tied to this beverage in the Hadith, where *khamr* often appears as a masculine noun[23] and is cast into a wholly negative light.

In addition to the six *khamr* passages, the Qur'an also relies on the root *s-k-r* to signal an earthly intoxicant (*sakar*),[24] the state of intoxication (*sakra*)[25] or drunkenness (*sukara*),[26] or the act of making someone or something inebriated (*sakkara*).[27] On rare occasions, the word *rahiq*[28] is used to depict a purest, sweetest, most excellent of wines,[29] and *ma'in* in reference to a cup of pure drink taken from a flowing stream.[30] Although this "pure drink" does not necessarily refer to wine per se, the text notes that what comes out of this stream is a wine-like substance that does not intoxicate (*nazafa*).[31]

Why would the Qur'an have to state that this beverage does not intoxicate, unless, of course, in another context, there was some question about its integrity? Interestingly enough, the root *n-z-f* (like some forms of *s-k-r*) can also mean to exhaust or to make mad, which fleshes out the notion of intoxication to include a distorted state of mind that may be analogous to, but does not necessarily stem from, the overconsumption of alcoholic beverages.

Since the Qur'an employs a fairly large repertoire of words to refer to various types of wine and intoxicating beverages and to different states of drunkenness, philology suggests that the Qur'an expresses a highly nuanced and ultimately ambivalent attitude towards wine and its effects. The Qur'an's ambivalence in terms of diction is manifest on the level of content. As stated above, zigzagging across the various Suras in no apparent order and according to no obvious logic, wine simultaneously clouds the eye, stems from the hand of Satan, and serves as a paradisical reward for those righteous enough to enter the Garden of Repose. If a believer were to search the Qur'an for the answer to the question—"Am I allowed to drink wine?"—he could find many relevant passages to support a variety of stances.

Rather than impose a logical consistency where there is none, or demand the text to predict the findings of a legal code that took subsequent centuries to develop, we would do well to analyze the often opposing ways in which the Qur'an elicits wine and intoxication. Taking stock of how the Qur'an evokes certain truths through its ambiguous references to intoxicants lends much insight into how this sacred text constructed and mapped the cosmos, and what it ultimately demanded from those who called themselves "believers."

Given that later Islamic exegetes privileged a limited set of pronouncements on wine to support a universal prohibition, we will jettison the traditional chronology, which was constructed to support legal disposition rather than a discursive reconstruction,[32] for a more comprehensive scope of analysis. Generally speaking, the many references to wine and intoxication can be grouped together roughly according to topic: wine and its association with worldly order, and wine and its depictions of cosmic truth. In addition, it may be useful to note where wine does *not* appear when one would expect to find strong associations with it, namely, with certain biblical figures who are well-known for their drunken indiscretions. In addition to being more inclusive of all statements having to do with wine and intoxication, this taxonomical approach reveals how the Qur'an's rather brief and often ambiguous references may not be understood simply as clipped legal statements stripped from their larger historical narrative, but rather as literary *topoi* used to underscore the limited repertoire of revelatory themes repeatedly restated with subtle variation throughout the text.

SOME VIEWS FROM THE WORLD: WINE AND GAMBLING

Sura 5:90–91 (al-Ma'ida) contains the strongest statement against wine. In this example, wine (*khamr*) appears in a list with gambling, idol-worshipping, and divination arrows, and is labeled an "abomination" from among the "acts of Satan":

> Oh, you who believe!
> Wine (*khamr*), gambling (*maysir*),
> idol-worshipping (*ansab*), and divination arrows (*azlam*)
> are an abomination (*rijs*) from among the acts of Satan.
> Keep away from them, so that you may prosper.
> Satan only wants to create enmity and hatred among you
> with wine and gambling,
> and to divert you from the remembrance of God, and from prayer.
> Will you not abstain?

Obviously, this passage leaves little room for interpretive maneuvering; clearly it would be difficult to bestow any positive elements upon a drink that is drawn from the hand of Satan. But what is the logical "glue" that bundles wine, gambling, idol-worshipping, and divination arrows together into a single package that is condemned?

The fact that all four items are referred to as an "abomination" (*rijs*) sheds some light on the underlying logic behind the condemnation. The term *rijs* is often used in connection with a variety of impure practices performed during the Jahiliya.[33] In general, it is tied to the punishment, penalty, or terror God lays upon the unbelievers.[34] Given their associations with slaughtered beasts, at least some of the items on the list may have been tied to pre-Islamic sacrificial practices.[35] *Maysir*, for example, a game of chance that utilized divination arrows (*azlam*)[36] or otherwise, was played in order to win one of the ten parts of a slaughtered animal, which may have been some kind of blood sacrifice offered to pagan deities.[37] *Ansab* both refers to the blocks of stone upon which the blood of victims sacrificed to idols was poured,[38] and to the stones representing deities in pagan cults.[39] Wine, like the other three components of the list, most likely played a part in pagan sacrifice as well. Their association with one another is thus historical and contextual rather than revelatory or divine.

Mention of these "detestable" practices draws a sharp distinction between those offering animal sacrifices in the Jahiliya (literally, the period of "ignorance"), and those offering animal sacrifices during the time of the revelation. Because an animal is slaughtered in both rituals, the difference between the two would have to lie in the means and the ends. For example, the Qur'an establishes cattle and camels as acceptable sacrificial victims; however, the text is careful to state that the name of God must be pronounced over the victim, and that it is not the blood or meat that reaches God but rather fidelity of the heart.[40] In this light, it is easy to see how the Qur'an uses these four items as a kind of literary trope to distinguish the "true" believers from the "false." Those ignorant enough to consume camels or cattle sacrificed to pagan gods would be the false, and those knowledgeable enough to partake in the meat over which God's name was read would be the true.[41]

This connection with sacrifice, however, still remains somewhat speculative; the text never states specifically what is problematic about these four practices. In the second half of the passage, wine and gambling are segregated from idols and divination arrows as those practices Satan produced in order to create divisions among the community, and to cause individuals to forget God and prayer. Again, the text never provides a reason as to why wine and gambling require further elaboration. Perhaps the audience would have known immediately why idols and divination arrows would have been condemned but would have been less clear about wine and gambling. Or, perhaps idols and divination arrows were tied to specific acts in specific contexts while imbibing and gambling were readily detached from a sacrificial context. Whatever the case, the Qur'an supplies little explanatory evidence as to why wine and gambling should be avoided, and also fails to enumerate punishments for ignoring its recommendations. What these verses do strongly assert, however, is that wine and gambling are ethically corrosive and socially destructive. As such, their practice thwarts divine order.

This clear condemnation in Sura 5:90–91 (al-Ma'ida) is never again repeated or reiterated in the Qur'an. The second passage (Sura 2:219–220 [al-Baqara]) that pairs wine with gambling is at best ambivalent:

> They ask you about wine (*khamr*) and gambling.
> Tell them, "In both is great sin (*ithm*) and profit (*manafi'*) for men.
> But their sin is greater than their profit."[42]

Even though this passage states that their sin is greater than their profit, here the suggestion lingers that one can (and perhaps should) somehow benefit from both wine and gambling.[43] Unfortunately, the criteria for distinguishing when wine or gambling serves as a benefit or sin are never given.[44] This lack of clarity could easily confuse those who are not in the know.

To compare the two passages, Sura 2:219–220 (al-Baqara) makes an ethical claim by simply introducing the two items of wine and gambling while giving only a brief commentary on their ratio of sin to profit. It merely states the obvious. Because their sin is greater than their profit, wine and gambling should be avoided. Sura 5:90–91 (al-Ma'ida) fleshes out this ethical justification and adds a social and cosmic dimension by suggesting that wine, gambling, and some additional items should be renounced, because they fall among the abominations of Satan (cosmic), create divisions of hatred among men (social), and divert them from the remembrance of God and prayer (ethical). By linking the condemnation to both worldly and cosmic orders, this Sura makes the strongest statement against wine.

However, even such strong pronouncements do not provide the legal basis upon which these accusations can be made, nor do they explictly state why wine should be clumped together with the other items in the first place (although, as mentioned above, there is an implicit association with pre-Islamic Arabian—or perhaps anti-Qur'anic—sacrificial practice). Instead, these two Suras present single impressions or reminders that this list of worldly items and activities somehow oppose God and are to be renounced by those who wish to maintain their proper status in relation to the divine. To embrace them is to stand apart from the community of believers, and so from God.

In sum, these two Qur'anic passages remind believers of what is divinely true through everyday items present in their immediate surroundings, all of which serve to elucidate and evoke further the revelation of God. In other words, the Qur'an does not prohibit wine as a *substance* in these gambling verses, but rather uses it as a means to evoke how the world must operate in order for it to reflect—rather than oppose—divine truth, and what humans must do in order to maintain this appropriate relationship with God.[45] If the text wanted to establish a legal precedent by banishing wine, gambling, idols, and divination arrows, then why weren't these items listed with carrion, pork, and blood, and clearly prohibited?[46] In addition, if the Qur'an were providing an exhaustive list of what was prohibited to believers, then why would the list stop at four (or seven, if carrion, pork, and blood were included as well)? As stated above, wine and gambling, or wine, gambling, idols, and divination arrows serve as literary tropes that evoke revelatory truths; namely, that the Qur'anic God requires the complete and uncompromised attention of those who accept his revelation, and that to embrace these impure practices is to deny his revelations and accept all that is opposed to the one true God.

WINE AND PRAYER

The ethical mischief produced by wine in these gambling verses is further illustrated by Sura 4:43 (al-Nisa'), where its effects apparently hinder one's ability to execute an appropriate ritual prayer in response to the divine mandate:

> Oh, you who believe! Do not draw near prayer
> when you are intoxicated (*sukara*) until you know what you are saying;
> nor when in a state of defilement until you have washed yourselves.
> When you are ill, or travelling,
> or when you have relieved yourselves
> or have had intercourse with a woman,
> and you cannot find water, take clean sand
> and pass it over your face and hands.
> God is benign and forgiving.

Strikingly, this passage groups intoxication with natural bodily functions such as sexual intercourse, urination, and defecation.[47] What do all of these items have in common? Each of these activities—drinking, sexual relations, urinating, and defecating—is not an impure act in and of itself, but only becomes so in *relation* to ritual activities.[48] Intoxication itself does not present a problem until one becomes drunk and then tries to pray. Yet, after a limited fashion, the effects of intoxication will wear off, and presumably one can safely re-enter the ritual arena. The same is true for sex, urination, and defecation. In these cases, sand or water, rather than time, is sufficient enough to remove the impure excretions. But like intoxication they are conditions that do not present permanent or serious danger to the believer's ritual competence.

If ritual ablutions of any kind are not aimed at rectifying certain impure acts, but rather address the general failing of human beings to control their bodily acts,[49] then the inclusion of wine in this list of bodily activities makes more sense. As Kevin Reinhart has suggested, both sand and water provide a kind of "envelope" or seal that coats the body after those "border lines" have been ruptured as a result of some sort of loss of control, like a seminal excretion.[50] In the case of intoxication, this "loss of control" takes the form of a lack of concentration or proper focus, which eventually must be regained before someone can return to reciting his prayer. Once control is regained, either through water, sand, or sobriety, the borders are sealed, order is restored, and the ritual can be safely performed. In other words, intoxication leaves no permanent stain that requires some kind of punishment or ritual rectification, and may, in fact, be acceptable as long as it is confined to non-ritual contexts.

Contrary to Suras 5:90–91 (al-Ma'ida), and 2:219–220 (al-Baqara), intoxication in this passage only becomes a problem when it interferes with the execution of a proper ritual. And, even when drunkenness does occur, the dangers it creates do not seem to have any lasting effects. The chaotic potential caused by one muttering prayers while drunk simply disappears when one eventually finds his way back to sobriety, or to the right state of mind. This rather lenient view towards intoxication stands in sharp contrast with the later legal tradition, where wine and other intoxicating drinks, along with pigs, dogs,[51] carrion, blood, excrement, and the milk of animals whose flesh is not eaten are turned into "actual" impurities—that is, impurities that stem from items with a perceptible body—and flatly prohibited.[52]

The primary concern in this passage, however, is not with wine as an impure *substance*, as held by the later tradition, but with the potentially dangerous *effects* of intoxication on human intent and understanding at the time of prayer. The issue here is not whether one should drink, or even if one should become drunk, but rather what happens when intoxication clashes with ritual prayer. The text assumes that intoxication, like urination, defecation, and seminal emission, is already a natural part of human life. The question is not how to avoid such a state per se, but what to do upon entering it during an inappropriate time or circumstance.

SIGNS AND INDICATORS: WINE AND GNOSIS

The only wholly positive treatment of an *earthly* intoxicant said to be derived from grapes and dates appears in Sura 16:66–69 (al-Nahl), a Sura which glorifies inebriating drinks by turning them into one of God's special signs to his community of believers. Although describing an earthly wine, the Qur'an has little interest in regulating social or ethical behavior with these verses, but with evoking a particular insight into the divine. As such, the text treats this intoxicating beverage in a positive fashion:

> In the cattle there is a lesson for you:
> We give you a drink that comes from their bellies,
> between their bowels and blood,
> pure milk, pleasant to drink;
> And in the fruits of the date-palm and the grape-vine
> you obtain an intoxicant (*sakar*) and good food.
> In this [saying] are signs for those who understand.
> Your Lord inspired the bees to make their homes
> in the mountains, trees, and hives built by men.
> Eat from all fruits and follow the paths of your Lord.
> A drink of many colors comes out of their bellies—medicine for men.
> In this are signs for those who understand.

What is peculiar about the verses in Sura 16 (al-Nahl) is the very phrase "in this are signs for those who understand," a refrain that follows mention of intoxicants, good food, and a "drink of many colors . . . medicine for men." How can an intoxicant serve as a sign for those who understand? The concept of "sign" (*aya*) in the Qur'an is multifaceted. The Qur'anic "sign" can refer to many things: the ark as the token of Saul's kingship;[53] the sun and moon as indicators of day and night;[54] and the wonders of nature either as signs of God's power and glory,[55] or as portents that serve as warnings.[56] Signs are also synonymous with miracles,[57] accounts or stories that tell of God's strength and power,[58] and, of course, the verses themselves that relate such signs.[59] In the above example, clearly the "intoxicant" acts as a sign to ignite deeper understandings of God's greatness.

Passages similar to those in Sura 16 (al-Nahl) are plentiful in texts held sacred by other Abrahamic traditions, and comparisons among them shed some light on the verses at-hand. For example, Genesis 27:28 states the following in reference to wine: "May God give you of the dew of heaven, and of the fatness of the earth, and plenty of grain and wine." Psalm 104:14–15 presents a comparable view: "You cause the grass to grow for the cattle, and plants for man to cultivate, that he may bring forth food from the earth, and wine to gladden the heart of man, oil to make his face shine, and bread to strengthen man's heart." Although God has freely given wine as a gift for men to enjoy, these two passages do not suggest that this beverage is some kind of "sign" that leads one to a deeper or more accurate understanding of the divine. Nor do they eliminate, as in the Sura above, the role of man as *essential* cultivator. Although humans benefit from the natural bounties that are rightfully theirs in the Hebrew Bible passages, they must still cultivate the natural resources that God has bestowed upon them. In the Qur'anic verses, this step is bypassed as God is elevated to both Creator and producer of all the agricultural wares humans freely consume.[60]

Rather than enumerate the wonderful gifts God has given to his creation, the "sign" phrases that appear in Sura 16 (al-Nahl) suggest a kind of Qur'anic gnosis or gnosticism in the sense that certain objects were believed to hold deeper meanings for those who knew how to perceive them. What do we mean by a Qur'anic *gnosticism*? Generically speaking, gnosticism refers to those religious systems that emphasize knowledge (*gnosis*) as an essential means to salvation.[61] However, in popular thinking "gnosticism" is a term used to describe Christian heretics who disagreed with the tenets of orthodoxy. In other words, gnosticism came to be identified as a separate (Christian) tradition in and of itself that directly opposed an already established "orthodox" position (that is, "Gnosticism" with a capital "G"), rather than a system of thought or interpretation that developed within a number of different traditions.

Because gnosticism became identified with a *Christian* heresy, it is not surprising that "gnostics" would be defined in terms of the language, symbols, and ideas of that particular belief system. However, this does not mean that gnosticism in Judaism or Islam, for example, would have to take on these same characteristic features. Unfortunately, by making gnosticism into a "religion" in and of itself, it is difficult to talk about its presence in other traditions. Perhaps this is why gnostic elements in Islam are rarely examined, except, of course, in the context of fringe, minority, or heretical groups such as the Shi'ite extremists.[62]

While "typical" gnostic imagery that focuses on the presence of messianic figures, the ontological separation of the Unknown God from the bumbling Creator, or the emphasis on individual, spiritual prowess is noticeably absent from the Qur'an, the fact that milk, wine, food, and a "drink of many colors"[63] are all signs for those who know draws sharp distinctions between those who can grasp the true, hidden message, and those who cannot. In other words, lurking within certain natural elements like the fruit of the vine is a kind of divine test used to separate those who properly interpret or "know" the signs from those who cannot see beyond the drink itself.

Presumably, those who quaffed an intoxicant for its effects without the deeper awareness of its divine origins would remain forever separate, on earth and in the next realm, from those who readily recognized the true power behind such a potent beverage. Here, the recognition or knowledge of the consumer, rather than the social context, serves to separate the true believer from the false. Although the Qur'an does not glorify inebriation per se in this passage, intoxicants themselves, like milk and honey, readily work as signs capable of facilitating insight into divine truth.

This Sura, which clumps together such liquids as milk, honey, and wine, could well be titled "al-Nahl" (The Bee) to highlight the polyvalency of these substances as the bee, too, is a categorical anomaly. For purposes of comparison, it is useful to examine a related tradition—Zoroastrianism—which casts the bee in a similarly ambivalent light.

Zoroastrianism divides the animal kingdom into two categories: those creatures that provide benefit and sustenance to human beings, and those that inflict harm. In the dualistic belief system of Zoroastrianism, the former kinds of creatures further the universal cause of the good, while the latter further the cause of evil. However, in Zoroastrianism there are some life forms, such as bees, that have the ability both to harm and benefit man (not unlike wine as it is described in Sura 2:219–220 [al-Baqara]).[64] Where do bees fall when the world itself must be strictly divided into two opposing forces? Bees, whose sting causes great pain but whose honey brings forth sweet pleasure and nourishment, embody both poles. Obviously the insect cannot be split easily into good and evil pieces. Therefore, much care is taken in Zoroastrian legal texts to separate the positive *qualities* of the bee from the negative.

Although the Qur'an does not advocate a dualistic universe, it does recognize that certain items in the world can embrace both positive and negative qualities simultaneously, depending on the perspective taken. For example, while the effects of intoxication in certain contexts can cause one to lose sight of God and prayer, as is the case in Sura 5:90–91 (al-Ma'ida), the fruit of the vine can still be considered a divine sign for those who properly reflect (or have the correct insight) in Sura 16 (al-Nahl). Like the treatment of bees in Zoroastrianism, Sura 16 (al-Nahl) ponders the positive attributes of something whose qualities in another situation may take on the opposite characteristics.

Rather than systematically separating the positive qualities from the negative, the Qur'an relies upon interpretive frames of reference to dictate what aspect of wine must be emphasized to further one's understanding of or reaction to the divine. In this way, wine can either point to God's goodness or to human failings. Depending on whether it appears as one of God's signs that points to the glories of his creation, or to something that is sorely mishandled by the creation, as is the case when one becomes drunk before prayer, wine appears in the Qur'an as both a sign for those who understand as well as an act of Satan. In different contexts—cosmic, communal, or ethical—wine either reflects divine truth or distorts it.

In either case, whether wine is portrayed as being good or bad, or whether its appearance in the Qur'an serves to instill wonder or fear, it must be emphasized that the Qur'an is not making a case for the legal status of wine. Rather, wine is a rhetorical trope that has the cumulative effect of revealing some fundamental truths about the relationship between believers and their God through the interplay between objects and their perceptions.

WINE AND PARADISICAL VISION

Wine and wine-drinking also surface as prominent themes in Qur'anic depictions of the apocalypse and subsequent afterlife. Not only does wine play a significant role in the actual destruction of the world, but it also serves as one of the glorious rewards the righteous receive when they bask in the pleasures of Paradise. As in the passages on wine and gambling, or wine as a sign for those who understand, wine and intoxication appear in apocalyptic and paradisical imagery to remind or warn; to incite feelings of unspeakable awe or absolute dread. Again, the Qur'an uses wine to evoke the appropriate response to the divine rather than present a legal statement on how this *substance* should be treated.

To contrast sharply with its paradisical vision, the Qur'an casts wine in a wholly negative light when the text describes the destruction ushering in the Day of Judgment:

> Oh, you people, fear your Lord.
> The great upheaval of the Hour indeed will be severe.
> The day you see it, every suckling female shall forget her suckling,
> and every pregnant female shall deposit her burden.
> You shall see men drunk (*sukara*), yet they are not drunk (*sukara*).
> God's chastisement is grim.[65]

On Judgment Day men will seem drunk, but not because of any alcoholic beverage. Here, the last blast is portrayed as a reversal or upheaval of the natural order of things; women who bear and suckle children will turn against their natures and abandon their young. Men, locked in a state of mental confusion that normally results from the consumption of alcohol, experience something much more sinister: a complete loss of control, a kind of madness from which they cannot be aroused. On the Last Day, all boundaries between order and chaos, sanity and insanity, and life and death are swept away with one blow; no one can escape the nightmare of a world without distinctions. The lesson to be taken from this passage is clear: If boundaries ultimately separate men from God, what happens when the lines are removed and God asserts his physical presence in the human realm? For any believer concerned about his ultimate status, the image is not inviting. Such references to drunkenness, which itself breaks down the fundamental boundaries of perception, are key in evoking the proper response on the part of those who believe.

Immediately beyond this chaotic, confused apocalyptic moment lies the tranquil and stable Garden of Repose, an ideal state where wine plays the role of divine reward. Wine makes a remarkably positive appearance in Sura 47:15 (Muhammad). Here, "rivers of wine (*khamr*)" are promised to the righteous ones privileged enough to reside in the Garden. In this paradisical moment, wine itself becomes a "joy to those who drink," and stands in direct opposition to the beverage served to those who are destined for the Eternal Fire: a boiling water so hot it cuts the bowels to pieces.[66]

Along with lounging next to rivers of wine, those individuals righteous enough to meander through the Qur'anic Paradise are allowed to imbibe as much wine as they please:

> Shadows will bend over them,
> and low will hang the clusters of grapes.
> Passed round will be silver flagons and goblets made of glass,
> and crystal clear bottles of silver,
> of which they will determine the measure themselves.[67]

However, the text is very careful to note that the wine the privileged consume is of an *uninebriating* vintage.[68] In fact, the overconsumption of this paradisical drink is portrayed as having the exact opposite effect of what one finds when "men are drunk, yet not drunk." Unlike the tortured men blinded by confusion and drunkenness following the final destruction, those virtuous enough to recline on the soft, supple couches after the earthly destruction and quaff unrestricted amounts of wine will receive a sense of *clarity* from their drink; a sharper vision by which the righteous can discern and appreciate the beauties of Paradise.

Those reaping their heavenly rewards will be served by immortal youths with "bowls and decanters, a cup full of purest drink (*ma'in*); they will receive no ache from it, nor will they suffer intoxication (*yunzafu*)."[69] Elsewhere in the Qur'an the chosen ones once again pass around "a cup full of purest drink (*ma'in*), white, delicious to those who drink, wherein there is no sickness (*ghawl*), nor will they suffer intoxication (*yunzafu*) from it."[70] Rather than wallowing in a hazy, heavenly state of drunkenness, these denizens of Paradise can quaff as much wine as they desire with none of the usual side effects. Their vision is not blurred. They do not fall into madness. The truth remains clearly seen. In Paradise, the believer's repose is not disturbed by nature's ambiguities. Presumably, the bee's sting no longer hurts just as wine no longer intoxicates.

In many respects, the gnostic signs depicted in Sura 16 (al-Nahl) are fully realized in the paradisical ideal. In the case of wine, the sign ultimately becomes signified. These paradisical images of wine are exempla of the perfected state of existence that awaits the righteous ones after the earthly world has been destroyed, or, perhaps, what should exist in the here and now if all of its precepts were only realized. Here, in its ideal form, wine is essentially stripped of its ambiguous characteristics and turned into an invariable, immutable beverage, the consummate reward for those permanent residents of the heavenly Gardens who managed to escape a treacherous, shaky world where men can readily be turned into stones. While marginal behaviors or concerns must be tolerated to varying degrees on Earth—an already shifting ground split between the two extremes of Paradise and Hell—they simply have no place in the projected ideal, for they would threaten its very coherence and perfection.[71]

This perfection resurfaces in Sura 83:25–28 (al-Mutaffifin), which states that those who followed the righteous path of God "will be served the choicest wine (*rahiq*), sealed (*makhtum*) with a sealing (*khitam*) of musk." With these verses, the Qur'an uses the concept of the "seal" to suggest a kind of fixed state free from the vagaries of a timebound world in which nothing more can transpire. Other Suras demonstrate this notion of permanence when they state that God sets a seal over the hearts and ears and eyes of the unbelievers, so that they cannot comprehend or accept the revelation from God.[72] Sura 33:40 (al-Ahzab) names Muhammad the seal of the Prophets, the consummate Prophet who will be succeeded by no other messenger. With his final seal, God's communication to the world is made complete. Just as all these examples point to finality, permanence, and perfection, so, too, does the paradisical wine that is "sealed (*makhtum*) with a sealing (*khitam*) of musk" suggest a beverage resistant to change and imperfection.

Wine is not the only thing stripped of its ambivalent qualities in the ideal paradisical state. The Qur'an consistently portrays the ideal realm as one in which any kind of ambiguity has no place. In Sura 56 (al-Waqi'a), the righteous ones who consume the uninebriating drinks are also accompanied by women frozen in a constant state of virginity, the wide-eyed *houris*.[73] These permanently chaste maidens avoid the stigma placed on any unmarried woman who is no longer a virgin, a status which poses a categorical anomaly that cannot be tolerated in the perfected world. This passage also reflects a strong desire for virgins to remain virgins; clearly, sexual activities in the Qur'anic Paradise will do nothing to transform a maiden to a matron. Further evidence supporting a Paradise intolerant of change or imperfection appears in the same Sura: Those who reside in the ideal realm will, in fact, be attended by servants "forever young" (*mukhalladun*).[74] Even the process of growing old will not be allowed to mar a Paradise immune to decay.

With its descriptions of Paradise, the Qur'an repeatedly depicts an ideal world where everything has achieved complete conformity to the revelation. Sura 47 (Muhammad) describes the Garden of Repose as having streams of water that will not putrify or decompose (*'asin*), rivers of milk whose taste will not change, and streams of honey that will remain forever cloudless (*musaffan*).[75] As in the case of wine, *houris*, and all the young servers, the paradisical walls serve to insulate water, milk, and honey from the threatening forces of (earthly) decay and transformation. While Sura 16:66–69 (al-Nahl) only pointed to the cosmic ideal with mention of water, milk, wine, and honey, Sura 47 (Muhammad) realizes it with reference to these same liquids, only in their perfected forms.

To summarize, the Qur'an uses intoxication in its apocalyptic visions to evoke fear, and wine in its descriptions of Paradise to incite simple truths about the believer's perfected existence. In the Qur'an's depictions of the Day of Reckoning, the damned who shun the truth are like those too drunk and confused to see the world around them or to understand their place in it (including their standing in relation to God). Here, with its visions of drunkenness on that Final Day, the Qur'an is not talking about a behavior resulting from the overconsumption of alcoholic beverages, but is making a stronger epistemological claim: Lose sight of the revelation, and you will lose sight of all that binds you to self, world, and cosmos.

In opposition to this apocalyptic confusion, those who embrace the truth with great clarity see the world as it should be when all conforms to the revelations of God. The Qur'anic Paradise is, in many ways, a projection of an idealized Earth. Its images are those of the world, only in perfected form. It is the place where world and cosmic order become indistinguishable from one another, once and for all. Therefore, while the heavenly wine may be "delicious to drink," it has lost all of its intoxicating potency. Within the uncertain earthly realm, the Qur'an repeatedly demonstrates how wine and intoxication can be ethically, socially, and therefore *cosmically* destructive. In a place where nothing stands to oppose the revelation, wine sheds its ambivalent and potentially negative qualities, and becomes a pleasurable drink like any other.

WINE AND THE PROPHETS

In addition to the gnostic passages, this explicit evocation of divine truth in the face of worldly ambiguity occurs outside the paradisical realm in only a few other instances. The Qur'an relates stories about certain key prophetic figures who, in their biblical contexts, had strong associations with wine and intoxication. While drunkenness and other questionable behaviors appeared with great frequency in biblical texts, these activities apparently compromised the Qur'an's insistent and consistent depiction of God's messengers as moral models for humanity, as ethical paradigms. While not completely without fault, the Qur'anic prophets do stand head and shoulders above the rest of the population by virtue of their role as God's messengers. And, as bearers of God's own word, these messengers must appear as unblemished as possible, as clean and pure receptacles for the transmission of sacred revelation. Therefore, we find a complete absence of wine and intoxication in association with individuals who, in the Judaic and Christian traditions, were all too familiar with the pleasures of the vine.

The argument that the Qur'an has no tolerance for behaviors that might conflict with its concept of God's true messenger is clear in the cases of Noah, Lot, and Jesus. In all the Qur'anic stories about Noah,[76] not one mentions his bout with drunkenness. The only criticism of Noah appears in Sura 23:25 (al-Mu'minun), which states that the chiefs of Noah's people accused him of being a "man possessed,"[77] but this is considered a lie. Drunkenness is never mentioned in association with Noah, not even in the context of a polemical argument or accusation. The absence of intoxication is curious, given the fact that it is such a prominent theme in the biblical version of the Noah story, as well as in its Jewish and Christian exegesis.[78]

In Genesis 9:20–23, note the following vignette describing Noah's infamous moment of indiscretion:

> Noah was the first tiller of the soil. He planted a vineyard, drank of the wine, became drunk, and lay uncovered in his tent. Ham, the father of Canaan, saw the nakedness of his father, and told his two brothers outside. Then Shem and Japheth took a garment, laid it upon both their shoulders, walked backwards and covered the nakedness of their father; their faces were turned away; they did not see their father's nakedness.

The story goes on to make a political point about the future of Canaan. The biblical account has Noah playing a variety of roles, none of which necessarily complement one another: Noah is the tiller of the soil in a new age; a lover of wine and the not so obvious pleasures one derives from lying naked in a tent; and an astute politician. In the Qur'an, there is only partial reference to the first. Noah is a prophet of God in a new age whose message is to warn his contemporaries to worship the one God:

> The people of Noah too, rejected their apostles.
> "Will you have no fear of God?" said Noah,
> their compatriot, to them.
> "I am indeed your true apostle. Fear God and follow me.
> For this I demand of you no recompense, for none can reward me
> except the Lord of the Universe.
> Have fear of God and follow me."[79]

The second has no place in the Qur'an because the predecessors of Muhammad would not have indulged in such compromising behaviors as drunkenness and voluntary exposure. The third, which involves the political rivalry between Israel and Canaan, has little meaning in a Hijazi context. The prophet's life is spun as generically as possible; neither his distinctive features, his fickleness, nor his foibles are left to mar the purity of the message.[80]

The attempt to present prophets or other significant figures as moral models for humanity is repeated in the case of Lot. As if Noah's indiscretions in the Book of Genesis were not enough, Lot continues, if not exceeds, the bad behaviors instituted by his noble but fallible predecessor:

> Now Lot went up out of Zo'ar, and dwelt in the hills with his two daughters, for he was afraid to dwell in Zo'ar; so he dwelt in a cave with his two daughters. And the first-born said to the younger, "Our father is old, and there is not a man on earth to come in to us after the manner of all the earth. Come, let us make our father drink wine, and we will lie with him, that we may preserve offspring through our father." So they made their father drink wine that night; and the first-born went in, and lay with her father; he did not know when she lay down or when she arose (19:30–33).

The story goes on to explain how the younger daughter also made her father drunk so that she, too, could have intercourse with him. As a result of these escapades, "both the daughters of Lot were with child by their father."[81] The Hebrew Bible reveals startling flaws in Lot's character: He, with great temerity, took up with his two daughters, and he was foolishly tricked by his own offspring, resulting in descendants borne of incest. Lot was weak; as a result, his integrity was compromised, his seed soiled.

In contrast to the biblical account of Lot's human failings, the Qur'an presents this character as a champion of righteousness and morality who was deeply dedicated to God. Sura 15:61–79 (al-Hijr) tells the story of how Lot was visited by a group of God's messengers. These messengers told Lot to leave with his family, for they were about to destroy the city and its inhabitants. As Lot fled for safety, the people stayed behind; actively engaged in immoral practices, unaware of their impending doom.

> Verily by your life they were utterly confused
> in their drunkenness (*sakuratihim*).
> So they were seized by the mighty blast at break of day;
> and We turned the city upside down
> and rained on them stones of hardened lava.[82]

Quite a contrast to the Genesis account. In the Qur'an, the clear head and righteous behaviors of Lot are set off against the drunken confusion and moral turpitude of those who were about to be destroyed. The message here has little to do with Lot. Lot is merely the mouthpiece, who, on cue, serves up the following prophetic maxim: Keep to the path of God, and you will be spared.

When wine *is* mentioned with a biblical character, as in the story of Joseph and his fellow prisoners in Sura 12:36–42 (Yusuf), it is in a rather ambivalent but wholly innocuous manner. For reasons that are not quite clear, we find Joseph sitting in a prison after resisting the wife of 'Aziz's seductive advances. Accompanying Joseph in prison are two unnamed men, who tell him dreams they had the previous night. One man dreamt he was "pressing wine" (*a'siru khamran*), the other that he "was carrying bread on his head, and the birds eating thereof." After some lengthy discussions about the glories of Allah, Joseph finally interepretes the dreams in Sura 12:41 (Yusuf). According to Joseph, the one who was pressing grapes would eventually pour out wine (*khamr*) for his lord to drink; the one carrying bread, however, would "hang from the cross, and the birds will eat from off the top of his head." Interestingly enough, in Sura 12:42 (Yusuf) the one pressing wine—the one who would ultimately be saved—somehow manages to forget his promise to mention the imprisoned Joseph to his master. So, although wine appears as a favorable indicator in the dream, Joseph's positive interpretation does him little good.

Moving to the New Testament parallels, we might expect the Qur'an to mention wine in association with Jesus, given the many references to wine, grapes, and the vine in the Gospels. In the Synoptic Gospels, for example, Jesus passes around bread and a cup filled with the fruit of the vine, which represent his body and blood, both of which serve to seal the terms of the new covenant.[83] In John, even though Jesus calls himself a vine, his father a vinedresser,[84] he no longer uses cultivated products like bread and wine to incarnate his flesh and blood. Instead, Jesus radically bypasses all metaphorical language and cryptic imagery in order to assert that "my flesh is food indeed, and my blood is drink indeed."[85]

In the Qur'an, however, Jesus only asks the Lord for a "table well laid with food from the skies," a sign for those who may have doubted the powers of God, or his ability to work miracles through those human beings whom he has chosen.[86] Here, there is no reference to wine, no cryptic or concrete minglings of Jesus' flesh and blood with the food on the table, nor any foretellings or forewarnings of an apocalyptic event. The absence of a "eucharistic"-type feast goes along with the majority of Qur'anic statements about Jesus. He, like his prophetic predecessors, had only a message, rather than a beverage, to serve.[87]

These revisions suggest that prophetic figures in the Qur'an are uniform and interchangeable; they are paragons of moral stability. Qur'anic messengers are not like the Noah and Lot of the Hebrew Bible, naive, erratic, and often gullible men, servants of a wrathful, merciful, but oftentimes remiss God whose patience is continuously tested—even by his chosen instruments. Nor are Qur'anic prophets the charismatic, kaleidescopic visionaries like

Ezekiel and Daniel, who from the margins call upon the people to set straight their path. The Qur'an's prophets also stand opposed to the semidivine, self-aggrandizing figures favored by the New Testament. The Qur'an, for example, would shudder at the portrait painted by Matthew of John the Baptist, a peripheral character who wore only a leather girdle around his waist, ate nothing but locusts and wild honey, and had this to say about a coming prophet:

> I baptize you with water for repentance, but he who is coming after me is mightier than I, whose sandals I am not worthy to carry; he will baptize you with the Holy Spirit and with fire. His winnowing fork is in his hand, and he will clear his threshing floor and gather his wheat into the granary, but the chaff he will burn with unquenchable fire.[88]

Obviously, neither John nor his successor is one who would blend in with the crowds. Instead, Qur'anic prophets represent what humans should be in their perfected, moral form in an ideal world. As ethical models of piety and relentless espousers of "right belief" they are without divine aspiration, fantastic vision, or human fault. Thus, Noah and Lot are stripped of, among other things, their drunken bouts, and Jesus his role as Divine Savior.

While the embarrassing details of drunken behaviors in the Pentateuch often required later exegetical repair,[89] the Qur'an avoids the problem of having to account for unseemly or dangerous behaviors on the part of God's messengers by simply eliminating the potential for them to occur. Interestingly enough, even the stories about the postdiluvian Noah that appear in later Islamic writings do not contain any information about his drunken behaviors. Al-Tabari, for example, mentions his exposure, but not his intoxication:

> Ibn Humayd: Salama: Ibn Ishaq: The people of the Torah claim that this was only because of an invocation of Noah against his son Ham. This was because while Noah slept his genitals were exposed, and Ham saw them but did not cover them.[90]

A more detailed version appears in *The Tales of the Prophets of al-Kisa'i*, where once again Noah's nakedness is noted, but not his drunkenness:

> It is said that one day Noah came to his son and said, "My son, I have not slept since I boarded the ark, and now I desire to sleep my fill." So saying, he put his head on Shem's lap and went to sleep. Suddenly a gust of wind uncovered Noah's genitals; Ham laughed, but Shem jumped up and covered him.[91]

According to this version, Noah did not stretch out naked because he was too drunk to know any better; rather, he was simply too fatigued by his noble journey on the ark to feel his garments being swept away by a quick puff of wind.

In sum, the Qur'an treats the presence of a prophet not as an aberration or eruption in the historical flow, but rather as a moral exemplar reflecting a stable, ethical cosmos. From the bosom of the community he will emerge, and to the midst of the community the prophet will return, carrying God's message to a wayward people who will invariaby reject the message and messenger. Thus, the string of prophets throughout the Qur'anic history are all spun with the same thread; no knots, no kinks, and no breaks can mar the integrity of the message. The faces, names, and places may change over time, but the message, and the form in which it takes, remains the same. The exception to this rule is, of course, Muhammad, who brings the final message that will presumably be heard, once and for all. With the sacrifice of idiosyncratic behavior for generic representation, and the supplanting of anomaly by static homogeneity, the Qur'an asserts what the ideal human should be, both on Earth and in Paradise. By holding the prophet up as the consummate human form, the Qur'an carves out one of the few places on Earth where the real reflects the cosmic ideal.

By eliminating any mention of wine with certain key biblical figures, and turning these figures into moral paragons, the Qur'an asserts a few fundamental themes about the nature of God, his revelations, and the status of the human being in relation to that revelation. In addition, by viewing all of God's messengers through the same typological lens, the Qur'an evokes the divine realm through that of the human. In the case of the prophets, what stands flawed in the human realm is made to conform to a more perfected moral form, and what overreaches in the earthly sphere is muted down to an appropriate level below that which is divine. Since wine has the potential to destroy morality or elevate one's status to that of God, it presents an unnecessary danger to those prophets who already face the difficult task of transmitting a perfected revelation in an imperfect world.

IN WINE ARE SIGNS

As stated above, the Qur'an's discussion of wine and intoxication can be broken down into two separate categories: its consumption on Earth, and its consumption in Paradise. Clearly, in the earthly realm, the Qur'an treats wine and intoxication with a certain ambivalence. Wine may not be strictly forbidden, like carrion, blood, or pork, but clearly it is ethically and socially destructive. From this worldly perspective, wine creates divisions among men, and diverts them from God in a number of disturbing ways. As a result, wine on Earth has the potential to corrode what is ontologically true, and should therefore be avoided in specific contexts where such damage could occur. In addition, sobriety characterizes the Qur'an's prophets, who, as moral models, could not engage in any activity that would disturb the worldly and cosmic orders. Not surprisingly, the Qur'an only treats earthly wine in a positive fashion when it uses this liquid to signify certain truths about the divine. From this vantage point, wine has little to do with ethical or social norms, but with displaying cosmic order, and it is glorified as such.

While this ambiguous treatment of wine allows the Qur'an to evoke certain understandings about what humans should know about the divine, and how they should respond to him, it interferes with the text's projected vision of an ideal state—Paradise—where divine truth is made manifest. Given the descriptions of wine in Paradise, only substances (and beings, for that matter) immune to the vagaries of change, and resistant to multiple meanings or interpretations can be tolerated in the utopian Garden where the righteous ones will be rewarded once and for all for following God's "straight path." A drink that is simultaneously an abomination and a hindrance to prayer would not qualify for entry into this absolute realm for it would undermine and threaten the cosmic order. In addition, the Qur'an no longer needs to use wine as a sign to evoke certain human responses to the divine in Paradise, for those who have entered the Garden presumably have realized all they need to know.[92]

In its incongruous depiction of wine, the Qur'an distinguishes sharply between what is real and what is ideal: the earthly realm of uncertainty, and the perfected domain of stability. Through its revelatory language, or prophetic discourse, the Qur'an defines and redefines the parameters of a cosmic and world order, using the very evidence of nature to incite a fixed repertoire of divine truths that lie within, yet transcend, human reality, in order to guide believers toward proper understanding and action. However, as the evidence above demonstrates, the Qur'an's views on wine have the tendency to shift radically, depending on whether it is used to elicit social/ethical norms, evoke issues of ontology, or both. In addition, the Qur'an rarely indicates its shifts in viewpoints; it is often difficult to know what frame or frames of reference the text employs for reading these various statements on wine. Multiple interpretations seem possible, especially when the proclamations are viewed side by side, or when one takes a practical stance and asks "Am I allowed to drink wine?"

It is this deceptively simple question that must be worked over and over, again and again, in the Hadith, which bypass all visions of Paradise to enlist wine in their efforts to create an orderly world that stands as a realization of what is ontologically true.

2

Finding the Perfect World

Analytic Discourse and the Quest for Order

In the Islamic tradition, Hadith are generally regarded as accounts of what Muhammad said or did, or his approval of what was said or done in his presence.[1] These traditions were not immediately recognized as divine law; they were considered a subsidiary authority to the Qur'an. The Hadith attained their limited command beginning in the latter half of the eighth century, when scholars and theologians started to embrace the notion that the *Prophet's* way of life should be emulated as a "perfect example" (*sunna*).[2] The idea that the Prophet's life could serve as an infallible source of law was best articulated by Muhammad b. Idris al-Shafi'i, who argued that Muhammad's actions were inspired, and should be viewed in tandem with the Qur'an as a source of divine will.[3] Al-Shafi'i based his reasoning on Sura 24:52 (al-Nur), which states that "[w]hoever obeys God and his Prophet, fears God and does his duty to Him, will surely find success."[4]

As records of an ideal life, the Hadith collections contain a variety of information by and about the Prophet ranging from what he said about dogs, divorce, and Hell to how he trimmed his beard, prayed in the evenings, and traveled to the distant heavens, where he met with such lofty figures as Moses and Jesus.[5] Whether or not the Hadith should be taken as actual historical accounts of what Muhammad (or one of his companions) said or did,[6] or as collections of normative statements regarding how believers should behave (or both, to varying degrees) is not relevant to this study. What is of primary concern here is *how* the Hadith articulate, legitimize, and institutionalize the behaviors of what they assert to be their "perfect example" for the benefit of the community.[7]

Unlike the Qur'an, the Hadith are consistent (with only a handful of exceptions) in their condemnation of wine and other intoxicants. Although they still find wine to be an ambiguous substance, they no longer treat this ambiguity as having any positive qualities, rhetorically or otherwise. Instead, wine—and more specifically the intoxicating effects of wine—become a source of danger that must be contained. Curiously enough, the Hadith do not simply state once and for all that the Prophet prohibited wine (as one would expect in a case in which the elimination of ambiguity is of the utmost concern) but rather repeat the same message over and over again through an assortment of fixed literary structures, all of which further elaborate and refine what must be condemned.

Reading through the various Hadith traditions, we miss the vivid images of wine as a sign evoking the magnificent divine or the brilliant splendors of Paradise, and we no longer hear of the benefits and pitfalls of wine's positive and negative qualities. The Hadith seek only to identify, define, and contain what is ethically (and therefore cosmically) corrosive. As a result, the Hadith present the Prophet (or one of his companions) setting up lists of prohibited ingredients from which wine was made, doling out formulaic punishments for wine-induced transgressions, and playing a role in a number of scenerios that all lead to God's sending down revelations that "prohibit" the consumption of wine. Given these repetitive statements of an earthly prohibition, the Hadith obviously view form as important a literary choice as content when dealing with questions of ambiguity. But how does the form of the prohibition contribute to the elimination of wine's ambivalency?

In general, the Hadith employ two distinct literary forms—the analytic and narrative (which will be discussed in chapter three)—to isolate and control wine's ambiguous status through its condemnation. By endlessly restating the prohibition through a limited set of literary forms, analytic discourse seeks to align the earthly realm with that of the divine while maintaining the fundamental separation between the two. This alignment is not directed toward bringing God into the world nor putting humans on the level of the divine, but toward organizing the world so that it best reflects what is ontologically true. There can be no room for ambiguous substances like wine in an orderly world, for they would contradict and undermine the very nature and structure of the cosmos. If the world is full of danger and uncertainty, then what does that say about the "ideal" realm this world reflects?

In the Hadith, analytic discourse formats the discussion of wine into lists (including fixed sets of numbered elements), patterns of deductive reasoning, formulaic repetitions, and parallel structures. These literary forms organize, divide, and arrange the world so that it properly reflects and supports the permanent and enduring patterns of divine law. Analytic discourse does not project this divine order and logic onto the discussion of wine through sets of external laws or philosophical suppositions, but rather shows the actual proscription internal to, and indistinguishable from, the rhetorical forms through which the prohibition is spelled out. By condemning a substance of such profound ambiguity, humans are not only affirming the laws of the world, but the order of the cosmos. In addition, by the same logic, if one denies the prohibition one is not simply transgressing human law but is also at odds with the *entire* cosmos.

LISTS AND LIST MAKING

The Hadith rely heavily on lists and list making to generate the prohibition of wine. A list contains items that are joined together because they share some common trait or traits that are either logically apparent, or culturally construed. In other words, by virtue of including or excluding one item or another, lists assert an underlying ordering principle that permits contiguity. The list, therefore, by its very nature generates a hierarchy of order: The lower level projects what traits the items on the list share; the upper what governing rule their like traits produce.[8] More specifically, based on their shared traits, the items on the list produce a governing rule, which, in turn, is capable of assessing any item not on the list that may possess some of the same taxonomic traits. Order not only reigns from the bottom up, but also from the top down, creating a system capable of classifying any object or action that might appear in the natural, divine, or human realms.

Individual items on the list embody the qualities of the list as a whole, and therefore the authority of the governing rule. As a component essential to the creation of the general rule, and as an integral whole that reflects the governing law, any item on the list becomes a fixed standard by which one can compare other objects to determine whether or not they should be included in (or excluded from) the category. More importantly, by linking the specific to the general, and by elevating the status of the general to that of a *divine* mandate, the list serves to link all that is natural or human with all that is divine.

By stringing like substances together under general rules and linking general rules with divine precepts, the Hadith show natural law and human logic to reflect the cosmic order. In this sense, the Hadith do not force the human world into conformity with divine truth by external command, but simply underscore what is *already* ontologically true. In other words, by setting up lists, the Hadith purportedly reveal the preexisting patterns of uniformity that are set to the contours of the divine itself. Through the self-conscious process of recording and uncovering these eternal patterns, the Hadith claim not to jeopardize, modify, or manipulate what has been divinely ordained, but simply to bring it to light.

Metonymy

In order to see how the Hadith use lists to classify the natural world so that it reflects cosmic order, note the following example from the collection of Abu Dawud:

> Qutayba b. Sa'id: al-Layth: Yazid b. Abi Habib: 'Ata' b. Abi Rabah: Jabir b. 'Abdallah heard the Prophet say in the year of the victory, when he was in Mecca: "God forbids the selling of wine and carrion and pig flesh and idols." And it was said, "Oh Prophet, what do you say of the fat or lard of carrion, which is used to coat ships, grease leather, and make light for the people?" He said, "No, it is forbidden." Then the Prophet of God said, "God struggles with the Jews, for when he forbade them fat, they calculated its cost, and sold it in order to eat its price."[9]

While on the surface this tradition appears to state a simple prohibition against the selling of some questionable substances, much more can be discerned upon closer scrutiny. A detailed examination of this passage reveals not only a list of items forbidden by divine mandate, but also a breakdown of one of the items mentioned into smaller components that must also be prohibited, and a polemical pronouncement against the Jews.

As noted in chapter one, the Qur'an links together wine and gambling in Sura 2:219 (al-Baqara), then adds idols and divination arrows to the list in Sura 5:90–91 (al-Ma'ida) to remind people to stay away from those things that interfere with God, prayer, and the maintenance of a unified community of believers. The underlying purpose of stringing these items together in the Qur'an is not to give a definitive statement on the legal status of wine and other items in the natural realm, but rather to evoke the deeper, prophetic point that divisions within the community further separate the true believers from the one God.

Like the Qur'an, Abu Dawud's tradition also contains a list with items resembling those in Sura 5 (al-Ma'ida), but this list differs in that its function is metonymical, rather than evocative.[10] It presents a general rule—

items that are prohibited for one purpose (selling) in a particular community cannot be used for another—then seeks to support this rule through a display of items that share the same traits.[11] If one is prohibited from selling carrion, then one should not derive benefit from the fat and flesh in other ways. By analogy, then, one should not use pigs, idols, or wine for other purposes because their selling has been condemned.[12] Each item, therefore, becomes a manifestation of the governing law, a fixed standard by which to compare other objects to determine whether they should be included in, or excluded from, the general category.

The metonymical character of this passage is further evident in the breakdown of carrion into its constituate parts, all of which are then forbidden. Just as the logic of the general mandate dictates the prohibition of selling putrefying flesh, so, too, does the prohibition of this type of flesh itself penetrate deep down into the fat and the lard, covering all other aspects of their potential profit or use. Similarly, the rule can be reversed and expanded outward into all aspects of human life, from defining commercial relations with other communities (as suggested by the criticism of the Jews) on up to the relationship between a notable group of believing individuals and their God. Clearly, those individuals and communities who engage in such forbidden practices will forever "struggle" with God.

As a result of this ordering principle, wine, carrion, pigs, idols, and humans are made subject to the same underlying laws. The purpose of this list is not simply to make statements about what items cannot be sold, or that one should not benefit further from what is prohibited from being sold, but rather to establish and assert "consistent and enduring patterns of relationships among diverse and changing concrete things or persons."[13] These patterns, which have the potential to include all items on Earth within a single, coherent, taxonomic system, hold little tolerance for ambiguity.

While Abu Dawud's passage enumerates contraband items, it is also concerned with separating the community of believers from those who share like practices and beliefs, namely, the Jews. The polemic with the Jews encoded within the lists is similar to earlier Jewish pronouncements on the very same issues as *they* legally hone the boundaries between themselves and the Gentiles. Compare the similarities between Abu Dawud's tradition with the following Mishnaic passage:

2:3 A. These things belonging to Gentiles are prohibited, and the prohibition affecting them extends to deriving any benefit from them at all:

B. (1) wine, (2) vinegar of Gentiles which to begin with was wine, (3) Hadrianic earthenware, and (4) hides pierced at the heart.

C. Rabban Simeon b. Gamaliel says, "When the tear in the hide is round, it is prohibited. [If it is] straight, it is permitted."

D. "Meat which is being brought into an idol is permitted."

E. "But that which comes out is prohibited."

F. "because it is like *sacrifices of the dead* (Ps. 106:28)," the words of R. Aqiba.

G. Those who are going to an idolatrous pilgrimage—it is prohibited to do business with them.

H. Those that are coming back—they are permitted.

2:4 I A. "Skins of Gentiles and their jars, with Israelite wine collected in them—"

B. "they are prohibited, and the prohibition affecting them extends to deriving benefit from them at all," the words of R. Meir.[14]

By using a similar set of items to generate a comparable mandate that condemns the selling of what is prohibited, the new community of believers was able to assert its own claims to truth as the righteous practitioner or custodian of God's law on Earth. Abu Dawud's passage, therefore, firmly locates the place of the Islamic community at the pinnacle of its monotheistic heritage through the very ways in which it distinguishes the commercial practices of Muslims from those in the outside world. The power behind this polemical move lies not in the fact that this statement was perceived as a new interpretation of God's law, but rather as an old mandate that had been properly reinstated after having been misused by the previous guardians of God's will.

Numbers and Numbering

The Hadith also create order and symmetry by setting up lists with fixed numbers of items that are prohibited. Numbers in these examples often have mnemonic significance. Given that the Hadith were likely transmitted orally before being written down, the numbers most often used in reference to the prohibition of wine are two, five, and ten. Generally speaking, the Hadith employ these numbers to list the substances from which wine is made, or to describe every possible way in which wine is forbidden.

For example, the number *two* appears in a description about the origins of wine:

> Ahmad b. Muhammad: 'Abdallah b. al-Mubarak: al-Awza'i & Ikrima b. 'Amir: Abu Kathir al-Suhaymi: Abu Hurayra: The Prophet said, "Wine (*khamr*) comes from these two trees: the date palm and the grape-vine."[15]

On the surface, the purpose of this passage lays out what wine (*khamr*) is made of. However, the somewhat cryptic reference to the two trees and the pairing of the date-palm with the grape-vine suggest that this passage held other meanings as well. For example, some Hadith trace the "two trees"—and thus the prohibition itself—back to the birth of humanity, when Adam fell from the Garden. In the earthly realm, Adam struggled with Satan (Iblis) over the rights of ownership to several of God's gifts to man:

> 'Ali b. Ibrahim: his father: some of our companions: Ahmad b. Muhammad and Sahl b. Ziyad: Ibn Mahbub: Khalid b. Jarir: Abu Rabi' al-Shami said: I asked Abu 'Abdallah about the history of wine; how its lawfulness and prohibition came about, and at what point the prohibition came down upon wine. He said: When Adam fell from the Garden, he craved its fruits, so God sent down two vines of grapes. He planted them. When they burst into leaf, produced fruit and ripened, Iblis, whom God had damned, came and put a wall around the two plants. Adam said, "What are you doing, O cursed one?" Iblis said, "They are mine!" Adam said, "You are lying!" So they accepted the Holy Ghost [to moderate] between them. When they eventually got to him, Adam told him his story. So the Holy Ghost took a mixture of stuff from the fire and threw it upon them and upon the branches of the two grapevines until Adam thought that nothing would remain of them. Iblis, whom God had cursed, thought the same. He said, "I'll enter the fire whenever you enter," for two-thirds had gone, and a third remained. The Ghost said, "What has burned off of them [the two-thirds] shall be be Iblis' (God curse him!), and what remains is for you, O Adam."[16]

The two trees may also have strong associations with Noah and the replanting of life after his journey on the ark. Several Islamic traditions explicitly put two grape-vines in the hands of Noah, and place him in combat with Satan over the right to cultivate these plants.[17] Through their associations with Noah, who replanted them in the postdiluvian world, these "two trees" could also represent goods that are further separated from the divine as they result from human cultivation and not divine creation. In any case, along with serving as a mnemonic device, the analytic presentation of "these two trees" may simply be a way to create balance and symmetry in the world.[18] In addition, by stating that one should not be consuming wine made from grapes *or* dates, the tradition further refines what is to be condemned. This passage is directed at those in the minority who vociferously claimed that the Qur'an was referring solely to wine made of grapes, and that all other intoxicating beverages made from other materials were permissible.[19]

The number *five* also surfaces in traditions that further clarify the definition of wine (*khamr*), as illustrated in the following passage:

> Hafs b. 'Umar: Shu'ba: 'Abdallah b. Abi 'l-Safar: al-Sha'bi: Ibn 'Umar: 'Umar: Wine (*khamr*) is made from five things: raisins, dates, wheat, barley, or honey.[20]

In addition to elaborating what substances fall under the heading of "wine" (*khamr*), this tradition and others like it also hold that five items can produce wine simply because five was an easy number to be counted on the hand.[21] According to the form and content of this tradition, wine did and always will come from five things: no more, no less. Different items may replace others on the list as long as the set ordering principle remains the same, that is, as long as "wine is made from five things." For example, Ibn Babawayhi presents a similar version of the above tradition, but mentions grapes instead of wheat.[22] By linking the form to the content, that is, by limiting the sources of wine to the fingers on a single hand, the Hadith are able to establish permanence and stability in the natural, human, and divine realms.

The Prophet's curse upon all those involved in the drinking, buying, or selling of wine in any way takes the following *ten*-fold form:

> Ali b. Muhammad and Muhammad b. Isma'il: Waki': 'Abd al-'Aziz b. 'Umar b. 'Abd al-'Aziz: 'Abd al-Rahman b. 'Abdallah al-Ghafiqi and Abu Tu'ma: Ibn 'Umar: The Prophet said, "I curse wine (*khamr*) on ten points: its owner, the one who presses and the one for whom it is pressed, the one who sells it and the one who buys it, the carrier of it and the one for whom it is carried, the one who eats its price, the one who drinks it, and the one who serves it."[23]

The number "ten" matches the fingers on two hands, again a way to count and keep track of what is important. In the above statement—a statement that exhausts every individual who could have any association with wine, or any situation in which wine could have been passed from hand to hand—ten becomes a sign for all that is fixed, set, and enduring. Just as there are no more fingers to be counted after the number ten, there are no more points on which wine can be cursed. In fact, the *same person* (the buyer in one instance, the seller in another) is even counted twice in order to keep the number fixed at "ten."

In the examples of two, five, and ten, numbering both limits the amount of objects to be included in the system as well as establishes the ceiling that is to be reached. In other words, these numbers allow nothing else to be included, nor do they allow for anything to be taken away. In addition, they easily accommodate variation in content as long as the overall form or structure is maintained. Wine cannot be cursed for seven, eleven, or twenty-three points, for this would leave gaps unaccounted for in the overall symmetry. One would have to ask what has been omitted, or what prohibited drinks humans are consuming that have not been explicated. Therefore, the prohibition uttered through such set formulae leaves no open ends or gray areas in terms of how wine is to be treated.

Lists of numbered items associated with the fingers on a hand, or tied to significant events in sacred history ensure that everything in the human realm is ordered, structured, and accounted for. No stray substance or behavior can be left outside the all-encompassing taxonomic system, whether it appears in the past, present, or future. Enclosed in a formal structure which governs and is governed by the precepts of its own inherent logic, the numbered items, no matter what they are or how they might change, become set and enduring for all time. This certainty contributes to the creation and assertion of a stable and ordered world, a world that reflects—at least theoretically—its cosmic counterpart.

DRAWING CLEAR LINES OF DISTINCTION: FERMENTATION, MIXTURES AND VESSELS

In addition to the creation of lists, the Hadith condemn the conversion of any substance into an intoxicant, and advocate strict separations between objects so as to maintain order, balance, and distinction between the natural, human, and divine realms. For example, many Hadith on wine stress the avoidance of mixing two or more fruits together for fear that such an unsavory combination will produce an intoxicant. They also point out that steeping a specific type of juice in a certain kind of container will produce a potent and dangerous drink.

The need to separate like items from the unlike, the clean from the unclean, or the good from the evil through such practices as the observation of dietary laws, sexual taboos, purity rituals, or food preparation is a common feature of many traditions, including Judaism and Zoroastrianism.[24] However, while issues of purity generally revolve around the preservation of categorical integrity in both of these traditions,[25] the Hadith, which equate purity with stability and right intent, condemn the mixing of two or more substances in order to avoid their potential *conversion* into an intoxicating third. In addition, the Hadith prohibit the use of any vessel that may facilitate such a transformation of substances and the consumption of any substance that may have undergone the process of fermentation. Clearly, this concern over the alteration of substances has little to do with "matter out of place,"[26] but with a suspicion of the process of transformation itself and its resulting products, which may alter one's mind or one's status in the community of believers.

As stated above, separating and ordering earthly items (or preventing their transformations) through a strict, formulaic language reflects a strong desire to maintain the fundamental boundaries between God and man. The lines that are drawn between objects in the earthly realm are vital because they reflect the divisions between belief and unbelief, a community of true believers and other religious groups, and the more abstract and profound separations between what is true and false, or human and godly. By maintaining proper separations between items of the everyday, individuals are confirming their own beliefs, and the community of believers is, in effect, strengthening, solidifying, and legitimating its own position in relation to other religious communities. In addition, these believers are fortifying their connection with—in effect by asserting their separation from—the divine.

Fermentations

One of the primary concerns in the Hadith is to prevent the intentional or unintentional conversion of any type of fruit or liquid into an intoxicant. Anything that intoxicates is flatly prohibited in simple analogic fashion:

> Al-Harith b. Miskin: Ibn al-Qasim: Malik: Nafi': Ibn 'Umar said: Every intoxicant (*muskir*) is wine (*khamr*) and every intoxicant is prohibited.[27]

If every intoxicant is wine, and wine is forbidden, then all intoxicants must be condemned as well. In addition to anything that clearly falls under the heading of an "intoxicant," substances that undergo radical changes, whether they be caused by mixing, aging, or improper storage, are also rendered dangerous. Unable to be pinned down or categorized as a result of their conversion, these ambiguous, fermented substances threaten the natural order of the world, for they become points for potential chaos or disturbance which in turn threaten individual convictions, communal relations, and the often precarious relationship between the human and the divine.

This preoccupation with the qualitative change that takes place within a single substance is articulated in several traditions that further refine the definition of "intoxicant":

> Suwayd: 'Abdallah: Hisham b. 'A'dh al-Asadi said: I asked Ibrahim about juice (*al-'asir*). He said, "Drink it before it ferments and undergoes an alteration."[28]

> Suwayd: 'Abdallah: Shu'ba: Qatada: Sa'id b. al-Musayyab: "As for what is called wine (*khamr*), it is what is left after its cleanness is gone and all that remains is muddiness." He angrily admonished anything that is steeped until it achieved that kind of darkness.[29]

Just as substances that convert into wine or some other questionable liquid are forbidden, so, too, is the wine that converts one-step further into a third element in some Hadith proclamations:

> Yahya b. Yahya: 'Abd al-Rahman b. Mahdi: Zuhayr b. Harb: 'Abd al-Rahman: Sufyan: al-Suddi: Yahya b. 'Abbad: Anas: The Prophet was asked about the wine that takes the form of vinegar. He said, "No."[30]

Somewhat surprisingly, Shi'ite traditions take the opposite stand on this type of vinegar, and allow its consumption.[31] As a useful point in contrast, there is some discussion in the Mishnah and in the Babylonian Talmud about the transformation of wine into vinegar. However, unlike the Sunni and Shi'ite examples, the general interest is not in the *process* of conversion per se, but in defining the conditions under which the ingestion of vinegar is permissible. For example, some passages debate the buying and selling of a wine that converts to vinegar in the middle of the monetary transaction.[32] Others prohibit the use of a vinegar made out of Gentile wine,[33] and a third group focuses on the mixing of prohibited and permitted wines and vinegars, and under what conditions the combination of the two can be consumed or not.[34]

While the majority of Sunni Hadith do not advocate the consumption of any alcoholic drink, a few passages do allow beverages that may be on the cusp of fermentation to be drunk after they are diluted.[35] The concern in these passages is not to allow intoxicants to be drunk after they are watered-down, but rather to deal with a situation where one does not *know* whether or not something has fermented. The Prophet, for example, had to dilute the fermented fruit-drink (*nabidh*)[36] at Zamzam[37] three times before he was finally able to consume it.[38] However, it must be emphasized that the Sunni Hadith are unified in their blanket condemnation of the consumption of any *known* intoxicant and make many preemptive moves to insure that no one imbibes at unawares.[39]

Unlike the Sunni Hadith, the Shi'ite traditions deem that "not even water can make the unlawful lawful,"[40] suggesting a greater fear of substances that undergo some kind of intoxicating alteration. Any drink that exceeds its "proper bounds and intoxicates" is prohibited,[41] and if one knowingly or unknowingly consumes such a beverage, one is violating the divine sanction. This intense desire to free the world of all ambiguity is not surprising in a belief system that holds the natural realm on the constant brink of chaos; no wonder such strong measures were taken in these Shi'ite traditions to maintain stability.

Both the Sunni and Shi'ite prohibitions against any intoxicating drink oppose the positions on wine taken in related traditions, most notably Rabbinic Judaism, which offers a few useful points for comparison in addition to the ones mentioned above. The Babylonian Talmud, for example, does not advocate drunkenness, but does encourage the consumption of certain types of wine (in a prescribed amount) in certain contexts. As noted above, wine prepared by Gentiles was forbidden, for it may have been consecrated for idol worship (*yein nesekh*), or, even if prepared for ordinary usage, may have held the suspicion that it was consecrated for idols.[42] Wine produced by Jews, however, is permissible, as long as it was properly diluted.

The Talmud frowns upon the quaffing of "strong" wine since its consumption could lead to intoxication, which is condemned in certain situations. Therefore, unlike the majority of Hadith, this Rabbinic work advocates the cutting of wine with water so as to reduce its potentially dangerous effects.[43] Priests should not become drunk lest the Temple be rebuilt and they are called upon for services;[44] legal decisions should not be made by judges who are inebriated;[45] and prayer under the influence of wine is regarded as a proper one, but prayer in a state of intoxication is considered an abomination.[46] In spite of these stipulations, however, the Talmud still praises the use of wine in religious ceremonies, and considers that wine taken in moderation induces the appetite, is beneficial to the health (especially to the intestines), and in general, sustains and makes glad.[47] While the Talmud calls for moderation, but then must carefully examine and regulate the rather generous space between temperance and (over)indulgence, the Hadith have no tolerance for such gray areas, and simply condemn anything that intoxicates or may potentially intoxicate.

Mixtures

Given their views on fermentation, the Hadith lay down strict rules to prevent the deliberate or inadvertent creation of any type of intoxicant. The need to keep various fruits separate so that their union will not produce a dangerous intoxicant is illustrated by several groups of Hadith that determine which fruits can and cannot be mixed:[48]

> Yazid b. 'Abdallah al-Yamani: 'Ikrima b. 'Ammar: Abu Kathir: Abu Hurayra: The Prophet said: "Do not steep dried dates (*tamr*) and unripe dates (*busr*) together. Steep each one by itself."[49]

> Qutayba b. Sa'id: Waki': Isma'il b. Muslim: Abu 'l-Mutawakkil al-Naji: Abu Sa'id al-Khudri: The Prophet said, "Whoever among you drinks *nabidh* shall drink raisins alone (*zabib*), dried dates alone (*tamr*), or unripe dates (*busr*) alone."[50]

> Isma'il b. Mas'ud: Khalid (b. al-Harith): Hisham: Yahya: 'Abdallah b. Abi Qatada: Qatada: The Prophet said, "Do not make *nabidh* from ripening dates (*zahw*)[51] and fresh dates (*rutab*) [mixed] together, or from unripe dates (*busr*) and raisins (*zabib*) [mixed] together. Steep each one separately."[52]

Clearly, these examples demonstrate that *nabidh* (even the uninebriating kind) may be made from a single fruit but not from the mixing of two or more fruits together. Not only do the Hadith argue for the need to steep certain fruits separately in order to avoid the production of intoxicating mixtures (or even the very mingling of their juices), they also lay out the whole spectrum of possible combinations of fruits that must also be forbidden.[53] Although the majority of these traditions do not explicitly state why mixing two fruits together is problematic, a minority do provide a possible logic that underlies all: The mixing of two items produces wine (*khamr*), which is forbidden.[54]

It is important to note that a handful of traditions do exist that advocate the consumption of mixtures. Curiously enough, the authority of these rather lenient traditions are traced back to women. Note the role of the Prophet's wife, 'A'isha, in the following example:

> Musaddad: 'Abdallah b. Dawud: Mis'ar: Musa b. 'Abdallah: a woman from the Banu Asad: 'A'isha: The Prophet of God had raisins (*zabib*) steeped for him, and had dates (*tamr*) infused in [the drink], and had dried dates steeped (*tamr*), and raisins (*zabib*) infused in [the drink].[55]

This tradition and others like it that rest their authority on 'A'isha, however, are countered by others that use the Prophet's wife to refute the drinking of any type of mixture, whether it intoxicates or not:

> Abu Dawud: Harb b. Shadad: Yahya b. Abi Kathir: Abu Salama: 'A'isha: "The Prophet forbade the mixing of two things."[56]

While these traditions are thorough in their efforts to show what must be kept separate (except in the cases above), they never provide a clear reason why these particular mixtures should be avoided. Furthermore, the Hadith offer no clue why different types of dates and raisins are analyzed in rigorous detail while other potentially intoxicating mixtures are ignored. Is it possible to mix raisins with dried apples, or blackberries with peaches? The repetition of the prohibition of mixing specific types of fruits (to the exclusion of all others) suggests that once the formula is fixed, the content may vary as long as it conforms to these fundamental patterns exemplified by dates and raisins.

This condemnation of mixtures suggests that fruits (and other items as well) must be kept separate and intact on the horizontal (human) plane so that more profound or abstract entities are kept separate on the vertical (divine). By separating one fruit from another, whether it be dates, raisins, apples, or blackberries, believing individuals can avoid the production of a dangerous drink. Analogously, by applying the general rule of separations to other items and relationships in the world, believers can avoid instigating more profound chaos when fundamental boundaries are disturbed, and their status in relation to the divine is put into jeopardy.

Vessels

The need to maintain fundamental boundaries in the natural world is also apparent in the Hadith's prohibition of steeping dates or raisins, or the mixing of both, in certain types of vessels. The number of Hadith devoted to this subject is vast in comparison with other topics on wine and intoxication, which attests to the profound interest in issues of separation and transformation. Only a few representative examples need to be dealt with to illustrate the norm.

In general, the Hadith identify four types of containers in which different kinds of dates and/or raisins are prohibited from being steeped: gourds (*dubba'*), green jars (*hantam*), hollowed-out stumps (*naqir*), and vessels smeared with pitch (*muzaffat*). Some of these traditions cite all four receptacles in their statement of the prohibition;[57] more often than not, however, one,[58] two,[59] or three[60] vessels are mentioned, and then presented in every possible combination. General statements of the prohibition against a *nabidh* that intoxicates,[61] or the prohibition against the mixing of two kinds of fruits follow these proscriptions. The following tradition adds the condemnation of mixing two kinds of fruits to the list of prohibited vessels:

> Wasil b. 'Abd al-'Ali: Ibn Fudayl: Habib b. Abi 'Amr: Sa'id b. Jubayr: Ibn 'Abbas: The Prophet of God prohibited gourds, green jars, vessels smeared with pitch, and hollowed-out stumps, and the mixing of dried dates and ripening dates.[62]

Oftentimes skins tied at the mouth,[63] or vessels made of stone[64] are recommended as types of receptacles that may be used to make *nabidh*, although a handful of traditions do prohibit the use of skins along with the lists of containers mentioned previously.[65] In addition, some traditions state that the prohibited vessels noted above are permitted if no other type of container is available, as long as one does not consume an intoxicant.[66] For example, 'Abd al-Razzaq's collection contains two traditions that permit the use of green jars, as long as one does not drink the contents if they inebriate.[67] As with mixtures, the authority of these relatively lenient traditions rests on two females: the Prophet's wife, 'A'isha, and Umm Abi 'Ubayda. Aside from the variation in detail, however, all of these examples that permit or prohibit certain types containers attempt to limit the conditions through which an intoxicant could be created and consumed.

As in the case of mixtures, the Hadith provide no clear reason as to why these particular vessels were prohibited. Perhaps these vessels were forbidden because they contained pores, which allowed for unwanted impurities to seep in. Porous containers are strongly associated with impurities in both the Zoroastrian and Jewish legal traditions. For example, Zoroastrian theology sets up metals in a hierarchy according to their porosity; the more porous a material, the more susceptible it is to impurities. Gold is the most resistant, then silver, copper, tin, brass, lead, stone, turquoise, amber, earth, wood, and finally clay.[68]

In Talmudic traditions, the emphasis is also on the avoidance of porous vessels for storing wine. In these cases, the concern is for whether or not the vessel in question previously contained wine consecrated to idols. If wine made by Jews is placed into a porous container that once held Gentile wine consecrated to idols, then the Gentile wine locked inside the pores would seep back into the Jewish wine, thus contaminating the whole batch.[69] In both the legal traditions of Zoroastrianism and Talmudic Judaism, the organizing principle for determining whether or not a vessel should be used is its susceptibility to the transmission of impurities and, to a certain degree, the history of the container.

The Hadith, on the other hand, are not concerned with potential contamination by Gentiles or otherwise, but with a vessel's potential for converting a substance into an intoxicant. When certain fruit juices are stored for long periods of time in closed vessels such as clay jars, stumps, gourds, or pitch-smeared containers, they can transform into inebriating beverages. Skins, on the other hand, with their open mouths and porous coatings, allow for ventilation. Fruit juices are less likely to ferment in such an airy environment. As a result of their particular concerns, the Hadith advocate the use of open containers while the Talmud shuns them when they demonstrate a potential for the transference of contamination.[70]

Like the prohibition of mixing dates and raisins, or ripening dates and dried dates together, the stress in the Hadith is not on the individual containers that are prohibited, but rather on the general rule that calls for the proper maintenance of a substance's internal stability. If fruit juices are allowed to ferment, and one drinks them and becomes drunk, the boundaries between right and wrong become confused. Just as the internal stability of grapes and dates become corrupted through the process of fermentation, so, too, does that of the believing mind when mixed with wine:

> Musaddad: Yahya: Abu Hayyan: 'Amir: Ibn 'Umar: 'Umar stood up on the pulpit and said, "Now the prohibition of wine (*khamr*) has been revealed and this drink is prepared from these five things: grapes, dates, honey, wheat, or barley. *Khamr* is what disturbs (*khamara*) the mind."[71]

And, given that the essential boundaries on the vertical/divine plane are intricately tied to those on the horizontal/human, a rupture on one plane will surely wreak havoc on the other.

In the cases of mixtures, vessels, and conversions, the formulaic language used demonstrates, through a limited set of items and the combinations of those items, how the world is ordered, and how it must adhere to fixed sets of boundaries and separations. By limiting the opportunities for fruits to ferment, these traditions set up fundamental distinctions in the world to which all must adhere. Just as dates must be kept separate from raisins, or *nabidh* from green jars, so, too, must the true believer remain separate from fermented beverages, and those who advocate their consumption. Likewise, the prohibition itself serves to distinguish the community of believers from other, like-minded monotheistic communities, and ultimately, the need for and adherence to the prohibition segregates the human from the divine. Ambiguities do not represent, reflect, or properly articulate this cosmic order in any way, and therefore cannot be tolerated on the earthly plane.

The general rule stresses how everything in the world must be kept in its proper place and informs the Hadith's treatment of mixtures, vessels, and conversions. Through their formulaic language, these traditions demonstrate the ways in which the world was, is, and should be ordered, understood, and discussed. Ironically, given that *any* substance related to drinks and drinking has the potential to be plugged into the system, the fixed and static divine rule that stresses the maintenance of boundaries and order will always remain flexible enough—ironically *ambiguous* enough—to accommodate a variety of changing situations and conditions in the world.

REPETITION, PARALLEL CONSTRUCTION, AND THE CREATION OF SYMMETRY

The Hadith not only employ analytic discourse to create lists or formulaic constructions aimed at separating one item from another, but they also set up repetitive clauses or parallel statements that further structure and divide the natural world so that it conforms to the divine. In general, these two types of analytic discourse generate the means through which authoritative statements from the past can be carried over into the future so that new ideas, situations, or substances can be assimilated to the fixed parameters of the formula itself. By repeatedly articulating the punishment for transgressing the prohibition or by countering its effects with the proper corrective measures, the Hadith are able to contain the damage or imbalance caused by the misdeed. Through these established modes of speech, the Hadith maintain the order of the world and properly interpret and make manifest divine truth through the language of the world.

Repetitions

The Hadith collection of Ibn Maja provides an example of a repetitive clause:

> 'Abd al-Rahman b. Ibrahim al-Dimashqi: Walid b. Muslim: al-Awza'i: Rabi' b. Yazid: Ibn al-Daylami: 'Abdallah b. 'Amr: The Prophet said, "Whoever drinks wine and gets drunk, prayer will not be received from him for forty days. If he dies, he will go to hell. [1] If he repents, and God forgives him, but he drinks again and gets drunk, prayer will not be received from him for forty days. If he dies, he will go to hell. [2] If he repents, and God forgives him, but he drinks again and gets drunk, prayer will not be received from him for forty days. If he dies, he will go to hell. [3] If he repents, and God forgives him, but he does it again, it is *incumbent upon God* to make him drink *radaghat al-khabal* on the Day of Judgment." They said, "Oh, Prophet, what is *that*?" He said, "Sweat from the inhabitants of Hell!"[72]

As discussed in chapter one, the Qur'anic passages on prayer and intoxication suggest that anyone who has become drunk may return to prayer when "you are sure of what you are saying."[73] However, the question becomes when is one sober enough to resume worshipping the divine? What happens if one thinks he is sure of what he is saying, but then becomes confused once again in the midst of a recitation? In order to omit any possibility for error, and protect the realm of the divine from a human faux pas, the Hadith ensure that God ignores a drunken prayer for forty days.

What is the significance of forty days, other than the fact that it marks off a lengthy unit of time? For reasons not quite clear, the number forty appears with great frequency in the three Abrahamic traditions. For example, rains pummeled Noah and his friends for forty days and nights in Genesis.[74] In the Synoptic Gospels, Jesus was tempted by the devil for forty days in the wilderness.[75] Muhammad was forty years of age when he received the first revelation from God. In medieval Christian penitential documents, forty-day cycles of punishment are applied with great frequency to a variety of infringements. One sixth-century document doles out the following punishment for those clergymen who become intoxicated:

1. Priests who are about to minister in the temple of God, who through greediness drink wine or strong drink negligently, not ignorantly, shall do penance for four days but if they do so out of contempt of those who censure them forty days.
2. Those who become drunk from ignorance, fifteen days, from negligence, forty days, from contempt, three forty-day periods.[76]

In addition to chastising the drunk, the forty-day sentence—and often its cyclical application—is also applied to such crimes as kissing a virgin in secret,[77] losing a piece of the Eucharistic host (especially if a mouse were to consume it),[78] sinning with oneself,[79] consuming carrion,[80] stealing food,[81] and getting drunk and then vomiting the host,[82] to mention a few examples.

The Islamic tradition also doles out punishments in units of forty. The Shi'ites, for example, draw an argument from natural science to explain why God would not receive prayer for forty days from one who is drunk:

> Muhammad b. Yahya: Ahmad b. Muhammad b. 'Isa: Ibn Abi Nasr: al-Husayn b. Khalid: Abu 'l-Hasan said to the Prophet: [Is it true that] if one drinks wine, his prayer will not be received for forty days? [The Prophet] said: They speak the truth. . . . When God created man, he began with a drop of sperm that remained forty days, then transformed it into a clot of blood for forty days, then made it into an embryo for

> forty days. If someone drinks wine, his state of confusion will remain forty days, in accordance with the transformation of his nature. If one drinks during some of his meals, he remains in this confused state for forty days.[83]

This passage illustrates the appeal to regularity that is highly characteristic of analytic discourse. The forty days that inform the stages of procreation under natural law parallels the divine punishment one receives for drinking wine. Man is not only transformed from a drop of sperm to an embryo in a series of forty days, but so, too, will his drunken confusion remain for forty days, and prayer will not be received for forty days. By using forty as the divine ruler that partitions the world, uniformity is achieved on three levels: natural, human, and divine.

Likewise, through the series of repetitive clauses, Ibn Maja's tradition on drunkenness and prayer puts forth strict measures so that if someone becomes inebriated and then tries to pray, the proper action or punishment will be activated, and order will be restored. In this particular case, a cycle of forty days is set as the minimal amount of time it takes to make sure that the appropriate punishment has been given, and that one is sober enough to put forth a proper prayer. If one continues to press the boundaries of acceptable behavior, it will be incumbent upon God to strike the final blow.

Note that there is no justification as to why God will not accept the prayer; what seems to be the primary focus is the modus operandi for dealing with one who transgresses the boundaries of acceptable behavior, not just once, but three or four times. This established convention for determining the fate of drunken worshippers leaves no room for protest, compromise, or negotiation on the part of the divine OR human. It is "incumbent upon God" to bestow the final punishment on the Last Day.

By setting up a fixed system for regulating human error, the Hadith free the world from ambiguity of any kind. Every human is dealt with on an equal basis, and every transgression is denounced and punished according to set, universal rules. In such a system, harmony, stability, and predictability are protected by the overall formulaic structure, which serves to keep the human realm in line with the divine.

With its cycles of transgression, punishment, repentance, and limited forgiveness, Ibn Maja's text (*matn*) varies little throughout the Sunni collections of Hadith. For example, similar texts with unrelated chains of transmission (*asanid)* appear in the collections of al-Tirmidhi, al-Tayalisi,[84] and Abu Dawud,[85] and parallel texts with related *asanid* (to Ibn Maja's example) in al-Nasa'i[86] and Ibn Hanbal.[87] In each of these examples, the sequential and repetitive pattern described above appears almost verbatim. Variation exists only in terms of the vocabulary used to describe the type of drink that is to be consumed by the condemned ones in Hell. In each case, however, the external form remains the same.[88]

Other traditions leave off the repetitions and provide only one forty-day punishment for the drinking of wine. In Ibn Hanbal's collection, the Prophet states that not one of his people shall drink wine, for God will not receive prayer from him for forty days.[89] Through the omission of God's final blow, the punishment is eased, which ultimately points to a more lenient view of the sin itself. Other Hadith, however, take the exact opposite tact by trimming down the fourfold cycle. In these pronouncements people have only one chance to remain sober before God is obliged to make them drink pus from the inhabitants of hell (*tinat al-khabal*).[90] There is no second, or even third forty-day reprieve before one is forced to consume a liquid that is truly vile. Within the fixed frame of the forty-day punishment, and through the subtle play in detail, the Hadith debate how grave a sin wine-consumption is, and what is the best punishment for such a transgression.

The ability to debate such issues—or to present a viewpoint—within the context of a set formula is illustrated by many Shi'ite Hadith that conform to the formulaic pattern described above. While these Shi'ite Hadith adhere to the same forty-day repetitions, they are often peppered with elaborate explanations as to *why* wine cannot be associated with prayer, explicit descriptions of the violent behaviors that intoxication can trigger,[91] or with scintillating details of the horrific punishments bestowed upon the wine-drinker:

> 'Ali b. Ibrahim: his father: Ibn Abi 'Amir: Mahran b. Muhammad: some man: Sa'd al-Askaf: Abu Ja'far said, "Whoever drinks an intoxicant (*muskir*), his prayer will not be received for forty days. If he does it again, God will serve him *tinat al-khabal*." I said, "What is *that*?" He said, "Liquid from the pudendum of fornicators."[92]

Equally grim examples describe how wine-drinkers, their faces blackened, tongues hanging out, and saliva flowing down their backs appear on Judgment Day. These unfortunate souls will be forced to drink *tinat al-khabal* as well as their Sunni counterparts; however, this ubiquitous drink is defined not as the matter that seeps from those who dwell in hell, but as the pus that bleeds from fornicators, or the ooze that flows from a prostitute's pudendum.[93] In these and other Shi'ite examples, the mechanistic repetitions that highlight man's repentance and God's forgiveness exist, but the punishments are strongly emphasized by the elaborate descriptions and colorful detail, which reflect a deeper interest in individual transgressions, as well as a more general mistrust in wine as a substance.

These examples display a world view quite different from what appears in the Sunni traditions. In general, the Shi'ite world is less stable and predictable. Although the underlying modus operandi is similar to that envisioned by the Sunnis, the Shi'ites additionally believe that intoxication not only can, but will, set off a chain of violent actions that could disrupt the worldly and cosmic orders. As shown above, the punishment for consuming this beverage in the Shi'ite world is far more grisly and morbid than what the Sunnis had ever imagined, and therefore stands as a much stronger deterrent for anyone contemplating such a potentially destructive act as drinking wine.

Because the world is hovering on the brink of chaos, the Shi'ites must become more vigilent in their efforts to control those who consume intoxicating beverages. Wine as a substance poses a greater threat as well. For example, in the Shi'ite world view, one small drop of wine on one's clothes can incite unspeakable evils, as demonstrated in the following passage:

> Muhammad b. Yahya: some of our companions: Abu Jamila al-Basri said: I was with Yunus in Baghdad. I was walking with him in the market when a companion opened a bubbly beverage made from barley (*fuqqa'*). It foamed up, spilling over onto the clothes of Yunus. I saw he was distressed about the situation, [especially] around the time when the sun went down. I said to him [at that time], "Are you going to pray, O Abu Muhammad?" He said, "I don't want to pray until I go home, so I can clean this wine (*khamr*) off my clothes."[94]

Clearly, the Shi'ite Hadith suggest that wine is capable of poisoning and contaminating anything it touches. As this and other passages demonstrate, however, wine is only problematic for those who call themselves "believers." For those who stand outside the circle of faith, contact with such a potent beverage will cause no harm:

> Muhammad b. Yahya: Muhammad b. Musa: al-Hasan b. al-Mubarak: Zakariya b. Adam said: I asked Abu 'l-Hasan about a drop of wine (*khamr*) or intoxicating *nabidh* that falls into a pot holding a large amount of meat and broth. He said, "Pour out the broth and give it to the Jews and Christians, or to the dogs, and clean the meat." I asked: What if blood drops into it? He said, "The fire will eat the blood, God willing." I asked: What if wine (*khamr*) or *nabidh* drops into the dough, or what about blood? He said, "It is rotten!" I asked: Should [the dough] be sold to Jews and Christians, and [the situation] explained to them if they deem the drinking of it [blood or wine or *nabidh*] permissible? He said, "Yes." I said: What about *fuqqa'*? Is it dealt with in the same way if it falls into anything? He said it would be reprehensible for me to eat my food if a drop fell on any of it.[95]

Still preoccupied with issues of wine and prayer, and the selling of that which is prohibited, the Shi'ite traditions, unlike the Sunni, depict close encounters with chaotic forces and evil powers. Given their precarious political situation, tragic history, and minority status, true believers must adopt tighter controls to keep themselves separate from other religious communities and to protect the world at-large from impending danger and doom. While the Sunni traditions simply fill in the gaps and seal off the cracks that allow for questionable powers or ambiguous conditions that threaten this world by subjecting every behavior, object, and thought to the rigors of a divine logic and order, the Shi'ite Hadith embrace a more stringent regime with the hope of preventing the world from further succumbing to the forces of disorder. This concern is not surprising among believers whose history and vitality depends upon frequent and repeated divine interventions, and whose eschatological hopes make them triumph over all others in the end.[96]

This generalization does not suggest that all Sunni Hadith on wine present a completely generic, mechanized view of the world, or that all Shi'ite Hadith are concerned with arming themselves for the cosmic battle against chaos. Certainly many Sunni traditions offer moderately detailed explanations as to why wine and prayer should not be mixed,[97] and many Shi'ite traditions retain the simple forty day punishment formula without the shocking detail.[98] As a rule, however, both Sunni and Shi'ite traditions prohibit wine with prayer, but confer the condemnation through varied rhetorical means. These rhetorical variations in which the prohibition is presented point to some marked differences in religious orientation. While the Sunnis are concerned with uncovering and maintaining the divine order as it is reflected in the natural realm, the Shi'ites are preoccupied with ensuring that order can be restored once the boundaries are (inevitably) disturbed. It must be noted, however, that the many differences between the Sunni and Shi'ite traditions are not of *kind*, but of *degree*, as suggested by the adherence to and recognition of the same general sets of divine conclusions.

The fourfold formula makes another appearance in some descriptions of how wine-drinkers should be punished in the Islamic community. Not surprisingly, the ways in which serial drinkers are punished by God have an exact counterpart on Earth in terms of how they are to be treated by human authorities. Because uniformity must be upheld in both divine and human realms, it is not unusual to see the repetition of action and punishment in debates over how a wine-drinker must be dealt with on Earth:

> Ishaq b. Ibrahim: Shababa: Ibn Abi Dhi'b: al-Harith b. 'Abd al-Rahman: Abu Salama: Abu Hurayra: The Prophet of God said, "If he is drunk,

> whip him. If he becomes drunk again, whip him." Then he said, "On the fourth time, strike his neck."[99]

> 'Asim b. 'Ali: Ibn Abi Dhi'b: al-Harith b. 'Abd al-Rahman: Abu Salama: Abu Hurayra: The Prophet said, "If he is intoxicated, flog him. Then if he becomes intoxicated, whip him. If he becomes intoxicated again, whip him. Then, if he becomes intoxicated, strike him in the neck."[100]

Not surprisingly, the majority of Shi'ite Hadith has the wine-drinker killed on the *third*, rather than the *fourth*, transgression of the prohibition. This slight variation reflects less tolerance for this type of behavior:

> Al-Nasr: Hisham: Sulayman b. Khalid: Abu 'Abdallah: The Prophet said, "Whoever drinks wine (*khamr*), strike him. If he continues to drink, strike him. If he continues a third time, kill him."[101]

Both the Sunnis and Shi'ites debate how many times wine-drinkers should be whipped or struck (before they are killed). Some traditions advocate forty lashes for taking even a small sip of wine, others eighty.[102] Some traditions suggest that Jews and Christians may also be lashed the same number of times if they are found drinking outside of their home;[103] others state that these "peoples of the Book" should be beaten even if it is discovered that they are consuming wine in the home.[104] These examples provide valuable evidence concerning the extent to which Muslims allowed (or hoped to allow) the Jews and Christians under their care to observe the rituals of their respective traditions.

As in the case of wine with prayer, these formulaic repetitions emphasize the proper procedures through which punishments are dispensed. The Hadith rigidly limit the number of transgressions; once the limit is exceeded, the appropriate punishment for that particular action is explicitly spelled out. Rather than having to decide (or worse, guess) what should be the correct punishment, which may allow the infraction to spread and infect other areas of the cosmos, one can simply plug the sin into an ordered system that automatically doles out the appropriate punishment. The natural order and balance of the world can be justly and effectively restored time and time again, no matter what the transgression and no matter what idiosyncratic conditions might accompany it.

This fourfold system resurfaces again and again throughout the Hadith on wine and demonstrates the desire for a fixed and ordered world. Just as one can drink and repent three times before being punished by God on the fourth, and flogged three times before being killed on the last, so, too, can one drink a skinful of raisins that have been soaked for three days before it must be poured out on the fourth:

> Mukhalid b. Khalid: Abu Mu'awiya 'l-'Amash: Abu 'Umar Yahya al-Bahrani: Ibn 'Abbas said: Raisins were steeped for the Prophet, and he drank [the liquid] during that day, the next day, and the day after. Then he commanded that it be given to the servants to drink, or else be poured out.[105]

In each of these cases, the form provides a way to structure and regulate proper behavior. The three repetitions serve as a convenient way to remind people of what inevitably comes down on the fourth in either the natural, human, or divine realms. Subjecting all behaviors to such a cycle creates a universal conformity, and leaves little room for ambiguity or anything else that might disturb the natural order of things, which itself reflects, as well as properly articulates, divine truth. These formulae create a legal system in the human realm that is, in theory, self-sufficient, for it operates according to the projected notion of divine law.

Conditional Formulations

The Hadith also employ conditional formulations to declare how drinking wine in this world precludes consumption in the next. Rather than establishing order through repetitive cycles, these conditional formulations promise order through an ineluctable chain of causes and effects. In the Sunni Hadith, the lush descriptions of a heavenly Paradise in which wine is served under shady trees by youths with never-ending bloom so prevalent in the Qur'an have been replaced by stark legal proclamations. These simple declarations, which essentially relegate Paradise to the status of "reward" (as opposed to idyllic and ideal place) appear in the following form:

> 'Ali b. Muhammad: 'Abdallah b. Numayr: 'Ubaydallah b. 'Umar: Nafi': Ibn 'Umar: The Prophet said, "Whoever drinks wine (*khamr*) in this world will not drink it in the next."[106]

> Abu Zakariya Yahya b. Durust al-Basri: Hammad b. Zayd: Ayyub: Nafi': Ibn 'Umar: The Prophet said, "Every intoxicant (*muskir*) is *khamr*, and every intoxicant is forbidden. Whoever drinks wine in this world, then dies while he is addicted to it, shall not drink it in the next."[107]

> Yahya: Malik: Nafi': Ibn 'Umar: The Prophet said, "Whoever drinks wine in this world, and does not repent, will be prohibited from it in the next, and will not be served it."[108]

> Suwayd: 'Abdallah: Hammad b. Zayd: Ayyub: Nafi': Ibn 'Umar: The Prophet said, "Whoever drinks wine (*khamr*) in this world, then dies while he is addicted to it and does not repent, will not drink it in the hereafter."[109]

Each of these examples employs a conditional formulation to give slightly different takes on the single theme that if one drinks wine in this world, he shall not drink it in the next. The first example is the harshest; its simple statement of the punishment leaves no room for second chances. It remains unclear, however, whether or not one is sent to Hell for drinking wine (and therefore will not get to sip the heavenly drink), or to Paradise, where one will be denied the luxury of wine-consumption but will still get to wallow in the other pleasures available. If the latter is the case—and clearly the rest of the examples point in this direction—then Paradise is no longer the projected ideal that the Qur'an evokes so frequently, but rather an extension of the earth that is still susceptible to ethical perversion. This pessimistic view of the afterlife suggests that there is no ideal, but only an endless projection of the real where order must be preserved at all costs.

The second and third examples are more lenient than the first, despite its ambiguous position on the consumption of wine in the afterlife. In the second, only the repeated use (and abuse) of wine will impede one from drinking in the hereafter. In the third, repentance for past indulgences will allow one to consume freely after death. The fourth and final example is the most lax of all: One is prevented from indulging in the paradisical wine only if one dies while addicted to it and is without repentance.[110] In other words, one sip now will not destroy the chances of quenching one's thirst in the afterlife, as long as one is contrite before death.

In each of these examples, the conditional formulation serves to offset the effects caused by human indiscretion. The violations caused by drinking wine in this world are automatically balanced by a counter punishment in the next. The formula, which negates earthly misdemeanors through an appeal to heavenly punishments by simply inverting the wrongful action, maintains balance in the human realm by establishing a mechanism through which order is continuously reinstated. No matter what transgressions and punishments are plugged into the system, the formula allows for a damaged world to correct itself:

> Yazid b. Harun: al-Jurayri: Maymun b. Ustadh: al-Sadafi: 'Abdallah b. 'Amr: The Prophet said, "Whoever of my people dies while he is drinking wine (*khamr*), God prohibits him from drinking it in heaven. Whoever dies when he is adorned with gold, God will prohibit him from wearing it in heaven."[111]

While the substance may vary and change, the underlying order, as well as the logic and language used to articulate that order, remains the same.

Shi'ite traditions try to offset earthly abominations by adding detailed descriptions of horrendous tortures and punishments that await drinkers of wine in the next world to the underlying logical structure. Not unexpectedly, the Shi'ite Hadith allow *no* wine-drinkers entry into Paradise. Those who sip or guzzle intoxicants are expected to die with an extraordinary thirst, and enter Hell with this same unquenchable desire for cool and soothing liquids,[112] or once dead be forced to drink continuously from the tortuous, hot waters of Hell.[113] In the Shi'ite vision of the world, if someone dies with even a drop of this detestable substance lodged in his belly, he will call "forth from his grave in confusion; jawbone cracking, saliva flowing," and burst into loud laments.[114] Shi'ites also promise that the wine-drinker will stand disgraced before God, "face split in half, tongue hanging out, crying out with thirst."[115] Again, these Shi'ite traditions find wine to be much more of a threat to the stability of the world than do the Sunnis. Its drinking requires a much more stringent—and a more individually tailored—punishment to offset the powerful disturbances this substance causes in the world. Those who sample from the vine are equated with unbelievers, and God will punish them as such.

In general, both the Sunni and Shi'ite Hadith that put forth these punishments stress the need to maintain balance and order on Earth through a highly structured language aimed at bestowing earthly and other-worldly punishments on those who drink wine. By making the hereafter a place for punishments, rather than a source for pleasure, these Hadith differ radically from those Qur'anic passages that project an ideal, stable, and idyllic drinking scene for those who have shunned temptation and embraced the faith.

In fact, the Hadith rarely mention wine and its associations with these blissful, paradisical moments, which is peculiar given that unrestricted consumption could stand as an incentive for those who have yet to face Final Judgment. Even the link between drunkenness and the Last Day is ignored in most the traditions. Although one tradition does describe the apocalypse as a moment when general ignorance will prevail, knowledge will decrease, illicit sexual intercourse will increase, and alcoholic beverages will be drunk, the End Time appears as more of a generic backdrop used to highlight or contextualize a list of items that are prohibited, rather than an imminent force that will occur as a result of God's wrath upon his wayward people.[116]

The Hadith do not only employ conditional formulations to distribute punishments, but also to measure out the amount of wine that is prohibited:

> Qutayba: Isma'il (Ibn Ja'far): Dawud b. Bakr b. Abi 'l-Furat: Muhammad b. al-Munkadir: Jabir b. 'Abdallah said: The Prophet said, "Whatever intoxicates in a great amount, a small amount is prohibited."[117]

In other words, if a quart of wine intoxicates, then one sip is prohibited. Just because one needs to drink a lot of a particular substance in order to become drunk does not mean that a smaller (less-intoxicating) amount of that same substance can be consumed without worry. In fact, the opposite is true. The specific qualities and attributes of wine or any beverage like it remain the same whether it be a single drop, or an overflowing goblet. This passage suggests that intoxication itself is not the sole target of the prohibition, but any substance that has the *potential* to create such a confused state of mind. Because wine and other alcoholic beverages may potentially "disturb the mind," even the physicality of these substances is called into question, and condemned.

The prohibition against the consumption of any amount of intoxicating liquid—great or small—can be contrasted with Rabbinic Judaism, where wine is permitted to be drunk in a diluted state so as to avoid the effects of inebriation,[118] and distinctions are drawn between how much wine one can consume before falling under the influence of drink, and before becoming thoroughly intoxicated. In general, the Talmudic ratio of wine to water is three parts water to one part wine,[119] and one can drink less than a quarter log of wine and still give a legal decision.[120] If one consumes more than a quarter of a log, he is "under the influence" of alcohol if he can speak in the presence of a king, and completely drunk when he cannot.[121] While the Talmud would suggest that the consumption of a "small" amount of wine will cause no harm (even if a greater amount causes one to become confused), the Hadith take a more radical stance by asserting that any quantity is to be condemned. The Hadith's intolerance for ambiguity is clear in their comprehensive condemnation of the consumption of any measure of liquid with the potential to intoxicate. If the world is to reflect the cosmos, then there simply is no place for marginal—and inherently threatening—substances or actions.

CONSTRUCTING A WORLD THAT IS PERFECT AND PURE

In order to make manifest the set and enduring patterns that govern the natural, human, and divine realms, the Hadith that employ analytic discourse use different types of formulaic language both to flesh out the definition of the prohibition and to set the divine constraints, which can then be applied to ambiguous situations or changing circumstances. The fact that the grammatical structure itself takes on such a vital importance in the Islamic legal tradition is not surprising in a belief system that puts much emphasis on the sacred word,[122] whether it be the insistence upon its divine status, the observance of its proper recitation, or the preservation of its precise calligraphic form. By continuously imposing rigid, formal structures upon miscellaneous or ambiguous substances, the Hadith not only create an earthly realm that reflects the divine will, but also project a divine will that is in fact conferred by the rules of the world. In this way, the prohibition—in all of its structured manifestations—both mirrors and fashions what is divine.

Whether it be through their employment of taxonomies, metonymies, repetitions, or conditional formulations, the Hadith generate laws and draw philosophical conclusions that can then be applied analogously to a number of other situations and things. These laws and conclusions are *theological* in the sense that they strive to reveal and define what is true about the world and the cosmos. In this way, both analytic and prophetic discourses share a common goal, even though the interpretive strategies they employ to reach such a goal vary greatly. While the Qur'an preserves wine's ambiguity by continuously altering and shifting its views toward it in order to evoke that which is divine (along with the proper human response to that divine), the Hadith confer all that is true by negating this beverage (and its intoxicating effects) and containing it, as well as expanding and fleshing out its prohibition in ways that confirm the cosmic and earthly order. These variations in strategy demonstrate radically different modes of defining, understanding, and translating divine truth.

Cosmic truth as revealed and refined through prophetic and analytic discourse (respectively) has few weights or balances to ground it firmly in history, or to tie it with the specific identity of a community of believers. Because human society is a temporal society, it is not enough that the divine be conferred through evocation or analytic discourse alone. The order of the cosmos must also be translated and structured through what is familiar, that is, through the communal, historical, and *human* contexts provided by narrative discourse.

3

Links to a Sacred Past

Narrative Discourse and the Refining of Communal Identity

Given the Qur'an's aphoristic and anecdotal format and the level of abstraction we would expect from legalistic traditions exemplified by many Hadith, these forms of discourse lack the concrete details of setting, temporality and actants that we associate with narrative discourse.[1] The prophetic language of the Qur'an uses a minimal amount of physical or historical evidence to evoke the more profound dimensions of divine truth, and the Hadith's analytic structures employ only those details that contribute to the maintenance of an ordered and structured world. In addition, the assertion that the Hadith are written accounts of the Prophet's "exemplary life" (*sunna*) further reinforces the idea that these traditions are describing ideal conditions or behaviors, rather than standing as accurate reflections of particular historical circumstances.

In general, much of the human detail absent in these other sources is provided by those Hadith that embed normative practices and beliefs in short narratives, which imbue them with historical or communal significance. In short, these Hadith provide a meaningful framework or setting for the presentation of a particular position on—or lesson about—wine. Yet, given this didactic orientation, whoever or whatever may appear in the background has little influence on the final point presented. For example, how is *Abu Hurayra*[2] important in the events surrounding the Prophet's condemnation of fermented drinks?

> Hisham b. 'Ammar: Sadaqa b. Khalid: Zayd b. Waqid: Khalid b. 'Abdallah b. Husayn: Abu Hurayra said: I knew that the Prophet of God had been fasting. So I waited until the end of the fast with a drink (*nabidh*) I had made in a gourd, then brought it to him after it had fermented. He said, "Throw this against the wall! This is the drink of those who do not believe in God and the Last Day."[3]

This passage resembles many of the formulaic traditions discussed in chapter two as it too prohibits the consumption of fermented drinks made in gourds. Given that other Hadith make the same point without the construction of a brief narrative scene suggests that the presence or absence of Abu Hurayra has no influence on the creation or configuration of divine law. For what rhetorical ends, then, do the Hadith employ these abbreviated narrative scenes to situate the prohibition of wine?

In dealing with issues stemming from the ambiguous nature of wine, the Hadith that embed the prohibition of wine within a wider narrative context add an important human dimension to what is divinely true. Though inherently didactic in nature, this type of framing, which will be called "narrative discourse" (to contrast it with its prophetic and analytic counterparts), inextricably ties the condemnation of wine to the community as a whole by mixing in significant places, characters, and events that serve as paradigms for actual practice. These vignettes put a human face on the formulaic, analytic presentations of the more abstract, divine law.

With the added attention to human detail, a particular law—in this case, the prohibition of wine—is linked with the identity of the community itself. If communal identity is connected with the articulation of the condemnation, then whether one drinks or not becomes a clear marker separating those who believe from those who do not. Working out the ambiguity of wine through the insertion of historical detail, therefore, becomes one and the same with establishing the boundaries of the community.

In short, the prohibition of wine, as relayed through the characters, places, and events provided by the narrative becomes ingrained in the community of believers on three levels: individual thought and action,[4] communal event, and the course of sacred history. It is important to note that narrative discourse does not necessarily record the individual, communal, or sacred events that *actually* took place at a given moment. Although these affairs and episodes may certainly have occurred, their historical validity can never be confirmed. Through the process of organizing sets of discrete facts into linear tales, the stories depicting community affairs establish and legitimize normative practices and beliefs. As a result, they serve to bring the divine more closely in line with, or more accessible to, human thought and action. By operating on all three levels—individual, community, sacred—abstinence itself becomes a way in which to measure one's individual, or communal fitness to be the rightful proprietor of the divine message.

MYTHICAL NARRATIVES: PLACING THE PROHIBITION IN SACRED HISTORY

In general, the Hadith that use myths and mythical characters to lay out the prohibition of wine are not solely interested in the condemnation of alcohol, but, more importantly, they are preoccupied with navigating the community of believers through the vagaries of time and tradition to its rightful place at the head of all monotheistic faiths. Through the elaborate descriptions of the paradisical landscape and the detailed character pictorials provided by the brief narratives, the community of believers is not only given (limited) access to, or a privileged place in, the realm of the divine, but can appropriate the ongoing sacred drama begun with Adam as part of its own historical past. Through the supplemental details of time, place, and person furnished by narratives that frame wine's prohibition, each individual and, more importantly, the community as a whole becomes legitimated and sanctified as part of a unitary monotheistic history.

Muhammad's Rise to the Head of the Community

The effort to bring a *community* of believers in line with the divine is clearly illustrated in a pronouncement found in al-Bukhari's collection of Hadith, which sets the prohibition within an extended tale about the Prophet's rejection of wine:

> Abu 'Asim: al-Awza'i: Ibn Shihab: 'Ubaydallah: Ibn 'Abbas:[5] The Prophet of God drank milk then rinsed his mouth and said, "It contains fat." (Ibrahim b. Tahman: Shu'ba: Qatada: Anas b. Malik) He added, "I was raised to the Lote Tree and saw four rivers, two of which were coming out and two going in. Those which were coming out were the Nile and Euphrates, and those which were going in were two rivers in Paradise. Then I was given three bowls, one containing milk, another honey, and a third wine (*khamr*). I took the bowl containing milk and drank it. It was said to me: "You and your followers will be on the right path."[6]

In this passage, the negative view of wine appears in a short tale about Muhammad's refusal to drink this beverage on his night journey. In addition, because the Hadith often treat honey as a potential intoxicant, it is not surprising that the Prophet ignored this liquid as well.[7] The benefits of using narrative discourse to link divine truth with communal identity become clear when al-Bukhari's tradition is contrasted with a Qur'anic passage that addresses the same journey through prophetic discourse.

Although the night journey per se is never mentioned explicitly in the Qur'an, there are many references to a kind of esoteric, mystical journey or ascension into the inner workings of the divine will:[8]

> He reached the highest pinnacle.
> Then he drew near and drew closer
> Until a space of two arcs or even less remained
> When he revealed to his votary what he revealed,
> His heart did not falsify what he perceived.
> Will you dispute with him what he saw?
> He saw him indeed another time,
> By the Lote-tree beyond which none can pass,
> Close to the Garden of Tranquillity,
> When the Lote-tree was covered over with what it was covered over;
> Neither did sight falter nor exceed the bounds.
> Indeed he saw some of the greatest signs of his Lord.[9]

In contrast to al-Bukhari's narrative, this prophetic passage suppresses all details of setting, events, and characters in order to highlight an abstract point. Although the Qur'an mentions an ascension, it provides no clues as to where, when, how or even why it took place. This revelatory scene also presents a Lote-tree, but only as a sign that separates human knowledge from divine wisdom. Note also the Qur'anic passage does not attempt to establish any kind of normative, communal practice; the text offers no explicit pronouncement on the virtues of milk or the dangers of wine.

These cryptic visions and referential signs stand in direct contrast with the sharp imagery in al-Bukhari's narrative, which treats the night journey as an actual journey, and the Lote-tree an actual tree that marks the farthest distance to which a prophet was allowed to travel, a geographical post from which it was possible to identify the four rivers. Through his ability to see visually, identify verbally, and thus appropriate physically the surrounding landscape, Muhammad, the eventual proprietor of all he surveyed, serves as the protagonist who wisely chooses milk over the threatening alternatives. The Prophet thus becomes narrative exemplar of the proper way for the community.[10] By using narrative discourse to create a dramatic setting in which some sort of movement or action takes place in a concrete space, the Hadith give the community a solid and formidable place on which to stand.

Aside from carving out both a mythical and geographical space for the community of believers, the narrative version of the night journey also recounts Muhammad's sanctification as head of the community, an event absent from the Qur'an's rather esoteric take on a similar theme. In al-Bukhari's passage Muhammad's test does more than bring to light the glory of God's word; rather, his words and actions introduce a theme not found in the Qur'anic repertoire, that is, the essential role of prophetic ingenuity, initiative, and control in placing and keeping the community on the right path. Because he *decided* not to take the wine, the Prophet himself becomes directly responsible for steering the community in the right direction.

In addition, al-Bukhari's narrative of the ascent, unlike the Qur'anic version, also reinforces a normative practice that is intimately tied with the identity of the community through divine sanction. Because the *Prophet* refused to take the wine, all who believe and follow his example will also find themselves on the right path. The implication is clear: If the *Prophet's* one sip on the paradisical journey was enough to de-sanctify and de-throne an entire community, then any person's gulp in the here and now would surely have similar consequences. The story, then, serves as a means through which the tradition recognizes abstinence as an essential practice that further separates the true believer from the false.

In general, narrative discourse allows for ongoing arguments about the nature and boundaries of communal space, as well as how far humans are allowed to travel within it. Note what happens when al-Bukhari's tradition is contrasted with a similar narrative found in the collection of Ibn Hanbal:

> 'Abdallah: his father: Ruh: Salih b. Abi 'l-Akhdar: Ibn Shihab: Sa'id b. al-Musayyab: Abu Hurayra:[11] The Prophet said: The night I was made to travel, I was brought two bowls, one of milk and the other of wine (*khamr*). I looked at them, and took the milk. Gabriel said, "Thanks be to God that he guided you to the right path. Had you taken the wine, your people would have been led astray."[12]

Ibn Hanbal's tradition is similar to al-Bukhari's in terms of the basic narrative structure. The Prophet embarks on the journey, he is presented with some bowls of liquid, he takes one of them over the other, and is given word that his community would continue to flourish. However, in spite of these similarities in the basic "plot," as well as the general conclusion that wine (or honey) should be avoided, there are key changes in the details that put forth radically different points about the relationship between the Prophet and divine, and the role Muhammad was allotted as the course of sacred history was played out.

Noticeably, Ibn Hanbal's passage omits the description of Muhammad's nocturnal journey through *Paradise* and the Prophet's demarcation of paradisical space.[13] Second, in contrast to al-Bukhari's version, this account presents Gabriel as sole interpreter of the divine test. Third, rather than the simple message that "you and your followers will be on the right path" there is the statement "thanks be to God that he guided you to the right path." Finally, rather than the Prophet reaping his reward because he chose the right drink, Ibn Hanbal's version details how Muhammad avoided disaster because he was guided to spurn the wrong drink. The details in Ibn Hanbal's tradition suggest that in spite of his elevated status within the community, the Prophet, and by analogy, all subsequent leaders, have no power to shape or alter the course of divine history. Prophets or other leaders of the community are not, nor should they ever be, charismatic representatives of the divine, but must remain moral, human agents who conform to a divine will revealed. Only their greater intimacy with the contents of that "will" distinguish them from other believers.

Ibn Hanbal's account does not arbitrarily choose Gabriel to deliver the test results. His role as the bearer of the revelations to the Prophet is already mentioned in the Qur'an,[14] and his appearance here supports the argument that a *divine* intercessor is the only one who can relay God's message. In other words, Gabriel's presence in this tradition serves to offset the achievements of Muhammad, who, in spite of his status as Prophet, is still barred from directly influencing the course of sacred history.

The fact that God guided the Prophet to the right choice in beverage further supports this point. Al-Bukhari's tradition suggests the wondrous sights presented to and rightfully interpreted by the Prophet secure his privileged status as leader of the community. In Ibn Hanbal's tradition, the Prophet is not allowed to succeed on the basis of this own merits, but rather stands aside as God moves him and his community out of the way of potential disaster. While the success of the community is causally linked to the Prophet's correct choice in the first passage, Ibn Hanbal's version predetermines Muhammad's choice so that the community could follow no other path.

In spite of these differences, however significant, the narrative in both examples turns the night journey, which only exists in the realm of allusion in the Qur'an, into a concrete event in space and time. By contextualizing the journey, these Hadith tie the negative view of wine to the sacred history of the community of believers. Muhammad's repudiation becomes a paradigmatic act that points the way for all communities who wish to follow the right path and continue on as protagonists through the unfolding sacred drama.

On the (Dis)placement of Noah, Adam, and Eve

The effort to bring all of the various Hadith narratives to fixed, divine conclusions—such as the deliverance of God's law regarding the prohibition of wine—also appears in descriptions of other biblical characters or prophets not directly involved in the development of the *Islamic* community after Muhammad's death. Noah remains as a shadowy figure in the Hadith as he does in the Qur'an. No longer a vehicle for the message of monotheism nor directly related to the rise of the Islamic community, Noah, even when mentioned in regard to wine, is relegated to the status of an archetype, the personification of a law that states how questionable beverages may be drunk. Only when two-thirds (presumably the alcohol) is boiled off and a third remains can wine be safely consumed:

> Ishaq b. Ibrahim: Waki': Sa'd b. Aws: Anas b. Sirin: Anas b. Malik said: Satan fought with Noah in the vineyard. They agreed that Noah would have a third, and Satan two-thirds.[15]

This tradition, which summarizes al-Kulayni's account of how the Holy Ghost had to intervene in a raging battle between two headstrong personalities over some grape-vines,[16] ratifies communal practice through the appeal to sacred history. However, the Hadith are quite capable of establishing this same normative practice without mention of these two archetypes:

> Suwayd: 'Abdallah: 'Abd al-Malik b. Tufayl al-Jazari said: 'Umar b. 'Abd al-'Aziz wrote to us, saying "Do not drink *tila'* (a thickened drink made from grapes) until two-thirds is boiled off and a third remains. Every intoxicant (*muskir*) is forbidden."[17]

The absence of Noah and Satan in a tradition that draws the same divine conclusion suggests that many Hadith assert a legal point on their own authority while other Hadith presume through their allusion to a narrative tradition that sacred history has prescriptive force and thus can be rhetorically effective in legal contexts.

Not unexpectedly, Noah's role in the Islamic community becomes a more poignant point of interest in al-Tabari's *History* (*Ta'rikh al-rusul wa 'l-muluk*),[18] as well as in Muhammad's biography (*Sirat rasul Allah*),[19] composed by Ibn Ishaq and later edited by Ibn Hisham, which, as genres, are devoted to grounding the Islamic community more firmly within its monotheistic past and raising it to the summit of all that has gone before. Yet, even in these self-consciously historical texts, Noah's words and actions have little impact on the divine conclusions that are put forth. In al-Tabari's *History* and in Ibn Ishaq's reconstructed *Book of Beginnings* (*Kitab al-mubtada'*),[20] early Islamic chroniclers called upon the character of Noah in an attempt to connect "the two ancient histories known to them, that is, those of the Jews and the Persians, to serve as a unified history of revelation culminating in the final revelation to Muhammad."[21] Al-Tabari succeeds in elevating and unifying these histories by first establishing Noah's favor in the eyes of God;[22] then by mentioning how only Noah's descendants (Shem, Ham, and Japheth) survived;[23] and finally by raising the progeny of Shem and Japheth, the begetters of the Persians and Arabs, over Ham, the primal seed of the Sudanese, in the attempt to illustrate the superiority of the two great peoples of Islam (who share a common origin) over their subordinates.[24]

Note that even in al-Tabari's account, the moral character and actions of Noah are never questioned or evaluated. The narrative simply assumes and then recounts his role as a righteous servant of God, and therefore as an ideal prophetic predecessor to Muhammad.[25] As a result of Noah's privileged status, the quality and spread of his seed is scrutinized in minute detail.[26] As in the Qur'an, Noah's drunken bouts are never mentioned in al-Tabari's narrative since they would bear no real impact on the divine course of history, which has already been determined. Noah's drinking could only serve to introduce troubling questions about the moral character of one of God's most useful instruments. Although al-Tabari does record that "while Noah slept his genitals were exposed,"[27] this statement only enjoins against Ham, who fixed his gaze intently upon his father's bared organs but could not be bothered to cover them. This rather unfortunate incident has no bearing upon the subsequent direction of sacred history, but it does serve as an aetiology for the vagaries of cultural history, namely, that Ham—the Sudanese—became a slave to his two more righteous brothers—the Arabs and Persians—who had the moral presence to clothe and protect their father.

In contrast to the Sunni traditions' generic representations, Noah makes a strong appearance in many Shi'ite Hadith. Noah's prominence is not surprising given this minority group's interest in how a series of significant historical setbacks led to their loss of political legitimacy. A preoccupation with the transmission of political and religious authority also fuels the Shi'ites' keen interest in figures of the past.[28] Throughout history, the Shi'ites were thwarted from keeping political power (the *imamate*)[29] within the family of the Prophet. The brief reign of 'Ali from A.D. 656–661 was really only a partial caliphate not to be secured by 'Ali's eldest son Hasan, who also failed to assume a position of unquestioned leadership. It was, however, the martyrdom of Hasan's younger brother, Husayn, at the hand of a large army (that included many of his alleged supporters), that solidified the Shi'ite position that they have been denied their right to rule by unrighteous forces of opposition.

Given their keen interest in the relationship between past and current events, the Shi'ites hand Noah a critical role in bringing about the prohibition of wine:

> 'Ali b. Ibrahim: his father: Ahmad b. Muhammad b. Abi Nasr: Aban: Zarara: Abu Ja'far said: When Noah descended from the boat, he planted a vine; then, he returned to his family. Iblis came (God curse him!) and pulled it out. When Noah returned to his vine, he found that it had been torn out. Gabriel came to him and told him what Iblis had done. Noah said to Iblis, "What made you pull it out? By God, I planted a branch that was very dear to me, and by God I will not leave here until I replant it!" Iblis said, "And I, by God, will not leave until I tear it out!" So Noah gave him a third. Satan refused to be satisfied, so Noah gave him a half. Again, Iblis refused the offer, but Noah was not inclined to increase it. Gabriel said, "Noah is the best of what comes from your goodness, O Prophet of God." Noah knew that Gabriel had given him power, so he gave Iblis two-thirds. Abu Ja'far said, "You can take fruit-juice (*'asir*) and cook it down two-thirds and drink it, for that amount is Satan's portion."[30]

Although the Sunni and Shi'ite Hadith both use events and characters to contextualize a divine law, the ways in which this message is formulated reflects their fundamentally different orientations toward the world.

While the appearance of Noah and Satan lend further authority to a normative practice in the Sunni example, their cosmic battle in the Shi'ite tradition shows how precarious the line is between good and evil. If something else had been said or done (in this and in other cases), the course of history could have taken an entirely different path, a path not of goodness and light, but of darkness and despair. Or, perhaps more significantly, the winds of political legitimacy could have shifted and blown by way of the Shi'ites. Although God's will in this example bends in favor of Noah, the battle between Noah and Satan in the Shi'ite anecdote implies that humans must continuously struggle against the ever-present, ever-intrusive forces of chaos that threaten to overpower that which is just and good.

In short, the Sunni example simply presents the law against wine as a universal given that always existed. The details about Noah serve not to bring forth this point, but rather to support and illustrate it. In contrast, the Shi'ite example must delve into the details of the cosmic struggle that ultimately brought forth the prohibition. In this belief system, the prohibition did not preempt historical time, but came to fruition as a result of a battle between two opposing forces, or a distinctive set of events and circumstances. In addition, the role of humans in the cosmic drama becomes much more important for they now have the ability to alter the course of divine will. Shi'ite narratives must not simply articulate and maintain the order of the cosmos, but also must assess how the damage occurred, and then set straight the paths through which order can ultimately be restored.

Not only does Noah play a prominent role in establishing the configuration of the Shi'ite law prohibiting the consumption of wine, but so, too, do Adam and Eve:

> 'Ali b. Muhammad: Salih b. Abi Hammad: al- Husayn b. Yazid: 'Ali b. Abi Hamza: Abu 'Abdallah said: When God cast Adam out, he commanded him to till and cultivate, so he threw him some branches from the Garden. He gave him a date-palm, a grape-vine, an olive tree, and a pomegranate. Adam planted them in order to provide for his descendants, and to eat from its fruits. Iblis (whom God had cursed) said to him, "O Adam, what is this branch [referring to the grape-vine] that is unfamiliar to me? I was here before you; would you allow me to eat something from it?" Adam refused to let him, so Iblis came back after Adam died, and said to Eve, "Truly he wore me out with hunger and thirst!" Eve said to him, "What do you want?" He said, "I want you to let me taste something from these fruits!" Eve said, "Truly Adam entrusted me not to let you eat anything from this vine; since it is from the Garden, it is not proper for you to eat anything that comes from it." He said to her, "Squeeze something from it into my hand." She refused, so he said, "I shall [only] *suck* [these grapes], and not bite [into them]." So she took a cluster of grapes, and gave it to him. He sucked the grapes, but did not bite into them. When Eve was finally reassured [that he would not actually *eat* the grapes], he prepared himself to bite into them. However, Eve pulled them away from him. God revealed to Adam that the grapes had been sucked by Iblis, my enemy and your enemy. Therefore, the juice of the vine—that which the breath of Iblis stirs—is unlawful to you. Wine is prohibited because the enemy of God, Iblis, deceived Eve when he sucked the grapes, even though he did not bite into them. The grape-vine is prohibited from its very beginning to its very end, as well as the gathering of its fruits, and what comes from them.[31]

Here, Eve succumbs to the conniving pressures and erotic overtures of the wily Iblis. Because Eve was deceived and let the enemy of God suck freely from her fruits, the liquid of the vine was condemned for all.[32] Again, this passage leaves the reader with the distinct impression that the prohibition came about *because* of a particular sequence of human failings, or *because* of the result of a cosmic skirmish between right and wrong, good and evil.

Significantly, Eve is left out of the discussion of wine in the Sunni Hadith, although she does make an appearance with respect to wine in the reconstructed biography of the Prophet and in al-Tabari's *History*:

> Sa'id b. al-Musayyab: Yazid b. 'Abdallah b. Qusayt: I heard him swear by God that there was no doubt that Adam did not eat from the tree while he had all his senses. Eve plied him with an intoxicating beverage. When he became drunk, she led him to the tree, and he ate of it. When Adam and Eve sinned, God expelled them from the Garden and denied them the pleasure and honor which they had. He flung them down and caused enmity on the earth between them, Iblis, and the serpent. Their Lord said to them, "Go down as enemies, some of you against the other."[33]

Although Adam would not have taken from the tree if he "had all his senses" and the burden of the sin rests with Eve, who made him drunk and unaware of his reckless behavior, Adam must still pay the price for his partner's ineptitude. However, by shifting the responsibility from Adam to Eve, this passage also shows how the community of believers can be saved from complete destruction and despair. Since Adam was only deceived, he is still worthy enough to become the first prophet in a series of major prophets who made the pilgrimage to Mecca and to take his place as a revered predecessor of Muhammad.[34] This narrative cleverly manipulates the details of the Fall to deflect full accountability from the first prophet leaving Eve, a figure of no consequence in the transmission of prophetic authority, to bear ultimate responsibility.

Even though the story of Adam and his wife's Fall is included in the Qur'an, the text blames the overall distortion of the true knowledge of God as the primary cause for the descent from the Garden as opposed to a single, corrupt act performed by one of the participants in the drama:

> Then Satan whispered to them,
> to reveal to them that which was hidden from them
> of their shameful parts.
> He said, "Your Lord has only prohibited you from this tree
> lest you become angels, or lest you become immortals."
> And he swore to them,
> "Truly I am for you a sincere advisor."
> So he led them on by delusion; and when they tasted the tree,
> their shameful parts were revealed to them,
> so they took to stitching upon themselves
> the leaves of the Garden.[35]

Neither an act of deceit nor a bit of wine was used to lure Adam or his partner into tasting from the forbidden fruits; only the faint whisperings of

Satan, master of the chaotic powers of delusion and faithlessness—potent themes in the Qur'anic repertoire—caused this primal couple to be plucked from the Garden.[36]

In all the narrative versions of the Fall, the details (as well as the dramatic thrust) vary, but the conclusion remains the same: Adam and Eve were no longer welcome in the Garden of Eden. Through various explanations of how they were expelled, however, the narrative allows for debates over the causes for and significance of this event. The Shi'ite Hadith portray Adam and Eve as key figures whose actions offset the course of monotheistic history. The details of their lives link the present and future state of the Islamic community to all that has gone before. While there is some recognition of wrongdoing within the confines of the heavenly Garden in the reconstructed *Book of Beginnings* (and it must be remembered that these writings were *removed* during the 'Abbasid regime), efforts were made to preserve and assert the integrity of one of God's prophets by diverting the blame to his female consort.

Both Sunni and Shi'ite narratives that use myths and mythical characters to frame the prohibition of wine are not solely concerned with defining the status of alcohol, but are also interested in grounding the community of believers firmly within their monotheistic heritage. These Sunni and Shi'ite traditions address both these issues by first selecting a variety of images, characters, and ideas from sacred history. They then rework them into a new narrative structure that not only raises the community of believers to the pinnacle of the monotheistic tradition, but also inextricably links this privileged place to the condemnation of wine-drinking, thus, sealing the divinely authoritative, universal status of the prohibition. However, by using different types of narratives to accomplish this task, these traditions project a variety of understandings of how the lines should be drawn between the human and divine, as well as the strategies needed to establish, maintain, or restore order within each realm.

HISTORICAL NARRATIVES: A PROHIBITION CARVED IN EARTHLY STONE

While narrative discourse uses myths and mythical characters to embed the prohibition into sacred history and to glorify abstainers, more often than not narrative discourse also draws upon discrete characters and circumstances to place divine truth firmly within the reach of human history. This customization of the prohibition, disguised in the form of seemingly innocuous detail, combines sacred history with faithful action and communal practice, which ultimately allows for new elements pertinent to a changing world to be worked in with the basic statement of the prohibition while affirming its sacred status. The traditions dedicated to describing the conditions under which the prohibitions appeared, that is, traditions specifically concerned with Qur'anic exegesis (*Tafsir*), hammer home the prohibition with concrete details locked in religiously significant contexts.

Qur'anic Exegesis and the Arguments from Chronology

As shown in chapter one, wine's ambiguity serves to evoke divine truths in the Qur'an; truths that either spark insight into the greatness of God's goodness or warn of his terrifying wrath. Rather than establish the history, permanence, or precise terms of the prohibition, wine's ambiguity sheds light on the inner contours of God's word. As the community of believers began to grow and expand, however, many religious scholars came to view the separate, evocative Qur'anic vignettes on wine as contradictory. Their concerns are reflected in those Hadith and exegetical writings that attempt to articulate and clarify the Qur'an's position on wine. Traditions devoted to resolving the Qur'an's ambiguous position on this beverage isolated four distinct verses on wine from the Qur'anic repertoire and then asserted a chronological order for them that reflected a gradual progression towards a clear condemnation of this drink. The four verses (which obviously do not include all Qur'anic statements on wine) stand as *sequential* revelations that gained in strength and specificity over time in response to an audience that continually refused to change its wayward practices and beliefs.

The traditional argument goes as follows:[37] Wine, like milk and honey, was first glorified as a sign of God's grace and goodness to all mankind, as Sura 16:67 (al-Nahl) indicates:

> And from the date-palm and the grape-vine you obtain
> an intoxicant and good food.
> In this are signs for those who understand.

However, in the days of Muhammad the people of Mecca and Medina would frequently indulge in wine-drinking to the point of scandal. For example, several Hadith present stories that illustrate how Muhammad's uncle, Hamza b. 'Abd al-Muttalib, mutilated 'Ali's camels in a state of intoxication.[38] The commentaries also provide information on how Muhammad's companions held frequent drinking parties which ultimately caused them to commit faults in ritual prayer.[39] All of these events are said to have led the divine (through four revelations to Muhammad) to develop and project a negative attitude toward wine.

At first, this negative stance was declared halfheartedly in Sura 2:219–220 (al-Baqara):

> They ask you about wine and gambling.
> Tell them, "In both is great sin and profit for men.
> But their sin is greater than their profit."

This distaste for wine, however, became more acute in Sura 4:43 (al-Nisa') as people continued their wayward drinking habits, and drunkenness began to seep into ritual prayer:

> Oh, you who believe! Do not draw near prayer
> when you are intoxicated until you know what you are saying.

As other atrocities concerning wine became more and more apparent, Muhammad put the final cap on drinking with his presentation of the following revelation in Sura 5:90–91 (al-Ma'ida):

> Oh, you who believe!
> Wine, gambling, idol-worshipping, and divination arrows
> are an abomination from among the acts of Satan.
> Keep away from them, so that you may prosper.

The establishment of the progressively negative sequence as well as the addition of some contextual details to a group of discrete, evocative statements suggests that God's word was formed or revealed in response to a particular set of human circumstances. In other words, the revelation was worked out to completion through human event. In such a scheme, the divine word is not only made subject to the realm of human action, but also becomes more responsive and inextricably tied to the continuous flow of historical and communal affairs. By making cosmic truth more accessible to human need, narrative discourse counteracts the abstract legalities set forth by analytic discourse as well as the elusive, divine evocations set forth by the prophetic, which leave little room for individual or communal participation.

At least superficially, the entry of the revelation into the earthly realm seems to compromise the integrity of the divine word; a word that exists outside and independent of the natural world. However, the isolation and subtle rearrangement of bits and pieces of the revelation into a successive scheme actually preserves the word from the *appearance* of being tarnished by human meddlings. Since only a new sequence is imposed upon a presumably static set of divine words, the reordering process serves to insulate what is deemed to be the inimitable word of God from unauthorized human manipulations.

Through the process of their contextualization, these discrete Qur'anic statements on wine and the divine are given human form, and become vital components in the assertion and divine sanctification of the prohibition. Narrative discourse, therefore, removes the inherent ambiguities found in the Qur'anic wine passages, and makes the revelation more directly dependent upon and responsive to human thought and action without visibly altering the content or status of God's word.

Qur'anic Exegesis and the Arguments from Context and Condition

Many Hadith flesh out the context of individual Qur'anic passages on wine in order to link them with the identity of God's community as a whole. In general, there are three distinct types of traditions that fall under this heading. The first includes those traditions in which individual situations or actions brought forth a divine revelation on wine. In the few cases that fall into this category, the prohibition becomes a direct result of certain conditions and circumstances that take place in the human realm.

An example appears Muslim's collection of Hadith, when Sura 5:90 is said to have been brought down in response to a drunken feast that got a little out of hand:

> Abu Bakr b. Abi Shayba and Zuhayr b. Harb: al-Hasan b. Musa: Zuhayr: Simak b. Harb: Mus'ab b. Sa'd: his father: When the verses of the Qur'an came down he said, I came upon a group from the *ansar* and the *muhajirun*. They said: "Truly we shall give you food and serve you wine to drink." But that was before wine was prohibited. They brought me to a garden, where they had the head of a butchered and roasted camel, and a skin of wine. So I ate and drank with them. I said: "The emigrants from Mecca (*muhajirun*) are better than the Medinans (*ansar*)." The man took one of the jawbones from the camel's head and struck me with it until I had no breath left. I went to the Prophet and told him. So God sent down the following on the matter of wine: As for wine and gambling and idols and divining arrows, they are filthy things from the works of Satan."[40]

The fact that intoxication caused one to say something that might disturb the inner unity of the Islamic community creates a dire need—a ripe environment—for the appearance of the prohibition. In this polemical example, some drunk declared that the *muhajirun*, or the Prophet's "emigrant" followers from Mecca were superior to the *ansar*, or the men from Medina who welcomed and supported Muhammad. The Prophet then uttered his repudiation of wine. Obviously, such "drunken comments" aimed at degrading the *ansar* were countered by the prohibition in order to send a direct message to both groups that one is not better than the other and that the two must become a unified front. In this case, the prohibition is not presented in an abstract space far-removed from human thought and action, but rather articulated in response to a precise unfolding of a sequence of events. Within this dramatic moment, the condemnation of wine becomes inextricably tied to the maintenance of a unified community of believers.

A second, more common form of Qur'anic exegesis takes the opposite approach by suggesting that the prohibition came about as a formula that preceded, albeit continuously applicable to, human action. This kind of wine tradition appears in anecdotes that provide an opportunity for the reassertion of the prohibition. Rather than showing how a precise sequence of events or a peculiar situation provoked God to send down the prohibition, the narratives that fall into this category suggest that human action is forever subject to the fixed and static divine prohibition.

In these cases, the actions, words, and characters of the narrative have little to do with the appearance or form of the prohibition. The content and characters are simply molded in such a way as to accentuate, highlight, and support the prescribed prohibition. An example that uses persons, setting, and conversation to create a suitable context in which to assert the order of Suras 2:219–220 (al-Baqara), 4:43 (al-Nisa'), and 5:90–91 (al-Ma'ida), appears in a tradition from the collection of Abu Dawud:

> 'Abbad b. Musa al-Huttali: Isma'il (b. Ja'far): Isra'il: Abu Ishaq: 'Amr: 'Umar b. al-Khattab: When the prohibition of wine came down, 'Umar said, "Give us a satisfactory explanation about wine." The verse that is in "The Cow" came down (they ask you about wine and gambling; Say: In them is a great sin). 'Umar was called and (the verse) was recited to him. He said, "Give us a satisfactory explanation about wine." So the verse in "The Women" came down (O you who believe! Do not go near prayer when intoxicated). The imam of the Messenger of God, when the prayer was performed, would call out, "Those who are drunk should not go near prayer." 'Umar was called and it was recited to him. He said, "Give us a satisfactory explanation about wine." So this verse was recalled, "Will you not abstain?" 'Umar said, "We abstained."[41]

Only the negative utterances on wine are extracted from the Qur'an and put into this anecdotal form, which is not surprising given that they are said to have come down in direct response to 'Umar's pleas for clarity on the prohibition. Strikingly, the assertion of the proper sequence in which to read the Qur'anic revelations does not represent the gradual *unfolding* of the prohibition due to a set of historical circumstances, but rather the *presentation* of what already exists as a discrete unit in the divine realm. In this scene, 'Umar does not serve as the active agent who brings about the prohibition; he is only the mouthpiece who orders the Qur'an's random and evocative statements about wine. As such, he has no causal links to, nor influence over, the final shape the prohibition takes.

Although 'Umar plays a vital role in the history of the early Islamic community,[42] we have few clues in this passage as to what that role might be, let alone the details of the dilemma he faced that might have caused him to call for a divine response. The sole function of the appearance of 'Umar and his quest for clarity is neither to shed light on this character nor to reconcile a question of his own making. Instead, 'Umar appears to set up an authoritative scenario in which the divine sanction of the prohibition can be asserted and legitimated. In the end 'Umar becomes merely a rhetorical device that solidifies the vital relationship between the prohibition of alcohol and the identity of those who profess to believe.

A third type of tradition also uses the narrative as an illustrative backdrop for the prohibition, but plays upon contextual detail to push the prohibition in new directions. This third category contains a set of anecdotes that find Anas serving up alcoholic beverages in Medina when the prohibition came down:

> Ya'qub b. Ibrahim: Ibn 'Ulayya: 'Abd al-'Aziz b. Suhayb: Anas b. Malik: We had no wine (*khamr*) except a drink that you call *fadikh* (an alcoholic drink made from dates). While I was offering drinks to Abu Talha and so-and-so and so-and-so, a man came and said, "Has the news reached you?" They said, "What news?" He said, "Wine (*khamr*) has been prohibited!" They said, "Pour out these vessels, O Anas!" They did not ask about it, nor did they continue to drink it after (they heard) the man's news.[43]

Essentially, this passage provides a context for the assertion of the prohibition, and identifies the kind of alcoholic beverage that was consumed in Medina at the time wine was condemned. The tradition also extends the term "*khamr*" to include alcoholic beverages that go by other names or come from fruits other than grapes.

Other traditions maintain this basic narrative frame but subtly manipulate the details in order to refine further the general prohibition. By fleshing out the reaction of some nameless people to the announcement of the prohibition, the following tradition shows how the Medinese should not be blamed for drinking wine before they had access to divine guidance:

> Muhammad b. 'Abd al-Rahim Abu Yahya: 'Affan: Hammad b. Zayd: Thabit: Anas: I was the drink-server in the house of Abu Talha. Their wine (*khamr*) was a drink made from dates (*fadikh*) in those days. Allah's messenger ordered someone to announce that wine had been prohibited. Abu Talha ordered me: "Go out and pour out the wine!" I went out and spilled it, and it flowed through the streets of Medina. Some of the people said, "People were killed when it was still in their bellies." On that the divine revelation came: *For those who believe and do good things there is no blame for what they have eaten.*[44]

The simple inclusion of some background information about the environment into which the wine was poured provides an opportunity for the presentation and contextualization of another Qur'anic passage: Believers should not be blamed for past sins they committed in ignorance.[45]

The focus on context and detail also furnishes greater opportunity to examine wine's ingredients and to assert how these various fruits and their combinations must also be prohibited. Again, as in the example of Noah, an abstract, philosophical proposition is given human form through its association with a particular historical moment:

> Hisham: Qatada: Anas: While I was serving a drink to Abu Talha, Abu Dujana, and Abu Suhayl b. al-Bayda' made from a mixture of unripe (*busr*) and dried dates (*tamr*), wine (*khamr*) was made unlawful. I threw it away. In those days, when I was their drink-server, and the youngest among them, we considered this mixture to be wine.[46]

This narrative tradition uses the condemnation of the mixture of unripe and dried dates—a combination that appears frequently in analytic form—to describe the type of drink being served when the prohibition against wine was given. The narrative slips in this bit of formulaic detail to hone more finely the boundaries of the prohibition without explicitly or radically altering the basic sequence of events. By articulating what was being drunk when the prohibition appeared, the details of the narrative open up the basic condemnation of wine (*khamr*) to include other types of alcoholic beverages. This practice of adding analytic detail to widen the definition of "wine" is also apparent in several traditions that state that at the time the prohibition came down wine in Medina was made from five different things.[47] Through the insertion of these analytic descriptions, the prohibition is further refined and expanded to fit the specific needs or practices of a growing community.

These formulae, however, not only accommodate change, but continue to project permanence and order in a world vulnerable to the vagaries of history.

These exegetical passages show how narrative discourse extends the prohibition of wine into a variety of directions. At the same time narrative discourse spreads the divine law against *khamr* across numerous alcoholic beverages so, too, does it tie the prohibition itself to the identity of all who believe, which thereby plants the revelation firmly within the history of a single community. As a result, individual believers are identified by a prohibition that claims divine roots, and the community that abstains is elevated above and beyond others that profess to be the rightful inheriters of monotheistic truth.

NARRATIVE DISCOURSE AND THE LAYERING OF EXEGESIS UPON EXEGESIS

Once the prohibition has been established in the human realm, either through Qur'anic exegesis or by implicit acceptance, it becomes necessary to show how it is applicable to a variety of ambiguous substances or is relevant to a number of confusing situations and conditions that confronted the community of believers. For example, could alcoholic beverages be used to make certain types of medicines? Is it possible to dine with others who were drinking wine? Through the very manner in which they answer questions pertaining to the process of fermentation, the drinking and selling of wine, the use of alcohol as medication, and the often tense relationship between those who drink and those who abstain, the Hadith attempt to maintain divine law every bit as much as the content of their answers addresses the changing needs of a dynamic community.

A Place for Dwelling upon the Details of Fermentation

Many Hadith use a combination of both narrative and analytic discourse to further extend the divine prohibition into the world. Not directly preoccupied with contextualizing or interpreting *Qur'anic* wine statements, these traditions pepper the basic prohibition of wine, which is itself a form of exegesis asserted through arguments from chronology, with abstract propositions that allow for further elaborations of the law.

The combined effort between analytic and narrative discourse serves to define, augment, and flesh out an abstract law with historical fact and supplementary detail, which not only allows for further exegesis upon the *prohibition*, but also for the solidification of the prohibition with the identity of the Muslim community. Therefore, while the notion of "exegesis upon exegesis" may suggest that a tradition is one-step farther removed from its revelatory "source," it also means that it is one-step further extended into the human world, and therefore that much more pliable and open to the community's shifting circumstances and conditions.

The union between narrative and analytic discourse is clearly illustrated in those traditions that weave fragments of abstract propositions put forth by analytic discourse into a larger narrative frame and add a few key details in order to assert, legitimate, and expand the prohibition. Note an example from the collection of al-Nasa'i:

> 'Amr b. 'Uthman b. Sa'id b. Kathir: Baqiya: al-Awza'i: Yahya b. Abi 'Amr: 'Abdallah b. al-Daylami: his father Fayruz said: I went over to the Prophet, and said, "O Prophet, I am the owner of a vineyard, but God sent down the prohibition against wine. What should we produce?" He said, "Produce raisins (*zabib*)." I said, What should we make with the raisins? He said, "Steep them at breakfast, and drink the beverage for dinner; steep them at dinner and drink the beverage for breakfast." I said, "What if we wait until it becomes strong?" He said, "Do not put it in earthen jugs, but rather in skins. For if it stays a long period of time, it becomes vinegar."[48]

This anecdote can be broken down into its separate analytic and narrative components. The narrative frame sets up a context in which an individual asks the Prophet to resolve an economic crisis that would certainly befall the upper-class, wine-producing Syrian community as a result of the prohibition.[49] Oddly enough, however, the Prophet never provides a concrete, practical solution to this economic dilemma other than the vague order to produce raisins. Instead, the narrative frame is used to lay out several mandates as to how certain fruit drinks must be produced and consumed in order to avoid any suspect conversion.

Because this tradition already assumes the condemnation of wine, the only task that remains is to demarcate more broadly the boundaries of the prohibition so that the law appears comprehensive enough in its original state to be applicable to any situation that might arise within the community. The law must be shown to have *anticipated* all potential problems that might challenge its authority. In this example, the narrative not only allows for wine-producers to secure an alternative future for their vineyards, but also extends the prohibition of wine to include the condemnation of all beverages that have been steeped longer than a day, or those that have been produced or preserved in earthen containers.

The Hadith are able to demonstrate the pliability of the fixed law by placing one or more of these analytic statements into the various conversations or events that flow within the course of the narrative, and then modifying the supporting detail. Note the following example also taken from the collection of al-Nasa'i, which contains the analytic repetitions of steeping in the evenings and drinking in the mornings (and vice versa):

> Suwayd b. Nasr: 'Abdallah: Qudama al-'Amiri: Jasra bint Dajaja al-Amiriya: I heard all the people ask 'A'isha about *nabidh*, saying, "We steep dates (*tamr*) in the morning and we drink [what is produced] in the evening. And we steep them in the evening and drink [what is produced] in the morning." She said: "It is unlawful to get drunk, even if there was bread and water." She said this three times.[50]

Here, the prohibition is widened to include date-beverages that have been steeped for more than a day, and the state of drunkenness is further refined by the suggestion that not even bread and water can reduce or diminish its effect.

Both examples retain characteristic features of analytic discourse to apply order and certainty to the world, but sacrifice some of its more formalistic traits for the sake of the narrative flow. By placing the modified structures of analytic discourse within a concrete, human setting, these Hadith unite the orderly patterns of the universe with the precise wording, application, and *relevance* of the law in a particular community. For example, the preference for drinking out of skins has many analytic counterparts whose authority rests on the Prophet's words:[51]

> Abu Dawud: Hisham: Abu Zubayr: Jabir: The Prophet said that *nabidh* was mixed for him in a skin.[52]

> Muhammad b. al-Muthanna: 'Abd al-Wahhab b. 'Abd al-Majid al-Thaqafi: Yunus b. 'Ubayd: al-Hasan: his mother: 'A'isha said, "*Nabidh* was made for the Prophet of God in a skin tied at the top. What was steeped in the morning, he drank in the evening. What was steeped in the evening he drank in the morning."[53]

Several analytic traditions also mention skins in reference to spoilage[54] and several focus on further transformations of *nabidh*, particularly its change from wine into vinegar.[55] However, al-Nasa'i's narratives no longer focus on what the Prophet said or did, as is the case in the analytic examples, but on how the later community must translate or interpret what he said or did. The shift away from the Prophet's words and deeds towards the community's appropriation of the Prophet's acts and message reflects the move from the articulation of an abstract law to a communal, human practice.

Even though abstract laws are put forth through historical event and realized through human word and action, care must be taken in order to protect the word from human interference. These two narratives remain protected by two rhetorical devices, both of which have a tendency to universalize the law on wine. First of all, neither the Prophet (nor anyone else for that matter) takes an active role in the establishment of the prohibition. Characters only articulate the established proscriptions. Second, all characters, events, and actions are confined by, and subject to, the formulaic legal propositions which serve as the limits and boundaries of the law. The repertoire of narratives (along with the variation in detail) becomes relatively fixed; the outcomes always static. In addition to these two strategies, divine truth is further protected by its very appearance in narrative form. These narratives allude to direct analytic counterparts that are widespread and well-known. The narratives' reference to analytic pronouncements strengthens the authority of the stories about wine because these formulaic statements are believed to reflect the inherent patterns that structure both human and divine realms. As a result of this elaborate system of checks and balances, the law becomes more pliable while it continues to solidify its permanent, divine status.

A Context for Forbidding the Drinking and the Selling

The prohibition of drinking and selling wine is often depicted in passages that appear in the analytic/narrative combination. Malik's collection contains the following anecdote:

> Yahya: Anas: Malik: Zayd b. Aslam: Ibn Wa'la al-Misri asked 'Abdallah b. 'Abbas about what is squeezed from grapes. Ibn 'Abbas replied, "A man gave the Messenger of Allah, may God bless him and grant him peace, a small water-skin of wine." The Messenger of Allah, may Allah bless him and grant him peace, said to him, "Don't you know that Allah has made it prohibited (*haram*)?" He said, "No." Then a man at his side whispered to him. The Messenger of Allah, may Allah bless him and grant him peace, asked what he had whispered, and the man replied, "I told him to sell it." The Messenger of Allah, may Allah bless him and grant him peace, said, "The one who made drinking it forbidden (*haram*) has made selling it *haram*." The man then opened the water-skins and poured out what was in them.[56]

In general, Malik's tradition serves to clarify the question concerning what aspect of wine is prohibited. If such a beverage cannot be drunk, then can it be sold or traded, and, if so, to whom? A tradition from al-Darimi's collection raises the question as to whether or not that which is prohibited can be sold to Jews and Christians:

> Ahmad b. Khalid: Muhammad b. Ishaq: 'Abd al-Rahman b. Abi Yazid: Abu 'l-Qa'qa' b. Hakim: 'Abd al-Rahman b. Wa'la said: I asked Ibn 'Abbas about skins of carrion (*mayta*). He said, "Skin the carcass and clean it." I asked him about the selling of wine (*khamr*) to the non-Muslim People of the Book. I said to him: We have grapes from which I take wine. We sell it to the People of the Book. Ibn 'Abbas said, "I presented a man who was drunk . . . to the Prophet." The Prophet said, "Don't you know that God forbade wine?" The man called to his servant, saying, "Take this [wine] out to the market and sell it." The Prophet said, "Don't you know that its drinking *and* selling is prohibited?" I commanded [the wine] to be emptied in the street.[57]

Clearly this tradition takes the stance that one is not allowed to sell what is prohibited to anyone.

As noted in chapter two, a statement forbidding the drinking and selling of wine also appears in some of the many formulaic structures characteristic of analytic discourse including the setting up of lists and the recitation of ten cursed points. The situation presented in Malik's tradition, however, seeks to resolve *permanently* the issue of what activities involving wine are prohibited by embedding the law within an historical context in which the Prophet acted. This "dramatic" moment reflects a point in time when the complexities of concrete conditions were such that they "just happened" to reveal another dimension of the law.

Because the narrative presents the condemnation of wine at a set moment in space and time, the boundaries of the prohibition become inextricably associated with the actions and behaviors of a specific community and its Prophet. In addition, the narratives' reduction of actual daily reality to a set of abstract characters and events becomes the rhetorical trope crucial to constructing the law as *prior* to the scene created. In other words, the Hadith subtly introduce a tautology: On the surface, they present a static law that is forever applicable to human circumstances; in reality they are subjecting it to a radical process of transformation as they extend it to meet the conditions set forth by the narrative.

A Situation in which to Meditate upon Medication

The Hadith also repeatedly associate wine with sickness and disease. Just as one cannot buy or sell that which is prohibited so, too, is it forbidden to medicate with substances that have been condemned in other contexts.

Both Sunni and Shi'ite traditions proscribe the use of banned substances in different ways. Note the following Sunni example, which presents the basic law without any unnecessary narrative detail:

> Sahl b. Hammad: Shu'ba: Simak: 'Alqama b. Wa'il: his father Wa'il: Suwayd b. Tariq asked the Prophet about wine (*khamr*). He prohibited him from producing it. He said, "But it is medicine!" The Prophet said, "It is not a medicine, but a disease!"[58]

While the Sunnis use few details to lay out the basic statement that wine should not be used as a medication, the Shi'ites layer the basic proscription with graphic illustrations. Note the following two Shi'ite examples:

> 'Ali b. Ibrahim: his father: Ibn Abi 'Amir: 'Umar b. Udhayna said: I wrote to Abu 'Abdallah, and asked him about the man who had been sent medicine for hemorrhoids. He drank it not out of enjoyment, but because he needed the medicine. [Abu 'Abdallah] said, "No, not one gulp!" Then he said, "Truly God did not put a remedy or medicine in what he prohibited."[59]

> Muhammad b. Yahya: Ahmad b. Muhammad: Muhammad b. Khalid, and al-Husayn b. Sa'id: al-Nadr b. Suwayd: al-Husayn b. 'Abdallah: 'Abdallah b. 'Abd al-Hamid: 'Amr: Ibn al-Har said: I came upon Abu 'Abdallah when he was in Iraq, and he said to me: I went to Isma'il b. Ja'far, for he had been afflicted. So I examined what caused him pain. He told me, so I prescribed a medicine for him that had *nabidh* in it. Isma'il said, "*Nabidh* is prohibited, and I am one of those who do not cure with what is prohibited."[60]

What is present in these Shi'ite passages and absent in the Sunni examples is a greater attention to the behaviors and concerns of individual characters. For example, these passages give the impression that someone's problems with hemorrhoids or concerns over Ja'far's illness might actually have raised the issue of what to do about treatments using wine. Again, these personal references reflect the Shi'ites' interest in the wayward but potentially favorable flow of historical event and individual influence.

Despite their interest in idiosyncratic detail when conveying the underlying message, these passages still play a part in refining the prohibition. Although they never explicitly refer to it, these anecdotes appear to be commenting (negatively) upon Sura 16:69 (al-Nahl), which glorifies the date-palm and the grape-vine for their production of "an intoxicant and good food," or honey as a "drink of many colors . . . [that contains] medicine for men." With their many references to hemorrhoids and other diseases, however, these narrative snippets do not focus on how intoxicating drinks can serve as a kind of spiritual medicine for men, but rather convey the fact that the curative properties of a condemned substance should never be embraced. Many Shi'ite traditions even go so far as to provide curative recipes for making a *nabidh* that does not intoxicate:

> Muhammad b. Yahya: Musa b. al-Hasan: al-Siyyari: Muhammad b. al-Husayn: one who informed him: Isma'il b. al-Fadl al-Hashmi said, "I complained to Abu 'Abdallah about the gurgling that had befallen my stomach, and my lack of taste in food." He said to me: "Why didn't you take some *nabidh*? We drink it, for it makes food more palatable, and it suppresses the gurgling and gases from the stomach." I said to him: "Describe how you make the drink." He said: "Take a cubic measure of raisins, and steep them, then wash them thoroughly with water. Soak them, cover them, and then leave the liquid for three days and nights if it is during the winter, and if it is during the summer, a day and a night. Put [the raisins] in another pot, and pour water over them. Take the best of [what is there] and put that in a vessel, and take its measure with a stick. Then cook it gently until two-thirds of it evaporates and a third remains. Then put half a measure of honey into it, or take a measure of honey, then cook it until that increased amount evaporates. Then take some spices, crush them, shred them into thin pieces, and toss them in. Boil them until the whole thing bubbles, then take [the spices] out."[61]

Although there remains some semblance of analytic discourse in this recipe with its references to three days and nights and the boiling off of two-thirds so that a third (nonalcoholic portion) remains, the emphasis falls on the precise record of the ingredients and the preparation involved in the creation of an uninebriating medication.

Because these narrative traditions treat wine not as a prophetic sign but as a real substance, they can condemn this material product without explicitly contradicting or visibly altering the Qur'anic passages they engage. Through the concretization of a prophetic or philosophical concept, the prohibition, whose link to the Qur'an is not readily apparent but relies heavily on the skills of the later exegetes, is more readily absorbed into the practices and actions of the community. The prohibition thus takes firmer root.

A Point from which to Turn the Tables

The Hadith also expand the prohibition of wine to cover a variety of worldly situations (without explicitly doing so) by spinning all possible understandings of a single word or phrase into as many directions as possible. These traditions rely on metonymy by using key words from the Qur'an as sanctified, legal anchors to venture into new interpretive directions. For example, the Hadith collections contain several different types of analytic and narrative traditions that put forth the proposition that believers are not to dine at a table upon which wine is served. The mention of a table (*ma'ida*) refers individuals back to the Sura called by the same name which presents a number of injunctions that can be used to separate true believers from the false, namely, the Jews and the Christians, both of whom have misinterpreted the message. Sura 5:71–76 (al-Ma'ida), for example, states that the son of Mary was only a messenger, and that those who claim him to be a messiah are unbelievers. The Hadith's discussions of tables, which draw off these same Qur'anic themes of separation and distinction, range from the sanctioned etiquette of individual dining practices, to the legal issue of actually sitting at a table where wine is consumed, to the theological concern of what tables people should be sitting around on Earth if they want to get to Paradise. In these examples, the metonymic associations of the word "table" sanctify further exegetical elaborations by linking them (however loosely) to the divine revelation.

Examine an analytic presentation of the table that lays out licit dining practices for individuals who believe:

> 'Uthman b. Abi Shayba: Kathir b. Hisham: Ja'far b. Burqan: al-Zuhri: Salim: His father said, "The Prophet prohibited two sorts of dining practices: Sitting at the table (*ma'ida*) drinking wine; a man eating when he is lying flat on his belly."[62]

The following passage uses narrative discourse to demonstrate that no one should physically seat himself at a concrete table upon which wine is being served:

> A number of our companions: Ahmad b. Abi 'Abdallah: his father: Harun b. al-Jahm said: I was with Abu 'Abdallah in al-Hira when Abu Ja'far came to me. Some of the chiefs had circumcised their sons, prepared food, and had invited guests [for the celebration]. Abu 'Abdallah was on the right of me at the table (*ma'ida*), eating, and with him at the table were many men. A man asked them if they wanted a drink. He came back with a cup filled with drink (*sharab*). But when the cup went into the hand of one of the men, Abu 'Abdallah got up from the table. When asked why he got up, he said, "The Prophet cursed whoever sits at the table with one who drinks wine (*khamr*)." In the opinion of others, he cursed anyone who willingly sat at the table of anyone who drank wine.[63]

This rather intricate Shi'ite passage is concerned with the specific, real-life circumstances surrounding the law, as illustrated by the interest in individual action. This tradition can be contrasted with a similar Sunni hadith, which relies on a conditional formulation to claim that sitting at a wine-laden table is the moral equivalent to not believing in God and the Last Day:

> Muslim b. Ibrahim: al-Hasan b. Abu Ja'far: Abu 'l-Zubayr: Jabir: The Prophet said, "Whoever believes in God and the Last Day shall not sit at a table where wine (*khamr*) is drunk."[64]

All three of these passages send strong statements to Jews, Christians, and anyone else who would profess to believe in God and the Last Day, but would frequently dine at tables of various sorts where wine was freely, even ceremoniously, consumed. The prohibition, therefore, is clearly presented in order to separate those who submit from the rest of the peoples of the Book and other unbelievers.

The general association between wine-drinking and unbelief is repeated often in the Hadith and appears in a number of traditions that do not mention tables. A tradition in al-Darimi's collection, for example, makes the following proclamation:

> Muhammad b. Yusuf: al-Awza'i: al-Zuhri: Abu Salama: Abu Hurayra: The Prophet said, "The fornicator is not a believer when he fornicates, the thief is not a believer when he commits a crime, and the wine-drinker is not a believer when he consumes wine."[65]

Just as the Hadith prohibit dried dates from mingling with unripe dates, so, too, do they segregate questionable behaviors from true belief and transgressors from the faithful. True belief and wine-drinking are fundamentally incompatible. Like the Qur'an, the Hadith flatly condemn hypocrisy, another form of ambivalency or categorical corruption that further separates the world from the divine order.[66]

In spite of such strong condemnations, the Sunnis express some concern over what might happen to the community if every Muslim were actually banished for his wine-drinking, which suggests that reckless consumption was perhaps more prevalent than one might expect:

> Zakariya' b. Yahya: 'Abd al-A'la b. Hammad: Mu'tamir b. Sulayman: 'Abd al-Razzaq: Ma'mar: al-Zuhri: Sa'id b. al-Musayyab: 'Umar banished Rabi'a b. Umayya to Khaybar for wine-drinking, where he united with Heraclius and became a Christian. 'Umar said, "I will not banish another Muslim after him."[67]

While the prohibition may have separated true believers from Christians, it also forced many individuals who could not meet its requirements to seek new alliances with others more sympathetic to the pleasures and powers derived from alcoholic beverages.

Not unexpectedly, the Shi'ites profess a more pessimistic view of the wine-drinker's status in the community of believers and in the universe at-large:

> Abu 'Ali al-Ash'ari: Muhammad b. 'Abd al-Jabbar: Safwan: al-'Ala': some of our companions: Abu 'Abdallah: The Prophet said, "Do not treat a wine-drinker who is sick. If he dies, do not prepare him properly for his funeral. If he witnesses, do not bear witness to him. If he becomes engaged, do not allow him to marry. If he asks you about the faith, do not entrust him with it."[68]

This example completely excludes the wine-drinker from all activities vital to the maintenance of one's status in relation to the community, and by analogy to the divine.

In general, the Hadith concerned with dining practices convey the basic message that one who believes should not mingle with those who freely consume wine. Although each tradition centers its discussion around the table, some passages use it to regulate communal practice while others employ it to set up the boundaries between those who will and will not be allowed to enter Paradise. In each case, the fixed entity of the dining table, which is firmly rooted in the Qur'an, allows the prohibition of wine to become a distinguishing mark of one who believes. Once highly ambiguous, wine becomes the fixed line between true believers and those who may profess the same truths about God and the Last Day while quaffing goblets of fine drink.

TALES UPON TALES UPON TALES: SPINNING OUT THE PROHIBITION THROUGH THE COURSE OF HUMAN ACTION

The Hadith also articulate the prohibition of wine through brief stories designed to emphasize the evils of wine and wine-drinking. Ibn Hanbal's following example demonstrates the Prophet's disapproval of selling of wine by setting up an entire scene in which skins of wine are slashed in a public display of anger:

> Al-Hakam b. Nafi': Abu Bakr (b. Abi Maryam): Damra b. Habib: 'Abdallah b. 'Umar said: The Prophet commanded me to bring him a large knife. I brought one to him; he sent it off to be sharpened, and

> gave it back to me. He said, "Come along with me, and bring the knife." So I did. He went out with his companions to the markets of Medina, which held skins of wine (*khamr*) that were brought in from Syria. He took the knife from me and sliced open all the skins that were in front of him. Then, he gave the knife back to me and commanded his companions to follow me. He commanded me to finish off the rest of the market so that not one skin would remain whole. So I did it; I did not leave a single skin in the market unslashed.[69]

The Prophet in this Sunni tradition strongly resembles another figure in sacred history who went on a similar rampage in the marketplace. The Gospel of Mark has this to say about the outrage expressed by one dismayed over what he believed to be a corruption of God's word:

> And they came to Jerusalem. And he entered the Temple and began to drive out those who sold and those who bought in the Temple, and he overturned the tables of the money-changers and the seats of those who sold pigeons; and he would not allow anyone to carry anything through the Temple. And he taught, and said to them, "Is is not written, 'My house shall be called a house of prayer for all the nations'? But you have made it a den of thieves."[70]

Throughout the legal literature, in this and other narratives, Muhammad's activities often parallel those of Jesus.[71]

Again, the point of Ibn Hanbal's passage and others like it is not necessarily to record when the prohibition came about or to establish its Qur'anic roots, but to validate its presence through a story that subtly connects the characters and activities of a community with those of sacred history. Because the narrative grounds the abstract prohibition into a tangible, human context, believers are able to participate with their Prophet in the sacred drama that surrounds the prohibition of wine. By following his example (and the example of his supporters), and pouring out the liquid that God has condemned, or throwing its containers against the wall, or slashing its skins sold in the marketplace, humans become directly responsible for upholding the law. Through their concrete demonstrations of the law, humans plant the revelation more firmly in the world.

In general, narrative discourse realizes several important goals. First of all, it humanizes philosophical propositions or abstract laws, making them more relevant and accessible to the community as a whole and integrating them more fully in human thought and action. Second, the narrative establishes a normative practice that sets those who abstain apart from others who may also believe in "God and the Last Day." Finally, it gives the word, which had been closed and sealed shortly after the death of the Prophet, a concrete form that allows it to be applied to new circumstances without compromising its divine and thus stable character.

ASSERTING THE PROHIBITION THROUGH PAST REDIRECTION: ADDITIONAL COMMENTS ON THE PORTRAYAL OF WINE IN THE *SIRA* AND *TA'RIKH*

Other early Islamic historical and exegetical texts articulate many of the same concerns about wine and wine-drinking laid out in the Hadith. In the first part of Ibn Hisham's *Life of the Prophet* (*al-Sira al-nabawiya*),[72] which is dedicated to describing the customs and practices of pre-Islamic Arabia before the coming of Islam, wine and wine-drinking are used both positively and negatively in the context of poetry to highlight the nobility of those who were soon to receive the divine word. Note the following poem from Dhu Jadan the Himyari, which describes the destruction of the castles of Baynun, Silhin, and Ghumdan in Yemen after the Abysinnian Domination:

> Peace confound you! you can't turn me from my purpose
> Thy scolding dries my spittle!
> To the music of singers in times past 'twas fine
> When we drank our fill of purest, noblest wine (*al-khamr al-rahiq*)
> Drinking freely of wine (*khamr*) brings me no shame.
> If my behavior no boon-companion would blame.
> For death can no man hold back
> Though he drank the perfumed potions of the quack.[73]

In this passage, the consumption of wine is associated with the honor and dignity of those who fought for their cause in battle and bravely faced death at the hand of their enemies. In this context, not even the noblest of wines was strong enough to soften the fear of inevitable death, although one certainly should not be ashamed to assuage the blow by drinking his fill.

Post-Qur'anic representations of pre-Islamic times also draw a strong connection between abstinence and oath-keeping. Sayf b. Dhu Yazan al-Himyari claims:

> Men thought the two kings had made peace
> And those who heard of their reconciliation found the matter very grave.
> We slew the prince Masruq and reddened the sands with blood.
> The new prince, the people's prince,
> Wahriz swore an oath

> that he would drink no wine (*musha'sha'*)
> until he had captured prisoners and spoil.[74]

Here, abstaining from wine until the promise had been fulfilled represents Wahriz's unflinching dedication to his people and to his cause: No wine will be drunk until the desirable result has been realized. In both these examples depicting pre-Islamic times, wine is never praised outright, but abstinence is used in the context of the overall narrative to highlight some honorable and venerable characteristics of those who lived a life as dignified and righteous as possible without benefit of the divine law. Wine is neither condemned nor glorified, but simply acknowledged as an integral part of the pre-Islamic milieu.

When the *Sira* shifts its focus to subjects and lands that are in the process of realizing, or have access to, the divine word, what is at best an ambiguous substance is now recast in a highly unfavorable light. It is important to note, however, that while the *Sira* portrays wine in a negative light, it does not articulate or dwell upon the *prohibition* of wine. Nor does it deal with the specific Qur'anic references that take a less than positive stance towards wine. For example, when the Prophet sends out deputations to teach the divine message, they are presented with lists of some of the major tenets of the faith. These tenets included statements about the good news of Paradise; the warnings of Hell; the authority of the Qur'an; the rites of the pilgrimage (*hajj*); the appropriate way to wear robes and hair while praying; the proper channels for resolving quarrels; the correct way to perform ablutions; how and when to pray; attendance in the mosque; the right amount of booty to extract; and the acceptance of Jews and Christians who were sincere in their conversions.[75] Noticably absent from this rather lengthy list is the prohibition of wine.

In spite of the fact the prohibition is never explicitly discussed, the *Sira*'s portrayal of wine suggests that alcoholic beverages were no longer tolerated in a post-revelatory world that equated abstinence with the acceptance of the final word of the one true God. This view is clearly illustrated in an example that has already been analyzed, that is, the story of Muhammad's night journey, and his receiving of the three drinks as a divine test. In the *Sira*'s rendition of the story, Moses, Abraham, and Jesus have assembled together when Muhammad lands in *Jerusalem*, where he then acts as their leader in prayer before demonstrating his inherent right to rule his community by acing the test. These details supplied by the narrative lend themselves to the obvious assertion of the privileged place of the new religious dispensation in relation to other traditions of the Book.[76]

Wine is also thrown into a negative light in those parts of the *Sira* devoted to recording Muhammad's battles and ultimate claims to political power. For example, wine is mentioned in a story about the conversion of 'Umar, who is said to have sold wine and reveled in drink before he heard the Qur'an and embraced Islam;[77] a tale about the salacious practices of an army about to get slain;[78] a discussion about a soothsayer who could only foresee the future—and therefore be of help to the Prophet's army—when sober;[79] a gory description about the horrors of the battle of Uhud;[80] a depiction of a soldier deemed militarily impotent because his horse became drunk on fermented barley-water (*al-madid al-mukhammar*);[81] and a wayward governor who was deposed by 'Umar because he composed a few verses that glorified drinking and poked fun at the present regime.[82] After the Prophet conquered al-Ta'if, a place well-known for its succulent wines,[83] he is said to have ordered the vineyards to be cut down.[84] Also, a rival prophet to Muhammad is believed to have ordered his people to drink wine and to fornicate, even though he reportedly upheld the tenets of the Qur'an.[85]

Even when the *Sira* uses wine-imagery somewhat positively in the context of poetic description, it directs the entire passage in which that description is embedded toward revealing the divine truth brought forth by the Prophet. Note the following ode recited at the time Ka'b repented to the Prophet:

> Su'ad is gone and today my heart is lovesick,
> in thrall to her, unrequited, bound with chains;
> And Su'ad, when she came forth on the morn of departure,
> Was but as a gazelle with bright black downcast eyes.
> When she smiles, she lays bare a shining side of teeth
> that seems to have been bathed
> once and twice in (fragrant) wine—
> Wine mixed with pure cold water from a pebbly hollow
> where the north-wind blows, in a bend of the valley,
> From which winds drive away every speck of dust,
> and it brims over with white-foamed torrents
> fed by showers gushing from a cloud of morn.[86]

Even though wine is used to highlight a particularly attractive aspect of a woman—her shining teeth—the fact that the poem goes on to talk about her ultimate deceit as a lover causes one to view this lovely and innocent smile with suspicion, for her intentions are the opposite of what they appear to be. The idea that appearances deceive and that one must not fall prey to such deception is further emphasized by the juxtaposition of this love poem onto lengthy adulations of the Prophet and the Qur'an. For example, Ka'b's long, erotic descriptions above are punctuated with lines like the following:

> I was told that the Messenger of Allah threatened me (with death), but with the messenger of Allah I have hope of finding pardon. Gently! mayst thou be guided by Him who gave thee the gift of the Koran, wherein are warnings and a plain setting-out (of the matter).[87]

The weaving together of these two seemingly disparate themes suggests that there is only one goodness and truth; when beauty fades away, and love is tarnished by deceit, all that remains in life is the struggle for what has been divinely inspired and ordained.

Al-Tabari's *Ta'rikh* shares many of the same overarching teleological concerns as the *Sira*, and therefore finds it necessary to show how ultimate success in the sacred drama is tied to abstention from intoxicating drinks. As noted above, al-Tabari does not include any information concerning Noah's drunken behaviors but makes Adam's consumption key in bringing forth his expulsion from the Garden (even though Eve gave him the fateful drink).[88] Like its presentation of Eve, the *Ta'rikh* records other scenarios in which women use wine as a tool to manipulate men to do their bidding. For example, a maiden plied the King of the Israelites with an abundance of wine so that in his drunken and lustful state he ordered John the Baptist's head to be cut off at her request.[89] In one tradition that is recorded but denounced, Khadija gave her father so much wine that he unwittingly gave her hand in marriage to the Prophet of God.[90] In addition, al-Tabari's traditions depict those individuals who turned away from a prophet's message—the descendants of Cain,[91] or the people to whom Noah was sent[92]—as wine-drinkers. The *Ta'rikh* differs from the *Sira*, however, in that it often uses the narratives to define and assert a number of established *legal* points about the prohibition of wine, while the *Sira* uses them to project an overwhelmingly negative view on the consumption of this beverage.

The following anecdote taken from al-Tabari's *magnum opus* fuses an all too familiar law with some contextual detail:

> According to Anas b. Malik: I was present in Jerusalem with 'Umar. While he was giving food to the people one day, a monk from Jerusalem came to him without knowing that wine had been prohibited. The monk said, "Do you want a drink which will be permissible according to our books, [even] when wine is prohibited?" 'Umar asked him to bring it and said, "From what has it been prepared?" The monk informed him that he had cooked it from juice until only one-third remained. 'Umar dipped his fingers into it, then stirred it in the vessel, divided it into two halves, and said, "This is syrup (*tila'*)." He likened it to resin (*qatiran*), drank from it, and ordered the amirs of the Syrian provinces to prepare it. He wrote to the newly established garrison towns (*amsar*), saying, "I have brought a beverage cooked from juice

> until two-thirds of it were gone and one-third remained. It is like syrup. Cook it and provide it to the Muslims."[93]

The two-thirds/one-third law is deeply embedded within an historical account aimed at describing the Caliphate of 'Umar b. al-Khattab when Jerusalem was conquered in the year A.D. 638, an event that had obvious relevance to the community as a whole. This account not only gives the community specific instructions on how to prepare permissible drinks, but also explores the relationship between the Muslims and the other peoples of the Book. For example, the fact that a *monk* brought a drink that was allowed according to "our books" suggests that the prohibition of wine—a law that ultimately distinguishes Muslims from other believers—is really contained in all the books that preceded the Qur'an thus cementing the status of the Qur'an as the cumulative word of God and the law as something to which even Jews and Christians must adhere. This passage illustrates again how an analytic law embedded within a larger narrative frame serves to tie abstract philosophical or prophetic claims together with the concerns of a particular community.

Another story in the same corpus weaves elaborate details about the prohibition of wine with the battles and political decisions that ultimately led to the success of the Muslims over the Quraysh:

> At the time of the afternoon prayer, Muhammad left the two villages and set up camp by the salt marsh. One of 'Ali b. Muhammad's six companions came to him at sunset prayer time and told him that his soldiers were indulging in inebriating drink, which they had discovered in al-Qadisiyyah. Accompanied by Muhammad b. Salm and Yahya b. Muhammad, 'Ali went to inform troops that intoxicants were not permitted, and from that day he declared wine (*nabidh*) illegal. He addressed them, saying, "You will be engaging armies in battle, so cease this indulgence in drink!" And they assented to his demand.[94]

Consumption and abstinence determined how battles were won or lost and, therefore, how sacred history played out in favor of Muhammad's community of believers. Through this short passage, the repudiation of any alcoholic beverage (and not just *khamr*) is linked with the identity of the community and becomes a necessary practice for anyone who considers himself a true believer.

The *Ta'rikh* includes other narratives that present a variety of situations through which the use and abuse of intoxicating beverages can be monitored,[95] and the proper punishments bestowed.[96] Occasionally abstinence from wine is set as one of the good qualities found in a man,[97] or drunkenness one of the concrete signs of moral depravity among those who, through the abuse of their political power, have turned against the word of God.[98] Oftentimes, however, the narrative provides the consummate environment in which to assert and clarify the prohibition. The following passage, for example, seeks to exhaust all the possible ways in which wine can be used through a story about a man taking a bath:

> According to al-Sari: Shu'ayb: Sayf: Abu 'l-Mujalid: They said: The news reached 'Umar that Khalid, once he entered the bathhouse where, after he had removed the depilatory agent, he had rubbed himself with a thick mixture of safflower and wine. So he wrote to him, saying "It has reached me that you rubbed your body with wine, but God has forbidden the drinking of wine or its use in any other way, just as he has forbidden sins committed in a direct or indirect manner. He has even forbidden the touching of wine unless you cleanse yourself of it immediately, just as he has forbidden you to drink it. So make sure it will not touch your body, for it is filth."[99]

Not only is it forbidden to medicate with or sell a prohibited substance, but so, too, is it forbidden to lubricate one's body with it. This passage implies that a person who merely touches wine enters a state of ritual impurity; an addition to this beverage's sins not found in the canonical Sunni collections of Hadith.[100]

In sum, both the *Sira* of Ibn Hisham and Tabari's *Ta'rikh* use stories or anecdotes that contain references to wine to make more general statements about the privileged position of the Islamic community as a whole, as well as to lend support to the authoritative status of the prohibition. In fact, from the time the *Sira* was composed and edited to the time al-Tabari began his monumental work, the negative stance on wine evolved to play a defining role in what it meant to a *Muslim*. Through the telling of these lengthy narratives, the prohibition is inextricably tied to those who have correctly interpreted God's final message.

NARRATIVE DISCOURSE AND ITS PROPHETIC AND ANALYTIC COUNTERPARTS

The treatment of wine through narrative discourse differs greatly from its prophetic and analytic counterparts with its accent on the human details that surround the prohibition. Narrative discourse, in contrast with the prophetic, does not treat wine as an ambiguous sign capable of evoking various and complex dimensions of the divine, but as a material substance able to incite profound iniquities. While the narrative—like the analytic—is concerned with projecting the fundamental patterns of universal law onto a wayward world through its discussion of such a potent substance, it accomplishes this in different ways by laying out the precise, concrete details surrounding the utterance of prohibition that will ultimately extend the abstract law well into human life. Because *'Umar* called his people to abstain; *Muhammad* chose the right drink; and *Abu 'Abdallah* himself condemned an alcoholic cure for hemorrhoids, those who mimic these paragons of true faith can also maintain and secure their place as the righteous and proper inheritors and proprietors of the revelation. Without a tangible human face in the prophetic and analytic literatures, divine law would remain distant, isolated, and detached from any community, which could result in its dissolution. In a world whose stability relies on its complete conformity to the divine, such a loss or decay would be of no small consequence.

4

A Brief Word on the Poetic Portrayal of Wine

The *prohibition* of wine was not a Qur'anic invention, but rather a strict legal proposition developed through analytic and narrative discourses that sought to "clarify" the revelation's ambivalent treatment of wine's ambiguities as a social and conceptual substance. This legal proposition implies a uniformly negative view of wine in the Hadith, although some attempts were made in vain to limit the severity of the prohibition through a variety of subtle exegetical strategies. For example, a minority of Hadith emphasize the dangers of *intoxication* over and against the particular vessel in which a drink is stored,[1] and in a few cases, which are always accompanied by a disclaimer, beverages fermented to varying degrees are grudgingly permitted.[2] Even though members of the Islamic community debated,[3] even flatly rejected,[4] the prevailing condemnation, the uniformly negative view of wine was still recognized and accepted as legal and binding.

Despite the unequivocal legal injunction against wine, the Islamic community still continued to mitigate its force. The wine imagery of the Jahiliya was a particularly rich source for rhetorical equivocation on matters of the vine. In the protected context of the "period of ignorance" (*jahiliya*),[5] the ambiguous quality of wine could evoke and celebrate a variety of sentiments about human existence without explicitly challenging the authority of the prohibition. It was well-known to believers that wine was a licit substance before Muhammad received the revelation. In addition, wine illustrates how the Jahiliya period often served as the vehicle through which the Islamic tradition turned the "pre-Islamic" into the "proto-Islamic," a kind of foil against which the articulation and superior state of the established community could be measured.[6]

As long as the glorifications of wine and the vine or the flagrancies of wine-drinking were confined to the time before the prohibition came about—a time that was pushed to the margins by the later tradition—they could be experienced vicariously without threat or challenge to the divine law. The time of the Jahiliya provided the perfect context for the imaginative consumption of wine because this period was itself deemed equivocal by the later Islamic tradition. Since the Jahiliya was portrayed both as a period of "ignorance" that was *necessarily* superseded by the divine law and as a "chosen" period worthy (and righteous) enough to receive the revelation,[7] it manifested an ambiguity within a temporal schema that readily assimilated the questionable practices of wine-drinking as well as wine's substantial ambiguity.

By preserving what was practiced in the past within the context of what must be superseded, condemned, but also curiously praised and glorified, believers who abstained could participate in wine with all its equivocal qualities—either the ecstasy achieved through intoxication, or the often sordid shamefulness that comes from a drunken stupor—while still observing the laws that rallied against any inherently ambiguous substance. Given that intoxication was often described and experienced through poetic *language* rather than actual consumption, and that this poetic language was itself confined to a period that was already pushed to the fringes of Islamic history, believers could openly embrace the dual nature of wine. This vicarious participation in the positive and negative qualities of wine softened the severity of a prohibition that exhibited, at least ostensibly, no tolerance for ambiguity of any kind.

Like its prophetic, analytic, and narrative counterparts, pre-Islamic poetry adds an important and vital dimension to the discussion of wine. While the prophetic evokes the divine, the analytic imposes a rigid structure upon the vagaries of human life, and the narrative paints that structure with a human face, the poetic preserves ambiguity and articulates wine's necessary—although highly suspect—relevance to human experience.

Vicarious participation in the praising and drinking of wine did not take place solely on the superficial plane of innocent reflection upon poetic description. It also occurred on the much deeper level of common human *ritual*, which represents a mode of experience not found in the other three genres. As Suzanne Pinckney Stetkevych has suggested, the poetry of the Jahiliya has been examined exclusively in terms of its presentation of static descriptions of Bedouin life; rarely have individual poems been analyzed for their overall, recurring paradigmatic structures and functions.[8] By undertaking a structural analysis of pre-Islamic poetry, Stetkevych has shown how these poems move beyond mere description to reflect the inherent patterns of ritual that dominate human life, most significantly, the rites of passage/initiation, separation/reintegration, male/female differentiation, and the distinctions made between purity and pollution, along with variations on these themes.[9]

The poetry's appeal to the very basic structures of human existence through an emphasis on ritual adds an essential, experiential dimension to the three genres of literature discussed above. This dimension is invoked on two separate levels: the level of description, which dwells upon the dual nature of wine through a display of sensual details; and the level of pattern, in which these details are placed within the context of the larger poetic structure.[10] Through his play on the ambiguous nature of wine, the poet creates meaningful contradictions or dichotomies that, when contemplated, bridged, or examined in light of the poetic whole, allow an individual to derive both personal, social, and universal meanings from his own reflections on some of the more complex and deeply rooted patterns of human life.

WINE AS CONCEPTUAL PARADOX

The study of pre-Islamic poetry is vast;[11] this brief discussion will only suggest how the poetic genre treated wine in a way that is fundamentally different from the prophetic, analytic, and narrative discourses. Unlike the authors or sources of the other three discourses, the Jahiliya poets preserve and even glorify the dual nature of wine. The poet explores the wide range of unbridled emotions sparked by intoxication and then contrasts these ecstatic yet melancholy feelings with ethical insights presented at the end of a poem. By privileging the ambiguous nature of wine rather than treating it as a problem to be eliminated, the poet can invoke the complex and often contradictory nature of human existence and offer some kind of resolution to this paradox.

This emphasis on human experience, which can be read empathetically (that is, on an individual level) or sympathetically (that is, as general meditations about the human condition), sets the poetic genre apart from the three discourses described above. Although prophetic discourse closely resembles the poetic in terms of its preservation of ambiguity, it differs greatly by subjecting details to a limited set of divine points, rather than using these diverse images to highlight the inherent patterns essential to human experience. The analytic, on the other hand, bears little resemblance to the poetic, for it tends to subject all idiosyncrasies to the same fundamental laws of the divine order. Narrative discourse holds some similarity to the poetic in terms of its interest in human detail. It, too, however, differs with its subjection of all detail to a limited set of divinely inspired paradigmatic models and themes.

The poetic genre, which sheds light on the multiple (but fixed or limited) dimensions of human existence through contemplation on the ambiguities present in everyday life, offers the perfect balance to these other types of formal language that reject idiosyncratic, sensual, and ambivalent expression. As such, these "pre-Islamic" poems that were privileged by the later tradition effectively, but indirectly (in a nonthreatening manner), opposed a divine prohibition that was deemed to be strict, oppressive, and unequivocal.

In the revelatory age many poets did criticize the prohibition directly and publicly through poems glorifying drunkenness and condemning Islam. Most famous of these protesters were the "libertines of al-Kufa," a group that included Bakr b. Kharija, a Kufan known for the lengthy time he spent in taverns drowning himself in drink and misery; Yahya b. Ziyad al-Harithi, who participated in drinking parties and orgies; and Abu Dulama, who hurled gibes against Islam while quaffing drinks in a saloon.[12] For those who wished not to be placed outside the community of believers or at odds with the one true God and his creation, the wine poems of the Jahiliya provided a shielded context in which to reflect freely upon the consumption of wine.

THE POEMS

The majority of the poems under consideration belong a group of classical Arabian poetry known as *qasa'id* (singular *qasida*). Most of the *qasa'id* belong to Arabia's most famous legendary poetry collection known as the "Suspended Ones" (*Mu'allaqat*). According to the Islamic tradition, poetry competitions took place in pre-Islamic Arabia during an annual fair near Mecca. The winning poems were ultimately embroidered in gold cloth and suspended from the Ka'ba in Mecca.[13] This legend, which drapes the poetry of the Jahiliya around what ultimately became the most sacred pilgrimage center in Islam, reflects the vital role of the Mu'allaqat in the later Islamic literary tradition, both in terms of theme and formal structure.[14] Given that the Islamic tradition embraces the "Mu'allaqat" as a revered category that both celebrates the period of the Jahiliya and serves as a foil against which true belief can be defined and gauged,[15] the poems that fall under this heading allow believers to participate in the sensual pleasures held by their predecessors while directing their gaze to a higher moral, social, and universal understanding.

In sum, the ambiguity of wine, with its play on opposed images, necessitates and facilitates the creation and establishment of some type of solution—in this case, the poet's realization of his personal limitations and social responsibility—both in terms of the structure of the poem as well as the poet's own emotion and experience. This play on ambiguity, however, puts forth a much stronger role in the Islamic tradition than simply an ability to spark a change in heart. Wine and intoxication lead to the squandering away of one's wealth and the ultimate alienation from one's tribe—actions that serve well to highlight the stereotypical characteristics of the Jahiliya. However, the social responsibility that comes out of the contemplation of one's sad predicament allows for a different take on this period altogether. The poets' creation of a social conscience from the recognition of personal limitations allows the later Islamic tradition to read into and portray the Jahiliya as both the ignorant *and* noble precursor to the revelatory era.

Labid b. Rabi'a

Labid's ode,[37] like Tarafa's, also follows the tripartite rite of passage model. The poem beings with a *nasib* that describes ruined dwellings and their departing women, one of whom is the poet's lover, Nawar. The journey motif follows, with an elaborate description of the poet's she-camel. The third stage, the boast, contains a drinking scene, a description of Labid's battle-mare, a gambling scene over the slaughtered camel and the sacrificial feast that followed, and a final word on the political prowess of the poet's tribe.[38] In Labid's ode, as in the case of Tarafa's, the wine passage has a dual function: It accentuates the isolation experienced by the poet, due to a lost love and separation from the community, and also serves as a kind of collective meal, a sacrificial, tribal feast.[39] By serving as part of a meal, "the mere fact of participating in such a drinking scene is an affirmation of membership in the community, that is, of aggregation."[40]

This tripartite pattern will become clearer upon closer examination of the following passage:

> And don't you know how many a night mild in its weather,
> Delightful in its sport and in its revelry,
> I spent as its convivial,
> and rushed to many a merchant's banner
> When it was raised and the price of wine was high.
> I paid a dear price for a wine
> in an aged and darkened wineskin,
> Or in a pitch-lined jug, ladled into cups,

its seal broken.
And many a morning draught of a pure wine
and a slave girl with a lute,
Plucking with her thumb on its taut strings.
My first cup I down before the cock
could crow in daybreak
To take a second when its sleepers woke.[41]

In contrast to the abandoned homes described at the beginning of the poem, the nights of revelry depicted above serve to counter the desolation and emptiness experienced by the poet in the opening scene. Despite the poet's social intercourse with singing girls and his fellowman through his consumption of wine, he has never felt more alone nor has he been set free from longing for his lost love. Wallowing in the state of wine's "forgetfulness," the poet is more acutely reminded of her absence. Moving beyond this liminal moment between isolation and celebration as well as loss and remembrance, the poet ultimately becomes reintegrated into his community. This communal emphasis is underscored by the association of the wine with sacrifice, which is sealed through several images laid out in the above passage. The first of these images is the blood-like color associated with the wine;[42] the second is the broken seal of the wine-jar, which relates to the broken seal of a deflowered virgin;[43] and the third is the notion of the morning draught, which points to the commensal aspect of the drinking passage.[44]

Through this sacrificial imagery, that is, through a return home to the tribe that is commemorated by the animal sacrifice, the immortality of the group, as opposed to the individual, is shown to be the higher good. Like Tarafa's example, Labid's ode aims to take the poet and thus the listener on a journey from the isolated depths of his inner self—or from the self defined by a lover's embrace—to the higher plane of the communal whole. Immortality is not achieved through the glorification of the self or by means of inner contemplation, but rather through the preservation of the tribe, which the sacrifice guarantees. Perpetuation of the tribe is valued; therefore, all action must ultimately be directed towards this higher good that rests over and above any individual aspiration or accomplishment.

In sum, in this example from Labid, the ambiguity of wine allows for movement towards a resolution of two extremes, a way to connect the poet from isolated thought and sensual pleasure to the final recognition and preservation of communal well-being, which is the supreme good. It also allows the poet to move between the opposite planes of loss and recovery: Loss of one's love and the painful memory of her, and more importantly, the loss of one's tribe and the remembrance of one's loyalty to it. It is wine's ambiguous status as a source of individual pleasure and pain as well as its function within a communal meal—a source of bodily sensation and communal responsibility—that allows it to facilitate the final movement, the closing of the gap between the liminal stage and that of tribal reintegration; the breach between self-isolation and communal obligation and participation. Again, as in Tarafa's example above, this duality of emotion and its resolution through the realization of social well-being further facilitates the Islamic tradition's understanding of the Jahiliya as both a time that required reform, yet was noble enough to receive the revelation.

'Alqama b. 'Abada

'Alqama[45] composed an ode that resembles the other two in that it opens with the remembrance of a beloved's departure, moves to the journey-phase, and concludes with the boast, which is introduced by a set of proverbs that ends with a wine song, horse-scene, and final pageantry.[46] In this ode, like that of Labid's, the wine-song takes on the formalities of a ritual that precedes a communal sacrifice:[47]

> I could well see the drinkers, among them a ringing lyre,
> men laid low by golden, foaming wine,
> The drink of a potentate,
> aged by tavernkeepers for a special occasion.
> It'll take you up and spin you around.
> For the headache it's a cure.
> A jolt of it won't harm you.
> No dizziness from it will mix in your brain,
> A vintage of 'Anah, a slammer,
> for a full year unexposed,
> kept in a clay-stoppered jug with a waxen seal,
> Glistening in its decanter,
> while a foreign-born page,
> mouth covered with a cotton band, pours it,
> Flagon like a gazelle high on the cliff face,
> neck and spout sealed with a linen sieve.
> Its keeper brings it out into the sun.
> It flashes white, ringed by branches of sweet basil,
> fragrance brimming over.[48]

Again, the placement of the wine passage before the final movement, the heroic boast in which the human struggle is affirmed while the two dominant forces of the human condition—fate and death—are contemplated, is strategic. On the one hand, the glorification of wine represents a certain celebration of life through the power of enhanced emotions and social contact. However, because the passage exploring the upper boundaries of joy *precedes* the final stage in which the lower limitations of life are also uncovered, the pleasure that is achieved becomes a double-edged sword since it is recognized that life's great joys are ultimately countered by death. As the poet himself describes this view of life in the verses that follow the wine scene, "whatever the stakes, the loser pays."[49]

'Alqama, like Tarafa and Labid, plays on the ambiguity of wine by first setting it up as one of the utmost pleasures in human life, and then connecting it with the bleak images of fate and death, which mark some of the lowest, inescapable experiences of human life. Pleasures can only be held in light of pain, life can only be recognized and experienced in light of death. As the poet lays out these opposites, he states: "On one side a spring-born calf is pleading, while on the other, the old camels, humps high, bellow."[50] Joy and sensual pleasure are set off to one extreme while fate and death are set off to the other. The drinking scene, which embodies these ambiguities, allows for the sharp contrast to be drawn between the two poles of opposites. With the realization of the limits of existence, both in terms of pleasure and pain, and of life and death, the poet is able to come to a new level of understanding about himself and his necessary place within his community. Again, as in the poems of Tarafa and Labid, the fact that community is emphasized over an individual's joy and sensual pleasure further parallels the dual nature of the Jahiliya itself. The Jahiliya not only embraced the undesirable qualities that necessitated the reforms of the coming revelation, but also those worthy and virtuous ones that in many ways already contained the seeds of what would later become Islam.

Maymun b. Qays (al-A'sha)

Like the models presented in the above examples, the ode of al-A'sha also follows the tripartite pattern of the *nasib*, *rahil*, and *fakhr*.[51] In this case, however, the theme of love becomes the dominant force that drives the poem forward. The poet begins with a long reflection on the woman (Hurayra) he desires but is unable to possess because she pines for another. In the second stage of the poem, al-A'sha replaces the conventional physical journey with a series of self-descriptive soliloquies designed to prove his love. One of these self-descriptions takes the form of a tavern scene through which al-A'sha demonstrates his social and sensual prowess:

I've been to taverns, my company a griller,
and sat hobnobbing with young men,
stern and hard like Indian swords,
who've known many a lover to perish of love's many woes:
I gently indulged them in curios of wit and jest
as we sat sipping bitter coffee,
and distilled wine from moist mugs—
wine of which their mouths never seemed to dry,
but forever called to the innkeeper,
"more wine"; and he, rolling up his shirt sleeves,
hurried back with
brimming flasks encased in red leather.[52]

Again, this scene stands in sharp contrast with the poet's isolation at the beginning of the poem; al-A'sha can revel with the best of them. However, as the poem progresses, the sensual value of wine and drunkenness is continuously questioned and ultimately replaced by a call for a pure love that lies above and beyond immediate, physical gratification. The point that wine hinders one's ability to see all that is true and good in the world is underscored by the following lines:

But see you yonder cloud
on whose edges lightning gleams like a flaming torch?
There's another behind it, and another,
huge and flashing,
surrounds it like a big bucket.
But from this joyful sight no revelry,
no drunkenness could ever distract me:
so I turned to those wine guzzlers in Durna, "Look at the flash"
but how could these guzzlers ever see?[53]

It is with this profound realization of nature's true beauty, a beauty that is not enhanced but rather marred by intoxication, that al-A'sha's emotions for Hurayra are transformed from lustful desire into a more pure and ethical love that can only be realized through moral conduct and self-control. This shift is evident in the last phase of the poem, where the individual value of self-control is raised to the level of a tribal ethic. Only through moral conduct and self-discipline is one free to judge others, as is demonstrated by the poet, who, having gained control over his own emotions, is finally able to launch a successful attack against his enemies.

The wine scene in this ode allows the poet to shift his focus from the gratification of his own immediate, sensual desires to the understanding and embracing of higher, ethical truths that draw him out of his isolation and hedonistic self-absorption, and place him squarely within the folds of the community. Because of his reflection on wine's ambiguous status as a beverage that both sharpens the senses of pleasure and pain, yet dulls them when it comes to envisioning a higher truth and beauty, the poet is able to examine his own life critically. The poet thus facilitates the shift from selfish desire to the realization of a purer form of love at the end of the poem. This ethical and moral evolution not only takes place within the individual and the tribe as a whole, but, by analogy, it also occurs within the flow of history as people move from the time of "ignorance" to that of Islam.[54]

THE OTHER SIDE OF IGNORANCE

The importance of poetry as a polemical or rhetorical tool in the period following the death of Muhammad is well-attested; this argument has been made in several long treatises on the subject and will only be summarized here.[55] In general, after the Prophet's death many poems appeared that were stylistically modeled after the pre-Islamic classical odes. These poems did not further the cause of the tribe, but the cause of Islam. For example, some poets glorified certain Muslim patrons who wished to be eulogized by mimicking the wine-imagery made popular by their Jahiliya predecessors.[56] So as not to confuse these later developments with the discussion of Jahiliya poetry, it is important to examine the poetry that appeared after the death of the Prophet.

While pre-Islamic poetry functioned as a kind of reenactment of tribal values, a ritual that enabled the tribe to face the impending forces of fate and death in an often brutal world,[57] the poetry that appeared during the Islamic period was panegyric: The poet no longer sung the praises of his tribe, but rather used the same kind of language and imagery to put forth the propaganda of a Muslim patron.[58] What sets apart these post-Jahiliya poems is the fact that they are dotted with a language that lacquers these patrons with familiar Qur'anic imagery and phrases, such as "the Guardian of the Faith" and "God's favorite."[59]

During the Umayyad times the Jahiliya wine-song branched off into an independent genre known as the *khamriya* (wine ode) and at this point functioned explicitly as a form of protest against the prohibition of wine.[60] While the poetic glorification of wine was used as a voice of dissent during this time, wine-imagery was also taken into the opposite direction by mystics who described their love for God through the language of intoxication.[61] Certainly both of these post-Jahiliya developments had much influence on the language of the prohibition as it was debated and refined in some of the later legal and exegetical traditions, and vice versa.

However, all of this is going well beyond the focus of this discussion. What must be kept in mind is that the poetry of the "Jahiliya," the poetry that traditionally preceded the prophetic revelation, lent another voice, another dimension, another possible interpretation to the other types of genres that disputed and discussed the same ambiguous substance. The fact that the poetry of the Jahiliya presented a viable—if not threatening—alternative to the views of wine presented in the Qur'an and Hadith is well-attested by the fact that the later Islamic tradition had most of these poets living long past a normal life span only to die during the time of Islam, a time when they would no longer be considered "ignorant" but knowledgeable in light of the new faith.

THE POETIC PRESERVATION OF WINE'S POTENT AMBIGUITIES

Poetic discourse dwells upon wine's inherent contradictions in order to evoke individual and social truths. Because drinking can be social yet solitary, it elicits a spectrum of sensual pleasures while noting the transience of such physical gratification. An individual, and by analogy the social whole, is forced to reconcile these two extremes by forming some ethical or moral realization about the self and its role within the community. Therefore, wine's ambiguities are continuously glorified and then thwarted as a way to facilitate the poet's—as well as the listener's—personal and social development, which in turn secures the life of the community.

The function of wine in poetic discourse may be better understood when compared to its role a related discourse; that is, that of the prophetic. Like the poetic, prophetic discourse highlights ambiguity in order to make a limited set of universal points. Although resembling the poetic in terms of structure and function, prophetic discourse differs greatly in terms of the kinds of truths it generates. For example, while poetic discourse uses the ambiguity of wine to evoke ethical and social order, the prophetic uses it to clarify and call forth divine truth. Rather than embodying the dichotomies of pleasure/pain, life/death, or social/antisocial, as portrayed in the poetic treatment of wine, wine in prophetic discourse actualizes that which is of God and that which is not of God. Bridging the gap between these polar opposites is not the individual who comes to realize the fundamental importance of tribal well-being, but the individual believer, who must recognize the difference between what is divine and what is not and make the right choice between the two.

In sum, the fundamental difference between poetic and prophetic discourse is not one of structure, but of orientation. With poetic discourse, not only are the images of wine rendered into physical, human terms, but so, too, are the truths they evoke. Through its play on the varied qualities and effects of wine, poetic discourse offers a viable alternative, or at least an element of mitigation, to the overwhelmingly negative treatment of this enticing but feared beverage that is more often than not found within the contours of a divine lesson rather than a human celebration.

This alternative view, which uses wine-imagery to underscore such fundamental issues as human understanding, growth, and tribal dignity (issues vital to human and communal life), could be successfully generated, protected, and preserved in a period as ambivalent as that of the Jahiliya. Drunkenness in the Jahiliya went hand in hand with numerous, unencumbered revelries with women, profound forgetfulness, and the squandering away of wealth. Intoxication, however, along with these other vices was readily overcome by moral choice, concern for tribal welfare, and an awareness of the higher, social good. Like drunkenness, the "ignorance" of the Jahiliya was readily checked by its unique strength and ability to receive and accept the divine word. Because of its profound ambiguity, wine not only allowed for twists of emotion and understanding within the poetry itself, but also for vital spins of interpretation put forth by the later tradition as it negotiated its barbarous but noble past.

5

Wine and Mystical Utterance

Upon its reflection of wine's many contradictions, Jahiliya poetry plays off the potent, sensual qualities of wine to condemn and celebrate a broad range of human experiences. Within the context of the Jahiliya, believers can participate in a kind of "vicarious consumption" experienced through poetic language. Poetry intoxicates; it does not violate. Similarly descriptive in nature, mystical poetry also uses wine's ambiguous nature to facilitate a certain type of experience. However, unlike the poetry of the Jahiliya, mystical poetry captures the experience of paradox itself—the essence of which it claims is divine—through wine and intoxication. Because mystical poetry attempts to describe a spiritual liberation, which is in itself indescribable, and to transcribe the ineffable—an inherent contradiction—images and metaphors that embody such contradictions become a staple of the mystic's poetic vocabulary.

The obvious parallels between mysticism and intoxication have long been acknowledged by scholars of religion, including William James, who writes:

> Sobriety diminishes, discriminates, and says no; drunkenness expands, unifies, and says yes. It is in fact the great exciter of the *Yes* function in man. It brings its votary from the chill periphery of things to the radiant core. It makes him for the moment one with truth.[1]

James goes on to say that while the depth of truth is revealed through the state of intoxication, sobriety leaves one with the distant memory of having engaged a profound state beyond what is readily apparent.[2] Intoxication, in that it brings about the awareness of another realm existing outside the dimension of normal consciousness, provides an obvious analogue to the

Sufi, who claims to have experienced such an ideal state in which the self is abolished and all is indistinguishable from the divine.

Likewise, then, sobriety—as adopted by the Sufi—becomes the place from which to traverse alterity, that is, to catalogue the shape and contours of that anomalous, intoxicated state seemingly devoid of self-conscious reflection. Although the mystic may claim otherwise, a perpetual state of intoxication or self-annihilation would hardly be desired, for there would be no point of contrast, no sense of normalcy or separation (sobriety) from which to reflect upon one's peculiar experience. Ironically, the Sufi can only be wholly aware of his loss of self and complete absorption into the divine when he has been severed from the place he longs to be. It is *only after* the mystic has restored his personal identity (or regained sobriety) that he can articulate fully the more desirable state of being (inebriation) in which the self is emptied of all that is not God. As such, intoxication and sobriety are particularly vivid and powerful images that hint at the mystic's quandry to lose his identity in union with the divine while remaining acutely aware of the details of his highly personal, individual experience.

In addition, wine, itself a subversive element within the tradition, becomes a useful metaphor for establishing the mystic's place in relation to other voices of authority. First, as stated above the Islamic tradition condemns wine and intoxication, because they break a number of physical and ethical boundaries, a radical act that threatens the very stability of the cosmos. The mystic himself, therefore, is not unlike this beverage and its effects for he, too, violates the recognized lines between human/divine, effable/ineffable, personal/impersonal, orthodoxy/unorthodoxy. Sufis, therefore, challenge both prophetic and analytic efforts to thwart instability and transformation as they freely and unrestrictedly move back and forth from a state of absorption (intoxication) to its necessary counterpart or antithesis (sobriety). For the mystic, true understanding can only be realized through an acceptance and embracing of the unresolved tension created by a selfless absorption into the divine and the continuous, self-conscious longing for and reflection upon that experience.

The Sufi also transgresses traditional, legal boundaries by privileging his own mystical experience over and above normative channels of authority. For example, both the mystics and the Qur'an talk about wine in relation to the divine and the heavenly Paradise. The paradisical vintage as described in the Qur'an is one that cannot intoxicate and therefore challenge the inherent stability and autonomy of the heavenly Garden that stands in direct opposition to a volatile world. However, while the Qur'an simply strips an earthly beverage of its subversive characteristics in order to create an ideal beverage for those who have followed the will of God, the Sufis convert these problematic qualities into metaphors that evoke non-tangible meanings capable of moving the true believer beyond the visually rich and stable Qur'anic Paradise (in essence an ideal earth) to an abstract, ineffable—yet strangely personal—encounter with the divine. The fact that this metaphorical language employs the properties of a *condemned* beverage to illuminate all that defies illumination ultimately allows the mystics to privilege their ideal resting place over and above the one prescribed by the tradition.

THE POETICS OF INTOXICATED LOVE AND SOBER REFLECTION

This study shall examine but a few representative examples from the vast corpus of relevant Sufi poetry. The mystics' desire to exploit every linguistic nuance and subtlety to express what ultimately cannot be said renders a large portion of Sufi work somewhat repetitive for our purposes. What will be included here are a few key examples that illustrate the mystical appropriation of wine-imagery. These examples come from the hands of two authors who are well-known for their extensive references to wine and intoxication: 'Umar Ibn al-Farid and Jalal al-Din Rumi.

'Umar Ibn al-Farid

Like many of his Jahiliya predecessors, Ibn al-Farid (A.D. 1182–1235), a native of Cairo,[3] explores the theme of a lover's longing for his beloved.[4] Ibn al-Farid departs from his famous forerunners in that his beloved is none other than the divine himself and the lover the mystic in search of what he desires. In a well-known wine ode (*khamriya*),[5] Ibn al-Farid uses wine and intoxication to evoke images of a pure contemplation unadulterated by individual, human thought.[6] Unlike the intoxicated state condemned in both the Qur'an and Hadith, the drunkenness he postulates, which preceded the creation of the vine does not disturb the mind, but rather produces a rare understanding not found on the level of earthly existence.

The poem opens by recalling a state of preexistence in which the soul was intoxicated on the wine of Divine Love:[7]

> (1) In memory of the Beloved we quaffed a vintage that made us drunk
> before the creation of the vine.
> (2) Its cup the full moon; itself the sun which a new moon causes
> to circle. When it is mingled with water,
> how many stars appear!
> (3) But for its perfume, I should not have found the way to

its taverns; and but for its resplendence, the imagination
would not have pictured it.
(4) Time hath preserved of it but a breath: it is unseen as a
thing hidden in the bosom of the mind.[8]

In these first four lines, the poet sets up two contrasting spheres that remain forever separate: the realm of truth, and the realm of ordinary material existence. As this section suggests, some (but not all) individuals have a sense that their souls are not where they should be. The soul's true state has somehow become trapped in the corrupting realm of existence, with only a distant memory of its pure origins. The source of one's true identity would remain forever hidden had the perfume and resplendence of a pure, Divine Love (here disguised as wine) not wafted through the recesses of the minds of those whose memories seek to recall their origins in that perfected, intoxicated state of preexistence.

The author's assertion of this sharp dichotomy—and strong hierarachy—between pure versus material reality becomes a recurring theme that is forwarded by images of wine and intoxication and informs the next four lines and the rest of the poem:

(5) If it be mentioned amongst the tribe, the tribesmen become
intoxicated without incurring disgrace or committing sin.
(6) It oozed up from the inmost depths of the jars (and vanished),
and in reality nothing was left of it but a name.
(7) If it ever come into the mind of a man, joy will abide
with him and grief will journey away.
(8) And had the boon-companions beheld the sealing of its vessel,
that sealing would have inebriated them without
(their having tasted) the wine.[9]

The potency of the metaphor of intoxication in lines five to eight stems from the fact that it is circumscribed by actual experience while transcending that very experience. Because an earthly intoxication can suggest the pleasures of lost inhibitions and a corresponding loss of self-awareness, one who has drunk wine from an ordinary vintage may find recognition in Ibn al-Farid's mystical visions. However, given that Ibn al-Farid's drunkenness occurred "before the creation of the vine," those earthly drinkers will soon find themselves quickly distanced from the deeper meanings of the poem. Their physical expectations would be sorely disappointed by Ibn al-Farid's *spiritual* intoxication.

Upon reading the poem, those who have become inebriated on ordinary wine will come to see that Ibn al-Farid's intoxication does not befuddle the mind, but, like the wine of the Qur'anic Paradise, produces a rare clarity.[10] Rather than stripping the beverage itself of its intoxicating properties, Ibn al-Farid retains the ecstatic emotion wrought by intoxication, but elevates this state of mind beyond an earthly drunkenness. Those who drink the pure liquid of Divine Love will lose their capacity for rational thought, but will not yield to those disruptive behaviors that often accompany a drunken state. In addition, one can become intoxicated without so much as taking a sip in Ibn al-Farid's vision. What these thwarted expectations suggest is that the poem is truly effective for those who have never taken a drop or seen an intoxicant, in other words, for those who adhere to the tenets of the tradition. Even the altered state of mind produced by an earthly wine—which itself expands, unifies, and says *yes* in its own way—must be rejected in order to liberate the self to what is truly real.

The poem continues in lines nine to twenty to list a series of miracles brought forth by the Divine Love masquerading as "wine."[11] This potent source of pure inebriation can raise the dead, heal the sick and disabled, cause one to regain his smell, keep a wanderer on the right path, inoculate against the venom of snakes, ward off madness, or lead a doubter to resolution—just to mention a few. Again, these qualities are not those normally associated with an earthly intoxication; in fact, these healing qualities point in the opposite direction of those behaviors or acts that stem from one sipping too much alcohol. Interestingly enough, many of the qualities mentioned in Ibn al-Farid's poem are those cited in several Hadith as reasons for *condemning* the consumption of wine and other alcoholic drinks.[12] Here, rather than disturbing the cosmic order, wine becomes a tool for restoring an ordered world, or at least allowing for a chosen few to escape a hopeless state of disorder.

By essentially reversing one's ordinary expectations, Ibn al-Farid is projecting what cannot be stated. "True" intoxication can only be understood through knowledge of its earthly form; however, knowledge of its earthly form constrains one's ability to experience what ultimately cannot be articulated. Only when one becomes aware of how the liberating effects of an alcohol-induced drunkenness actually bind the self to the material realm can one comprehend how an intoxication wrought by Divine Love can ultimately return the self to its true state.

Because the metaphor of intoxication is both limited by, yet transcends, actual experience, it provides the ideal rhetorical pivot around which the mystic can move back and forth between states of ecstasy (loss of identity and absorption into the divine), and sobriety (return of identity and the point from which to reflect). Without such a metaphor that necessitates two contrasting modes of experience (earthly intoxication and its pure, unadulterated form) and distanced reflection upon that experience (sobriety), the mystic could not exist, or at least could not voice the ineffable.

In line twenty-one, Ibn al-Farid fields an obviously rhetorical question that asks him to describe this mysterious and unusual wine, "for thou art acquainted with its description."[13] Here, we find the mystic's quandry fully articulated: Certainly Ibn al-Farid cannot describe in detail what cannot be described. To satisfy his inquisitor, he launches into yet another description of this wine's positive attributes but attaches certain qualifiers to each one that essentially negate each "positive." This act of bestowing traits and then negating them stems from the problem of giving the "ineffable" names which, in fact, do little to describe what actually is.

The ideal wine is, as Ibn al-Farid describes, "pure, but not as water; subtle, but not as air; luminous, but not as fire; spirit, but not (joined to) body."[14] What appears in his rather vague and somewhat contradictory descriptions is what Michael Sells has labeled *aporia*, that is, the presentation of a dilemma.[15] Sells suggests that one of the problems mystics face is that saying something *is* is saying something positive. Because the ineffable defies all words or categories, any positive statement is in need of some sort of negative qualifier that will move the ineffable once again outside the realm of human understanding.[16] As Sells argues, "the authentic subject of discourse slips continually back beyond each effort to name it or to deny it nameability. The regress is harnessed and becomes the guiding semantic force of a new kind of language."[17] Sells has labeled this act of pairing positive statements with negatives *apophasis,* a term which implies that a "saying must continually be unsaid, resulting in a tension that itself contains meaning."[18] Ibn al-Farid, by suggesting that wine is pure, but not as water is pure (and that a "true" intoxication is unlike an earthly one), uses *apophasis* to answer the question posed to him by not answering it.

Lines 23–30 continue along this line by presenting a series of paradoxes that attempt to illustrate the split of the cosmos into "pure" and material realms. The discourse discussing this pure wine was "eternally prior to all existing things" (23);[19] "through it all things came into being" (24);[20] it is a "wine without a vine" (26);[21] "before it is not 'before' and after it is not 'after' " (29);[22] "its grapes were pressed in the winepress ere Time began" (30).[23] These nonsequitors point to wine, a material substance, but describe it in terms that can only be associated with the immaterial. The poet demonstrates the paradox of describing the nonmaterial: it can only be *imagined* via a material signifier. As a result, while one can comprehend the realm of the real (of which this earthly realm is a mere shadow), one can never truly grasp its essence, for it is continuously constrained by the images used to project it.

The rest of the poem (lines 31–41) plays off the prohibition of wine by again reversing what is normally assumed. In line thirty-three, wine is not depicted as a great sin, but as "the greatest sin to renounce."[24] Here we have a direct challenge to the orthodox condemnation of wine. Those who seek the divine in the negation of ecstatic experience are truly at odds with cosmic truth. Wine is not a beverage that steers one away from truth, but rather moves one toward truth:

> (40) Joyless in this world is he that lives sober,
> and he that dies not drunk will miss the path of wisdom.
> (41) Let him weep for himself—whose life is wasted
> without part or lot in wine![25]

In startling contrast to those Hadith that recount the horrors facing those who die with a trace of wine upon their lips[26] (but without direct reference to those Hadith), these few lines advocate a constant state of drunkenness that violates no cosmic or earthly laws, but in fact restores the natural order of things. Here, all the negative qualities one expects from wine and wine-drinking are in fact reversed to the degree that they become positive and even *necessary* parts of one's true faith. With this interpretive twist, Ibn al-Farid is replacing traditional authority with his own experiential/non-experiential understanding of what is ultimately true, and how one is to gain access to that truth.

What this *khamriya* poem presents are series of paradoxes, thwarted expectations, and the rupturing of earthly and cosmic boundaries. True intoxication can never be captured through human language; only in the state of sobriety can the Sufi hint at the ineffable experience. Even though moments of ecstasy and true intoxication rely upon the contrasted state of sobriety for the realization of their potency and meaning, the mystic portrays sobriety as the flawed version of where he longs to be. However flawed this state may be, it serves as a key vantage point from which the Sufi can privilege certain understandings about the divine that often conflict with traditional interpretations. As illustrated above, such understandings include an ideal state of (pre)existence to which all those in the know (Sufis) must return, a dualistic vision of the cosmos, and a sense that intoxication, or the loss of self-identity, is the way to move from the material realm to the realm of spirit, or Divine Love.

Through the constant denials that his wine-imagery and metaphors of intoxication at all resemble their earthly forms, the mystic has an effective cover for his reinterpretation of the established tradition. Ibn al-Farid cannot be accused of being a revisionist of the tradition, because he would be the first to suggest that the images he uses to describe what essentially cannot be described are ultimately inadequate. What Ibn al-Farid actually *is* saying will never be revealed in any concrete fashion for any positive statement he may make about the ineffable is quickly denied and countered with a negative. The fact that *intoxication* is used as opposed to some other metaphor that would be equally inadequate reveals to some extent the mystic's interpretive agenda. The mystics' idiosyncratic use of wine's rhetorical character signals their exclusionary aims: only a select few can comprehend the irony and paradox of a wine that intoxicates and thereby perfects the believers' obedience to God.

Jalal al-Din Rumi

While Ibn al-Farid's meanings are somewhat veiled and cryptic, none cannot deny the message put forth through the ecstatic utterings of Jalal al-Din Rumi (A.D. 1207–1273).[27] While Ibn al-Farid has been accused of being far more reserved and cautious than his Persian companions,[28] no one could charge Rumi of mincing words. Like Ibn al-Farid, Rumi relies upon the common knowledge of earthly drunkenness to evoke an awareness of the kinds of effects Divine Love produces. However, once that image is evoked, Rumi quickly disassociates the purified version of intoxication from its flawed worldly counterpart so that the ideal may never be confused with the real:

> Like me, cut yourself off from sensuality's intoxication—
> behold its drunkenness in a camel!
> Know that in this world the drunkenness of sensuality is despicable
> compared to the angels' intoxication.
> Their intoxication dwarfs this intoxication—
> how should they pay any regard to sensuality?
> Until you have drunk fresh water, briny water is as sweet to you
> as light in the eyes.
> A single drop of heaven's wine will tear your spirit away
> from all these wines and sakis.[29]

While ordinary drunkenness can lend some insight into the kind of intoxication experienced by angels, Rumi is clear to note that this earthly type of inebriation pales in comparison and must be sacrificed to attain a higher form of awareness.

Like Ibn al-Farid, Rumi also uses images of wine and intoxication to contrast a flawed material realm accessed through exterior or superficial understanding with an ideal realm appropriated through inner (and thus more privileged) gnostic awareness or recognition. He claims, for example, that "the vulgar drink wine from the outside, but the gnostics drink it from the inside."[30] This wine, unlike all earthly wines, "will make you the master of meaning and deliver you from outward forms!"[31] The mere mention of such a drink is considered a danger to those who are "unripe," or ignorant, for their incomprehension will lead them away from inner truths to a wine that is "disgraced."[32] Similar to the beverage evoked in Sura 16 (al-Nahl) in the Qur'an, this radiant, illuminating wine of the mystics shifts the attention away from the material realm toward the realm of the divine. Unlike Suras 47 (Muhammad), and 56 (al-Waqi'a) however, wine no longer serves as a paradisical reward of any type, a static and fixed sign of an ideal order to which all things on Earth must aspire, but rather the essence of Divine Love itself. Again, these mystics rely upon the necessary but wholly inadequate metaphor of *human* inebriation as a means to gain access to the intoxication Divine Love evokes.

Like Ibn al-Farid, Rumi is accutely aware of the Islamic tradition's prohibition against wine, and supports that position by condemning also those earthly "wines of wretchedness"[33] that veil the intelligence. However, Rumi is careful to distinguish the wine wrought by Divine Love from ordinary alcoholic beverages:

> Hark, oh heart! Be not deceived by every intoxication!
> Jesus is drunk with God, but his ass is drunk with barley.[34]

Rumi's condemnation of ordinary vintages and his exhaltation of spiritual drinks presents a paradox to the reader. The potency of the wine metaphor lies in the fact that the tradition considers alcoholic beverages such dangerous substances. How odd to harnass and embrace the power of those dangerous substances which, under ordinary circumstances, can sever the relationship between man and God, and disrupt the order of the cosmos! By glorifying this drink prohibited for its transforming nature, the mystic himself is transgressing recognized boundaries and subverting ordinary experience to facilitate a loss of identity and ultimate absorption into the Divine. Like ordinary grapes that become wine, the mystic, too, undergoes a radical metamorphosis from individual believer to a "master of meaning,"[35] a connoisseur of Divine Love. As long as one clings to normal realities and expectations about wine and intoxication, he will forever be tied to the material realm, and forever excluded from the mysteries that behold one who becomes *truly* drunk. By engaging in the language of *mystical* intoxication, the Sufi can uphold the fundamental laws of the tradition while breaking them *symbolically*. This interpretive move allows him to privilege a new conceptual framework while claiming fidelity to established practice and belief.

Rumi, like Ibn al-Farid, also uses wine and intoxication to privilege certain types of believers (ascetic Muslims) over others (ascetic Christians). In line thirty-four of his *khamriya*, for example, Ibn al-Farid states that Christian ascetics were "intoxicated by [wine] without having drunk thereof!"[36] Here, the poet is asserting that the doctrine that God revealed himself in Christ represents only a portion of the truth, a truth that is only realized by *Islamic* saints, who proclaim the complete message that God is revealed in every atom of existence.[37] Similar to Ibn al-Farid's use of wine as a distinguishing criterion among Christian and Muslim mystics, Rumi argues that Jesus' community only drank grape wine while the community of the Qur'an consumed its pure, ideal form.[38] Both Rumi and Ibn al-Farid separate true believers from those further down the path to understanding through a subtle distinction in the vintage one drinks: those with access to a partial truth drink from an earthly vine, and those with full access quaff the ideal type. Oddly enough, while most Muslims see that reward coming to them in Paradise, the mystic has access to it in the here and now.

MYSTICAL LANGUAGE AND THE NON-RESOLUTION OF CONFLICT

While the poets of the Jahiliya seek to resolve wine's ambiguities in order to evoke certain individual and communal responses, the mystics take the opposite approach. The mystics prefer to exacerbate those gray areas; for them, truth lies somewhere in that which defies categorical understanding. Resolution of such ambivalencies will only lead one further away from true knowledge and experience; truth surfaces as one moves back and forth between the two polar opposites of sobriety/intoxication, experience/reflection upon that experience, and the material/ideal realms.

Like its prophetic, analytic, and narrative, and, to a certain degree poetic counterparts, mystical discourse also supports the prohibition of wine and concedes the dangers inherent in an earthly intoxication. An earthly intoxication will only lead one away from the true state of drunkenness which results in a loss of self and absorption into the divine. Anyone confusing the two states of mind is obviously not in the know, and will forever be tied to the muck and mire of the material realm. However, the fact that a prohibited substance is used to express an awareness of a God who vehemently opposes its consumption further strengthens the Sufis' authoritative voice, for they are suggesting that Divine Love transgresses all *human* boundaries, including those that theoretically establish his will. Using a condemned substance to make their point also allows the Sufis to use their *experience* of the two polar extremes as a means to penetrate divine truths not contemplated by ordinary believers who follow the literal meaning of the law. The fact that the Sufis do not advocate the imbibing of an earthly intoxicate illustrates their reverence for what is ultimately decreed by God; however, their privileging of such blasphemous imagery indicates their willingness to assert that true knowledge of God must go beyond the observance of his laws or the literal meaning of his texts.

Conclusions and Future Comparative Directions

THE FIVE DISCOURSES AS A WHOLE

The presence of prophetic, analytic, narrative, poetic, and mystical discourses in the early Islamic tradition translates an ineffable religious vision into concrete, human terms while asserting the proper interpretive mechanisms that would inoculate it from human interference or control. For example, prophetic discourse bestows wine with a number of different interpretive possibilities, but funnels the variations into two outcomes: Wine either evokes the glories of Paradise, or expresses an earthly transgression. While analytic discourse relocates a heavenly wine into its earthly context, it does so by tying it to the fixed structures of natural law that governs the universe itself. The narrative form links the discussion of wine with the vagrant life of the community, but does so by subjecting content to a divinely approved end result, no matter what the condition or context. Poetic discourse is no exception as it uses vicarious consumption for the restricted purposes of illustrating either the barbaric practices of a people who required the revelation, or the nobility of a people who deserved it. Mystical discourse also restricts wine-imagery to highlight a limited set of emotions. In this case, the actual consumption of wine is replaced with a metaphorical understanding of how its effects produce a particular, privileged understanding of the divine.

Although each type of discourse deals with some aspect of rendering the ineffable vision into human terms, each one taken alone is too limited to serve as the tradition's primary mode of interpretation. However, when the five discourses are netted together as a whole, they create a more flexible, productive, and accommodating interpretive dynamic. This dynamic translates the revelation into the language of the world through a variety of ways and means that resolve the problem of ambiguity without threatening the semblance of divine superiority and stability. What these five genres generate as a whole is a cluster of fixed paths or possibilities through which the revelation can be properly interpreted, translated, asserted, and elaborated.

Prophetic discourse serves to evoke a limited set of understandings about the divine. Given that wine can simultaneously evoke the glories of God's wonders in Paradise as well as instigate disunity among believers, its status as a licit beverage becomes clouded when order and structure (rather than divine evocation) become the primary focus of inquiry. When order and structure are privileged, then the substantive nature of wine—a nature that lends itself to the systematic purging of its equivocal qualities—becomes the more suitable focus for interpretive activity. Taken as parts of a single whole, these two types of discourse—prophetic and analytic—complement one another. Through formulaic language, analytic discourse provides the necessary, logical structures for interpreting the revelation while the prophetic divinizes the formulae (through indirect means), thereby preserving, evoking, and continuously asserting the true word of God. Just as the analytic does little to spark insight into the nature of God's will through wine-imagery, so, too, does the prophetic fail when it comes to determining whether or not something like "barley drinks" should be included under the category of "wine," and therefore prohibited. These insights serve to accommodate new inquiries into the nature of this beverage as well as present a more expansive repertoire of interpretive dimensions in which to demonstrate the power, authority, superiority, and *clarity* of a revelation that is, in fact, highly ambiguous.

Narrative discourse further rounds out the interpretive frame by grounding the revelatory experience in individual and communal life, giving it a much-needed human dimension. Through narrative discourse, humans participate in the presentation of the divine word, albeit without directly altering the revelation. As the narratives' adherence to the limited contexts and conclusions suggest, the divine word has already been given. Since any experience has been given a determined outcome, any human word, thought, or action depicted in these narratives is ultimately subject to a preexisting divine outcome. In spite of these constraints, however, narrative discourse is still able to put forth a decidedly human and communal translation of the revelation, which carves out a temporal and spatial dimension for the realization of the theophany that renders in communal terms what has been divinely evocated and logically construed.

Countering the Qur'an's evocative mode of understanding divine will as well as the logical and communal paths for interpreting that will, the poetry of the Jahiliya emphasizes human emotion, ritual, and experience. The human emotions generated from these poems, however, could only have been celebrated before the coming of the revelation. As such, they were experienced vicariously and evaluated according to the moral highs and lows of the age of "ignorance" into which the revelation had been poured. In Jahiliya poetry, intoxication embodies the necessary confusion that precedes one's understanding of his more elevated social role as part of the larger tribe. Wine, therefore, stands as a necessary ambiguity that ultimately facilitates a more noble understanding of one's place in the world; a social and moral good highly valued in the post-revelatory world. While Jahiliya poetry counters the other three genres with its emphasis on human emotion (although ironically it supports them in their suspicions of this drink), it also provides a much-needed respite from the severity of the prohibition by exploring some of the powerful dimensions of wine's peculiar effects.

Similar to the poetry of the Jahiliya, Sufi visions also mollify the severity of the prohibition by allowing for unrestricted contemplation on the physical effects of intoxication as a means to achieve mystical vision. Like Jahiliya poetry, mystical poetry draws deeply from human experience to evoke a more privileged perspective of one's place in the world. While the former locates the believer in terms of his social role, the latter focuses on his place in relation to the divine. Both, however, use wine to facilitate the necessary shift in one's understanding of self, community, and divine, and their interrelations. While those in the Jahiliya would actually consume wine to facilitate a changed perspective, mystics focus on the metaphorical quaffing of this intoxicating drink. By apparently glorifying a prohibited drink, these mystics point to an experience that defied human language and ultimately privilege that experience over and against more analytic channels of religious authority. As such, mystical discourse assuages the prohibition by actually asserting its value. The emphasis yet again on human experience—albeit a restricted form of that experience—stands in sharp contrast with the prophetic, analytic, and narrative forms of discourse which all leave the experiential dimension out of the equation. However, while the fact that the Sufis ultimately ridicule the actual consumption of wine places them within the confines of the tradition, their view that mystical experience allows them direct access to Divine Love shifts them to the margins.

The five discourses together demonstrate the privileged, varied, and authoritative ways in which the revelatory vision was translated into the language of the world during the early history of the Islamic tradition. One of the primary motivations behind the selection or privileging of these particular modes of interpretation was the recognition that the human realm was inherently and fundamentally distinct from that of the divine. What limits the interpretive possibilities of wine is an inherent concern toward observing and maintaining the strict lines between the human and divine, but at the same time limiting the depth of the cleavage so that the two realms retained a meaningful relationship. The fact that the discourses privileged were those that stripped an *earthly* wine of its potential to produce a physical experience of ecstasy and limited its ability to *transform* (itself as a substance or the minds of others) illustrates this point. An alcoholic frenzy did not serve to bond humans more closely with one another or with their God, but fundamentally corrupted those relationships. Any type of language—poetic, prophetic, narrative, formulaic, mystical—that contradicted this point was still preserved within the tradition, but dismissed, ridiculed, or relegated to the level of "entertainment."[1] While other "Peoples of the Book" may adhere to such utterances that glorified wine's inherent powers, true believers should not be swayed by its seductive forces.

The stability and flexibility of any tradition—its very life—is dependent upon the necessary combination of, and tension among, different types of discourse. The combination of diverse and often opposed elements that reflect variant interpretations of a divine message (or reflect disparate ways of rendering solutions to apparent incongruities that form under a single ideological rubric) ultimately allows for adaptation and expansion. A single mode of interpretation is simply not pliable enough or ambiguous enough to absorb or allow for change. However, the dialectical relationships between these various genres of literature can readily assert a "divine truth" without ever really capturing it, defining it, or locating it in one specific text or another. As such, the message and authority of these works are forever dependent upon their complementarity, which allows for limited yet flexible modes of interpretation.

It should not be assumed, however, that these five discourses are interchangeable. An obvious hierarchy has been established among them, with a preference for prophecy over poetry, didactic example over ecstatic vision, and teleology over dramatic moment. Given this hierarchy, the nature of the relationships between discourses becomes highly complex. Prophetic discourse, representing the word of God as relayed through his messengers, stands at the head of the interpretive ladder. While this type of discourse stands as the most authoritative, it is, ironically, the most ambiguous. God's views on wine are not stated clearly but require further clarification, which is only achieved at a secondary level of authority through the analytic's formulaic assertions of a divinely sanctioned, *Qur'anic* prohibition. Given that the analytic ties these formulae to divine decree *and* the fundamental laws of the world, the prohibition netted into the Qur'an through a subsidiary command takes on a universal status not to be challenged by human beings.

Undoubtedly, however, the realities of daily existence would have challenged a prohibition so far removed from human experience. Alongside the analytic in terms of its level of authority, narrative discourse allows for more flexibility (however limited) in the interpretive scheme by providing historical, social, and Qur'anic contexts for the placement of the prohibition. God requires the prohibition, but only does so in response to the actions of a wayward people. Humans should abstain from drinking alcoholic beverages not only because God's revelation requires them to, but (perhaps more importantly) because certain prominent members of the early Islamic community submitted to God's will and command. As limited as this flexibility is, narrative discourse still mitigates the interdiction by removing it from the distant realm of abstract, universal law and providing it with revelatory and contextual justification, both of which give humans direct and easy access to elevated exemplars upon which they should model their lives. As is the case with analytic discourse, the narrative clarifies the Qur'an's ambiguous view towards wine. In opposition to it, however, the narrative allows human beings to take a universal, abstract prohibition into their own hands, and become directly responsible for observing or transgressing it.

At the bottom of the interpretive ladder, the poets and mystics further expand this limited flexibility in the universal prohibition by indirectly supporting the prohibition but challenging the more acceptable, analytic channels of authority. In these marginalized discourses, wine becomes the necessary catalyst that moves individuals from one perspective to a more elevated state of mind or body. Although humans must ultimately reject wine and its effects for higher forms of individual, communal, or divine truths, these truths cannot be discovered without reflection upon this ambiguous, awe-inspiring drink. This integral connection between wine and human experience allows for further diminution of the divinely decreed, universal status of the prohibition in that it opens wine up to further contemplation of its physical effects. In both of these discourses, humans come to comprehend their own authoritative voice, for it is through their individualized experiences that truth is ultimately realized. This realization may not challenge the prohibition per se, but it does contest the idea that law resides outside the realm of individual human access or intervention.

It must be noted, however, that the Sunni and Shi'ite interpretative schemes vary considerably. In the Shi'ite works, we find a predilection for personalized drama and event. Humans have an ability to alter what has been divinely construed. While the Sunnis have constructed a world that is stable, fair, and well-insulated from human manipulation and control, the Shi'ites live on the brink of chaos; their world could be forever modified as a result of the events that took place in a single moment in history. One must be constantly vigilant in maintaining order to ward off tragic occurrences that may move humans further from where they should be in relation to the divine and in relation to other believers. Strikingly, while both goups observe similar interpretative hierarchies of authority, their views on the content and context of these discourses are radically different. The Shi'ite case well illustrates how alternative perspectives can be asserted within what appears to be a fixed set of divinely decreed interpretive rules.

SURVEYING SOME FUTURE COMPARATIVE DIRECTIONS

In concluding this study, let us explore a few directions in which a methodological focus on genre and interpretation might be taken, and discuss how this study could offer new insight into other topics within the Islamic tradition as well as unexplored areas of comparative religion. Wine provides a uniquely lustrous illustration for an examination of how a tradition deals with issues of ambiguity through unique strategies of interpretation. Might a "less-ambiguous" substance have served as an equally useful exemplum? Although wine, with an inherently dual nature that would naturally call forth some of the most extreme and creative of all exegetical strategies may indeed be the "mother of all ambiguous examples," other topics with less flamboyant profiles need not be excluded from this type of study. Such mundane topics as "facial hair" or "urine" or "bells" would serve equally well in the same capacity. As long as such issues as what to do about facial hair, or to what extent a stream of urine could pollute create points of contention or question (that is, ambiguity), one can assume they will be resolved, condemned, or modified through some of the same privileged types of language and interpretation that were used to deal with the ambiguous nature of wine.

In fact, the interpretive treatment of facial hair and urine offer some startling similarities with that of wine. For example, note the preoccupation with lists in al-Bukhari's collection of Hadith:

> 'Ali: Sufyan: al-Zuhri: Sa'id b. al-Musayyab: Abu Hurayra: "Five practices are characteristic of the Fitra (note only *four* are listed!): circumcision, shaving the pubic region, clipping the nails, and cutting short the mustaches."[2]

In the case of urine, one can already see some interesting comparative dimensions with wine in terms of how polluting liquids are discussed. Al-Bukhari preserves a series of traditions that place the same law—how water neutralizes the pollutant effects of urine—in a number of different contextual settings:

> Ya'qub b. Ibrahim: Isma'il b. Ibrahim: Ruh b. al-Qasim: 'Ata' b. Abi Maymuna: Anas b. Malik said: "Whenever the Prophet went to answer the call of nature, I used to bring water with which he used to clean his private parts."[3]

> Musa b. Isma'il: Hamman: Ishaq: Anas b. Malik said: "The Prophet saw a Bedouin urinating in the mosque and told the people not to disturb him. When he finished, the Prophet asked for some water and poured it over [the urine]."[4]

> 'Abdallah b. Yusuf: Malik: Hisham b. 'Urwas: his father: 'A'isha said: "A child was brought to the Messenger of God and he urinated on [the Prophet's] garment. The Prophet asked for water and poured it over the soiled spot."[5]

In each of these examples, the basic rule that urine can be countered with a splashing of pure water remains the same while the setting varies in each case.

In its focus on highlighting the strategies of interpretation privileged by a tradition as it struggles to deal with issues of ambiguity, this study differs from others that use objects as their focus for comparison. In general, the study of comparative objects yields little more than description. A more fruitful point of comparison is how traditions formulated different sets of solutions to similar sets of problems. Given this theoretical framework, rather than asking what is the role of wine in different religious traditions, one might inquire what types of interpretive strategies do traditions create to deal with ambiguous substances like wine? In this way it may be possible to analyze how traditions, at certain points in their development or through certain analogous texts, negotiated their boundaries through particular religious orientations that support or were supported by strategic choices in language.

In other words, the comparative focus must shift from recounting the similar conclusions all traditions seemingly draw from the same repertoire of religious forms to analyzing the different strategies traditions use to resolve similar points of contention. By highlighting comparative strategies, rather than the resultant objects of those strategies, the study of religions could be more inclusive of those traditions that do not display such apparent commonalities and be all the more open to entertaining a variety of religious expressions, even if they do not privilege the same common denominators. Only when criteria stemming from language, gesture, and exegetical ingenuity become the primary focus of comparison will every tradition be given a vital and valued place—an equal but different voice, so to speak—within the comparative project.

Notes

INTRODUCTION

1. Mircea Eliade et al., eds., *Encyclopedia of Religion* (*ER*), 16 vols. (New York: Macmillan, 1987), *s.v.* "asceticism," by Walter O. Kaelber.

2. H. A. R. Gibb et al., eds., Encyclopaedia of Islam (*EI*²), 2d ed., 9 vols. and supplement to date (Leiden: E. J. Brill, 1954–), *s.v.* "k͟hamr," by A. J. Wensinck.

3. James H. Charlesworth, ed. and trans., *The History of the Rechabites: Volume I: The Greek Recension,* Texts and Translations 17; Pseudepigrapha Series 10 (Chico, California: Scholars Press, 1982), 53.

4. Jacob Neusner, trans., "Tractate Baba Batra," in *The Talmud of Bablylonia,* (Atlanta: Scholars Press, 1992), 93. Reference cited by P. Crone and M. Cook, *Hagarism: The Making of the Islamic World* (Cambridge: Cambridge University Press, 1977), 157 n. 38.

5. Arthur Vööbus, trans., and ed., *Syriac and Arabic Documents: Regarding Legislation Relative to Syrian Asceticism.* Papers of the Estonian Theological Society in Exile, no. 2 (Stockholm: Dean Jakob Aunver, 1960), 27, 42.

6. Mary Douglas, *Purity and Danger* (London: Ark Paperbacks, 1985), 2.

7. Ibid., 5.

8. Ibid., 37.

9. Ibid.

10. Ibid., 40.

11. Ibid., 121.

12. Ibid., 161.

13. Ibid., 162.

14. Ignaz Goldziher's works under discussion are as follows: *Muslim Studies,* eds. C. R. Barber, and S. M. Stern, 2 vols. (Chicago: Aldine, 1968, 1971); *Introduction to Islamic Theology and Law,* trans. Andras and Ruth Hamori, ed. Bernard Lewis (Princeton: Princeton University Press, 1981).

15. A. J. Wensinck's works on wine include: *Concordance et indices de la tradition musulmane,* 7 vols. (Leiden: E. J. Brill, 1936–69); *EI*², *s.v.* "k͟hamr"; M. T. Houtsma et al., eds., *The Encyclopaedia of Islam* (*EI*¹), 4 vols. (Leiden: E. J. Brill, 1913–1934), *s.v.* "nabīd͟h."

16. Goldziher, *Introduction to Islamic Theology and Law*, 62.
17. Goldziher, *Muslim Studies*, vol. 2: 64.
18. Ibid., 59.
19. Ibid., 64.
20. Ibid.
21. The word "Ḥadīth" (which appears in its singular form) will serve as a collective noun for "traditions," or those recorded accounts of what the Prophet said or did, or his approval of what was said or done in his presence. The word "ḥadīth" in its lowercase form will be used to represent a single "tradition."
22. Goldziher, *Muslim Studies*, 62.
23. In al-Rāzī's commentary on Sūra 2:219 (al-Baqara) we find al-Shāfiʿī arguing that every intoxicating drink (*muskir*) is wine, and Abū Ḥanīfa stating that wine is simply the equivalent to a strong *grape* juice which develops a foam (as result of fermentation) (Fakhr al-Dīn al-Rāzī, *al-Tafsīr al-kabīr* (*Mafātīḥ al-ghayb),* trans. Helmut Gätje, *The Qurʾān and its Exegesis* [Berkeley: University of California Press, 1976], 100–209). Obviously, the former is going to take a much stricter and more inclusive view of the prohibition than the latter.
24. See Goldziher, *Muslim Studies*, vol. 1, 27. Goldziher points out some of the tensions between the customary practices of the pre-Islamic Arabs, and the rigid laws set forth by Muḥammad.
25. See Wensinck, *A Handbook of Early Muhammadan Tradition, s.v.* "wine"; and *Concordance et indices de la tradition musulmane, s.v.* "k̲h̲amr."
26. Wensinck states that "[t]he prohibition of wine, although unanimously accepted, gave rise to dissensions between the juridical schools, dissensions which are reflected in ḥadīt̲h̲ in historical disguise" (*EI*², *s.v.* "k̲h̲amr"). For further discussions of some of the dissensions among these early schools, as well as the presentation of some of the specific issues that were up for debate, see Ralph S. Hattox, *Coffee and Coffeehouses* (Seattle: University of Washington Press, 1985).
27. "Prophetic" discourse in many ways is analogous to what Jacob Neusner calls "symbolic" discourse. According to Neusner, symbolic discourse in Judaism provided a way in which "faith as confidence in God rather than faith as the statement of truth about God" could be conveyed (*Symbol and Theology in Early Judaism* [Minneapolis: Fortress Press, 1991], xiii). In other words, as opposed to theological propositions that yield syllogisms about who God is, or what God does, symbolic discourse, through evocative language, imagery, and the repetition of a few key words or themes, calls forth attitudes and emotions that support or reinforce these theological statements without *explicitly* doing so (id.).
28. Jacob Neusner coined the term "analytic" discourse in *Oral Tradition in Judaism: The Case of the Mishnah* (New York and London: Garland Publishing, Inc., 1987), 83. Neusner suggests that analytic discourse frames its ideas according to syllogistic patterns. Rather than evoking a fixed set of abstract, theological concepts through symbolic language, the analytic classifies and compares, infers and invokes, deduces and induces one case over against another in order to find the right rule for

each matter or situation in the world (id., 4). For Neusner, the text that best illustrates this kind of thinking is the Mishnah, which, when taken as a whole, constitutes a "coherent logic and topic, a cogent world view and a comprehensive way of living" (id). This comprehensive way of living ultimately creates a total system through which, in Neusner's scheme, *Israel* and its people are sanctified in both deed and deliberation (id.).

29. Neusner sees "narrative" discourse as rounding out the picture with the creation of stories that ground the sayings or abstract images produced by the other two discourses into an authentic historical past, a familiar setting, or a concrete moment (*Judaism and Story: The Evidence of the Fathers According to Rabbi Nathan* [Chicago: The University of Chicago Press, 1992], xv–3). With narrative discourse, the story becomes an effective and appropriate mode of thought people use in order to articulate and communicate their encounters with God on Earth (id., xi). While this work draws from the categories Neusner has created, it has made many modifications of these terms based upon their application to an Islamic context. In addition, it is important to note that while Neusner sets up these different types of discourses and explores them in their relationship to specific texts, he does not (as this work will) analyze them together as a whole, nor does he discuss their dialectical relationship within the context of a single tradition.

30. These genres also roughly correspond with John Wansbrough's five exegetical types that he argues were applied to Muslim scripture by its interpreters: haggadic (paraenetic, narrative), halakhic (legal), masoretic (linguistic), rhetorical, and allegorical. This essay will focus mainly on what Wansbrough calls the "haggadic," "halakhic," and "rhetorical," and will not take the view, as Wansbrough does, that these progress chronologically (*Qur'ānic Studies: Sources and methods of scriptural interpretation* [Oxford: Oxford University Press, 1977], 119–246). It is interesting to note that the early Islamic texts under consideration rarely rely upon allegory as a useful interpretive tool (except, of course, in the case of mystical writings, which tend to be marginalized to varying degrees by the orthodox tradition. See chapter five for more discussion on "mystical discourse").

31. By jettisoning the argument on Qur'ānic origins, I can adopt a neutral position over whether or not the Qur'ān was redacted at an early or late date. The debate, which centers on the problems associated with describing the relationship between, and historical formation of, Islamic scripture and the related but often radically opposed traditional texts—biographical (*Sīra*), exegetical (*Tafsīr*), legal (*Ḥadīth*)—and which has been approached from radically different perspectives, can be divided roughly into three camps: the traditional view (the Qur'ān was given piecemeal to Muḥammad during his lifetime, but was later codified during the reign of 'Uthmān), and the early- and late-date theories. The early-date theory has been articulated in detail by John Burton, who insists that the Qur'ān was redacted by Muḥammad himself and was thus contemporaneous with Muslim origins (*The Collection of the Qur'ān* [Cambridge: Cambridge University Press, 1977]). In light of this theory, traditional materials provide later interpretations of, and elaborations on,

this earlier text. The late-date theory, promulgated by John Wansbrough, takes the exact opposite approach to the same problem of textual incongruities. According to Wansbrough, "it was only after the articulation of the law as divinely decreed [i.e. in the third/ninth century] that a scriptural canon was established, the result primarily of polemical pressure" (*Qur'ānic Studies,* 227). Wansbrough's argument for the late dating of the Qur'ān is an argument based on typology; he is suggesting that because the Qur'ān itself contains a composite of "exegetical types," types he derives from examples taken from early Tafsīr, then it must have come *after* the formulation of these earlier traditions. While the categories he has identified as the principle types of scriptural explication are useful to this essay, I do not believe they necessitate a late redaction of the Qur'ān; they could just as easily fit into a paradigm of simultaneous development.

32. Gordon Newby, *The Making of the Last Prophet* (Columbia, SC: University of South Carolina Press, 1989), 11.

33. For further discussion on the subject of religious authority during the ʿAbbāsid period, see Gordon Newby, "Tafsīr Isra'iliyyat," *Journal of the American Academy of Religion* 47, no. 4S (1979): 685–697, and *The Making of the Last Prophet*; Barbara Freyer Stowasser, *Women in the Qur'ān, Traditions, and Interpretation* (New York: Oxford University Press, 1994); and *Islamic Jurisprudence: Shafiʿi's Risala*, ed. and trans., Majid Khadduri (Baltimore: The Johns Hopkins Press, 1961), 67–68.

CHAPTER ONE: QUR'ĀNIC VIGNETTES OF THE VINE

1. See Sūra 5:90–91 (al-Mā'ida), where wine is labeled an "abomination," and Sūra 16:67 (al-Naḥl), where it becomes "good food."

2. Sūra 20:113–114 (Ṭāhā) provides a good example of the Qur'ān's "self-proclaimed" agenda: "Thus have We sent it down: a Koran in the Arabic tongue, and proclaimed in it warnings and threats so that they may take heed and be admonished. Exalted be God, the True King!" (*The Koran*, trans. N. J. Dawood [London: Penguin Books, 1993]). See also Sūra 42:7 (al-Shūrā). In his most recent work, Fred Donner has classified the form and content of the Qur'ān into three distinct categories: the paraenetic, which puts forth ecstatic exhortations (appearing in rhymed phrases called *sajʿ*) to warn the audience of the Last Day and call them to believe in God and to do good works; the legal, which governs particular communal relationships and the association between believers and their God; and the narrative, which includes anecdotes about significant biblical and Arabian figures. Donner suggests that despite this diversity in form and content, the Qur'ān pronounces essentially one basic message that all humans must believe in the one true God. In other words, the text calls upon its hearers to be *pious* (*Narratives of Islamic Origins: The Beginnings of Islamic Historical Writing* [Princeton: The Darwin Press, Inc., 1998], 64–67).

3. Sūra 88:4–16 (al-Ghāshīya). See also Sūras 13 (al-Raʿd) and 51 (al-Dhāriyāt) for further images of that final day.

4. Sūra 39:5 (al-Zumar): "It was to reveal the Truth that He created the heavens and the earth. He caused the night to succeed the day and the day to overtake the night. He made the sun and moon obedient to Him, each running for an appointed term. He is the Mighty, the Benignant One." (Translated by Dawood).

5. Sūra 55:14–15 (al-Raḥmān).

6. Sūra 111 (al-Lahab).

7. See Sūra 26 (al-Shuʿarāʾ).

8. Sūra 4:144 (al-Nisāʾ).

9. Sūra 2:43 (al-Baqara).

10. Sūra 4:11–14 (al-Nisāʾ).

11. Sūra 4:43 (al-Nisāʾ).

12. Sūras 4:15–16 (al-Nisāʾ); 17:32 (al-Isrāʾ); 24:2–9 (al-Nūr); and 25:68 (al-Furqān).

13. Sūra 5:69 (al-Māʾida).

14. Sūra 5:51 (al-Māʾida).

15. Sūra 83:25–28 (al-Muṭaffifīn).

16. Sūra 4:43 (al-Nisāʾ); 5:61 (al-Māʾida).

17. It is this incongruity that turns wine into a sign of danger for later exegetes and legal scholars, who devote much time to containing its ambiguous earthly status. See chapter two for further insight into this issue.

18. The Qurʾān, like all sacred texts, contains many contradictions. Note its position on Jews and Christians, for example. In Sūra 5:51 (al-Māʾida), believers are told not to take Jews and Christians for friends; whoever does so is unjust in the eyes of God. However, in 5:69 (al-Māʾida), "those who believe, and those who are Jews and Sabaeans and Christians, whoever believes in God and the Last Day and does good shall have no fear nor shall they grieve." Another example of ambivalency is the Qurʾān's position on free will and predestination.

19. Sūra 16:67 (al-Naḥl).

20. Sūras 37:40–48 (al-Ṣāffāt); 47:15 (Muḥammad); 56:17-19 (al-Wāqiʿa); 83:25–28 (al-Muṭaffifīn).

21. Sūra 5:90–91 (al-Māʾida).

22. *EI*[2], *s.v.* "kh̲amr." The absolute form in Aramaic appears just twice in the Hebrew Bible, the first in Ezra 6:9 and the second in Ezra 7:22 (Francis Brown, *A Hebrew and English lexicon of the Old Testament with an appendix containing the Biblical Aramaic* [Houghton Mifflin, 1906], *s.v.* "khamr"). In each case, the God of Heaven demands a sacrifice of *khamr* (along with silver, wheat, oil, salt, bulls, and rams) in exchange for the well-being of the king and his heirs.

23. The Aramaic *khamr*, unlike its Qurʾānic counterpart, is also masculine.

24. Sūra 16:67 (al-Naḥl).

25. Sūra 15:72 (al-Ḥijr).

26. Sūras 4:43 (al-Nisā'), 22:2 (al-Ḥajj).

27. Sūra 15:15 (al-Ḥijr).

28. Sūra 83:25 (al-Muṭaffifīn).

29. Edward William Lane, *An Arabic-English Lexicon*, 8. vols. (London: Williams and Norgate), *s.v.* "r-ḥ-q."

30. Sūras 37:45 (al-Ṣāffāt); 56:18-19 (al-Wāqiʿa).

31. Sūras 37:47 (al-Ṣāffāt); 56:19 (al-Wāqiʿa).

32. For a discussion of the traditional chronology, see chapter three, pp. 65–67.

33. *EI*², *s.v.* "maysir," by T. Fahd.

34. For the passages on punishment, see Sūras 6:125 (al-Anʿām); 9:95 (al-Tawba); 9:125 (al-Tawba); 10:100 (Yūnus). Elsewhere in the text, we find pigs and idols depicted as "abominations." See Sūras 6:145 (al-Anʿām); 22:30 (al-Ḥajj) for such descriptions.

35. This observation was made by T. Fahd, *EI*², *s.v.* "maysir."

36. The divination arrows (*azlām*) were described as three: positive, negative, and blank. The *azlām* could also include such objects as pebbles, or dice (*kiʿāb*) (Franz Rosenthal, *Gambling in Islam* [Leiden: E. J. Brill, 1975], 74 n. 30).

37. Ibid.

38. Criticizing any tradition for something like idolatry is often used as a polemical tool against traditions with similar beliefs and practices. Note Sasanian Zoroastrian's criticism against Zurvanism for emphasizing Zurvan (Time) as the first principle over Ohrmizd and Ahriman, which put the good god into an unworthy position: "The countries are bewildered by deceptive idols, wall-pictures made of wood and stone! They fear Deceit, they prostrate themselves and pay homage to him. They have left the Father in Heaven and worship Deceit!" (Jes Peter Asmussen, ed., and comp., *Manichaean Literature: Representative texts chiefly from Middle Persian and Parthian writings.* [Delmar, New York: Scholars' Facsimiles and Reprints, 1975], 14).

39. *EI*², *s.v.* "nuṣub," by T. Fahd.

40. Sūra 22:33–37 (al-Ḥajj).

41. Interestingly enough, the idea that wine diverts men from the remembrance of God is prevalent in other sacred texts as well, such as the Hebrew Bible. For example, in Isaiah 5:12, we find the following verse: "They have lyre and harp, tambourine and flute and wine at their feasts; but they do not regard the deeds of the Lord, or see the work of his hands." We find another example in Joel 3:3: "I will enter into judgment with them there, on account of my people and my heritage Israel, because they have scattered them among the nations, and have divided up my land, and have cast lots for my people, and have given a boy for a harlot, and have sold a girl for wine, and have drunk it." As is the case with Sūra 5:90–91 (al-Mā'ida), wine's associations with gambling and other practices in Joel 3:3 serve as a kind of commentary upon those who stand outside of, or perhaps even in direct conflict with, the rightful community of believers.

42. Sūra 2:219–220 (al-Baqara).

43. Some commentators noted that the Qurʾān does not say that wine and gambling *are* sins, but that they contain sin. Thus, they conclude that wine and gambling are not explicitly prohibited by the Qurʾān (Rosenthal, *Gambling in Islam*, 78).

44. Some commentators have suggested that the winners of *maysir* would donate their slaughtered portions to their own people, and that some of the losers would purchase some of the parts that had not been won and give them to the poor. It is to this act of charity that these commentators attribute the "advantages" (*EI*², *s.v.* "maysir").

45. The idea that the Qurʾān did not strictly prohibit wine circulated among a minority of legal scholars and theologians who claimed that God did not actually forbid *khamr* in 5:90–91 (al-Māʾida) but indicated with some force that one should simply desist from using it (Ibn Qutayba [ʿAbdallāh b. Muslim], *Kitāb al-ashriba* [Dimashq: al-Majmaʿ al-ʿilmī al-ʿarabī, 1947], 17, as noted by Ralph S. Hattox, *Coffee and Coffeehouses* (Seattle: University of Washington Press, 1985), 50.

46. The items that the Qurʾān explicitly forbids (*ḥurrima*) include carrion, blood, pork, and whatever has been killed in a name other than God's. Also forbidden is whatever has been strangled, killed by a blow or fall, or by goring, or that which has been mauled by wild beasts or slaughtered at altars (Sūras 5:3 [al-Māʾida]; 16:115 [al-Naḥl]).

47. It is important to note that a similar passage on ritual impurities appears in Sūra 5:6 (al-Māʾida), but without mention of intoxication: "Believers, when you rise to pray wash your faces and your hands as far as the elbow, and wipe your heads and your feet to the ankle. If you are polluted cleanse yourselves. But if you are sick or travelling the road; or if, when you have just relieved yourselves or had intercourse with women, you can find no water, take some clean sand and rub your hands and faces with it." (Translated by Dawood).

48. The dangers of performing prayer under the state of intoxication are also suggested in the Hebrew Bible and in the Babylonian Talmud. Note, for example, the following biblical passages that forbid the use of wine when praying: "No priest shall drink wine when he enters the inner court" (Ezekiel 44:21); "And the Lord spoke to Aaron, saying, 'Drink no wine nor strong drink, you nor your sons with you, when you go into the tent of meeting, lest you die; it shall be a statute forever throughout your generations' " (Leviticus 10:8–9). For Talmudic examples, see Sanhedrin (22B), where priests are prohibited from taking wine lest the Temple be rebuilt while they are drunk, and they are called upon to perform their ritual duties.

49. Kevin Reinhart, "Impurity/No Danger," in *History of Religions* 30, no. 1 (1990):19.

50. Ibid., 20.

51. The Qurʾān does not deem dogs to be impure; like wine, the negative attitude towards this type of animal developed within the Ḥadīth, as can be seen in

the Chapters of *Ḥadīth* entitled "kalb." For further information on why dogs were thought to be unclean, see A. J. Wensinck, *Handbook of Early Muhammedan Tradition, s.v.*, "dogs."

52. *EI*², *s.v.* "nadjis," by A. J. Wensinck.

53. Sūra 2:248–249 (al-Baqara). These and the following Qur'ānic references for signs are taken from *EI*², *s.v.* "āya," by A. Jeffrey.

54. Sūra 17:12–13 (al-Isrā').

55. Sūras 7:105 (al-A'rāf); 30:19–29 (al-Rūm).

56. Sūras 2:164, 266 (al-Baqara); 26:64–68 (al-Shu'arā').

57. Sūras 3:49 (al-'Imrān); 13:38 (al-Ra'd); 26:154 (al-Shu'arā'); 43:47 (al-Zukhruf).

58. Sūras 2:252 (al-Baqara); 5:75 (al-Mā'ida); 12:7 (Yūsuf); 15:75 (al-Ḥijr); 34:19 (Sabā').

59. Sūras 3:108 (al-'Imrān); 6:124 (al-An'ām).

60. I would like to thank J. Andrew Foster for this observation.

61. Gilles Quispel, in *ER, s.v.* "gnosticism," puts forth the following definition: "Today gnosticism is defined as a religion in its own right, whose myths state that the Unknown God is not the creator (demiurge, YHVH); that the world is in error, the consequence of a fall and split with the deity; and that man, spiritual man, is alien to the natural world and related to the deity and becomes conscious of his deepest Self when he hears the word of revelation. Not sin or guilt, but unconsciousness, is the cause of evil."

62. For an example of gnostic influences in Shī'īsm, see Marshall G. S. Hodgson, *EI*², *s.v.* "ghulāt." According to Hodgson, the *ghulāt* were concerned with defining the nature of the imām's person. As a result of their speculations, different groups took the following positions: (1) the imām was the executor of the prophet; (2) the *imām* possessed prophetic authority himself; (3) the imām and Muḥammad possessed a spark of the divine light (*nūr ilāhī*) that was inherited from Adam on down through the line of prophets; (4) the imām represented the divinity as a lesser god on earth, or by infusion of the divine spirit in him.

63. Sūra 16:69: "*sharābu mukhtalifu alwānuhu fīhi.*" Note that the word "*sharāb,*" here used for a type of honey that was consumed for medicinal purposes, is often taken to mean alcoholic beverages or wine (Lane, *s.v.* "*sh-r-b*"). An alcoholic honey-drink (*al-bit'*) often appears on lists of prohibited beverages in the Ḥadīth.

64. Jamsheed Choksy, *Purity and Pollution in Zoroastrianism: Triumph over evil* (Austin: University of Texas Press, 1989), 15.

65. Sūra 22:2 (al-Ḥajj) (*Al-Qur'ān*, trans. Ahmed Ali [Princeton: Princeton University Press], 1984).

66. Sūra 47:15 (Muḥammad).

67. Sūra 76:14–21 (al-Insān), trans. Ali.

68. Note the distinction E. R. Goodenough suggests that Philo makes between the "dangerous physical drunkenness from wine and another drunkenness experience by "thousands" who have not touched wine at all" (*Jewish Symbols in the Greco-Roman Period,* vol. 6, bk. 2, *Fish, Bread, and Wine* [New York: Bollingen Foundation, Inc., 1956], 202). For Philo, as pointed out by Goodenough, "the bad effects of wine—such as folly, ignorance, and nudism—are unfortunately not limited to drunkards . . . the good effects of wine can become symbols of spiritual states, simplicity, receptiveness, and the catharsis of the soul" (id.). Philo has labeled the "good effects" of this particular spiritual state "sober drunkenness," a state of drunkenness that can take place without any consumption of wine at all (id.). Whether or not it is this spiritual state of intoxication that the Qur'ān is referring to is difficult to determine; the language, however, suggests some sort of catharsis on the part of the one who is being rewarded.

69. Sūra 56:18–19 (al-Wāqi'a).

70. Sūra 37:45–47 (al-Ṣāffāt).

71. Or, perhaps, one might argue that all temptations have been removed. Presumably in Paradise, one no longer is confronted with moral choices; within the walls of the Garden, there is only one option, one path available to those who are righteous.

72. Sūra 2:7(al-Baqara); 6:46 (al-An'ām); 45:23 (al-Jāthīya). These Sūras suggest that God has the power to shield certain individuals from his message; in other words, he selects a number of individuals to wallow ceaselessly in the mire of their disbelief while others he allows to be transformed by his words.

73. Sūra 56:22 (al-Wāqi'a).

74. Sūra 56:17 (al-Wāqi'a).

75. Sūra 47:15 (Muḥammad).

76. See Sūras 7:59–64 (al-A'rāf); 11:25–48 (Hūd); 26:105–120 (al-Shu'arā') for other illustrations of Noah serving as the vehicle for the message of God.

77. Noah is described as "*rajulu bihi jinnahu,*" meaning literally "a man possessed by jinn."

78. See, for example, the *Midrash Rabba: Genesis,* ed. and trans. Rabbi Dr. H. Freeman, and Maurice Simon, vol. 1 (London: Soncino Press, 1983), 290 (36.3. to .5.).

79. Sūra 26:105–109 (al-Shu'arā'), trans. Dawood.

80. For further elaborations on this creation of a "prophetic type," see Michael Zwettler, "A Mantic Manifesto: The Sūra of "The Poets" and the Qur'ānic foundations of Prophetic Authority," in *Poetry and Prophecy,* ed. James L. Kugel (Ithaca and London: Cornell University Press, 1990), 75–119. For similar arguments, see Michael Cook's *Muhammad* (Oxford: Oxford University Press, 1983), especially p. 32; and Marilyn Robinson Waldman's "New Approaches to Biblical Materials in the Qur'ān," *The Muslim World* 75, no. 1 (January 1985): 1–13, and *ER, s.v.* "*nubūwa.*"

81. Genesis 19:36.

82. Sūra 15:72–74 (al-Ḥijr), trans. Ahmed.

83. Matthew 26:26–29; Mark 14:22–25; Luke 22:14–20.

84. John 15:1.

85. John 6:54–55. By stressing carnal consumption, the author of John may be putting forth an ironic twist to the wholly symbolic meal presented in the Synoptic Gospels.

86. Sūra 5:113–115 (al-Mā'ida). When the disciples asked Jesus to have God send down a table of food, "they said: 'We should like to eat of it to reassure our hearts and to know that it's the truth you have told us, and that we should be witness to it.' Said Jesus, son of Mary: 'O God our Lord, send down a table well-laid with food from the skies so that this day may be a day of feast for the earlier among us and the later, and a token from you. Give us our bread, for you are the best of all givers of food'" (trans. Ahmed).

87. The Qur'ān is not always successful in its struggle to downplay Jesus' superhuman nature and charisma. Compare the Qur'ān's depiction of how Jesus is able to "speak from the cradle" in Sūra 3:46 (al-ʿImrān), and "breathe life into the dead" in Sūra 5:110 (al-Mā'ida) with its sharp insistence that Jesus is only a messenger in Sūra 5:75 (al-Mā'ida). Even though the text makes it clear that *God* is the one allowing Jesus to perform such miracles, the fact remains that such wonderous deeds were associated with *this* messenger and not some other apostle.

88. Matthew 3:11–3:12.

89. See note no. 78.

90. *The History of al-Ṭabarī, vol. 3, The Children of Israel, trans. William Brinner (Albany: State University of New York Press,* 1991), 11. The fact that a "history" would record how a prophet found himself in such a compromising position (however tame in comparison with the biblical version) is not surprising given that the purpose of narrative discourse is to provide continuity and legitimacy with links to a sacred past. In this type of discourse, events, characters, and places become of the utmost importance in establishing oneself as the increment in the tradition on which one stands. For further elaboration on this idea, see chapter three.

91. W. M. Thackston, Jr., *Tales of the Prophets of al-Kisa'i* (Boston: Twayne Publishers, 1978), 105.

92. Even though the Qur'ānic Paradise is a realm of perfection, the deity is rarely to be found. Even in the Garden, humans remain separate from the divine.

CHAPTER TWO: FINDING THE PERFECT WORLD

1. For a thorough description and discussion of the evolution of these early Islamic "traditions," see *EI*², *s.v.* "ḥadīth," by J. Robson.

2. Ibid.

3. Barbara Freyer Stowasser, *Women in the Qur'ān, Traditions, and Interpretation* (Oxford: Oxford University Press, 1994), 105.

4. Ibid.

5. For more on Muḥammad's "night journey," see chapter three.

6. Many Western scholars have come to the conclusion that most Ḥadīth did not originate with the Prophet, but were put into circulation at a later date in order to support the customs, opinions, beliefs, economic strategies, legal decisions, or political claims held by interested groups. These scholars accept that the Ḥadīth reveal more about the concerns of the place and time in which they emerged than the actual words and deeds of the Prophet. For examples of such approaches, see Ignaz Goldziher, *Introduction of Islamic Theology and Law*, and *Muslim Studies*; G. H. A. Juynboll, *Muslim Tradition: Studies in chronology, provenance and authorship of early ḥadīth* (Cambridge: Cambridge University Press, 1983); Joseph Schacht, *An Introduction to Islamic Law* (Oxford: Oxford University Press, 1964), and *The Origins of Muhammadan Jurisprudence* (Oxford: Oxford University Press, 1950). For a study that opposes these views, see Muhammad M. Azami's, *On Schacht's "Origins of Muhammadan Jurisprudence"* (New York: John Wiley and Sons, 1985).

7. Stowasser, *Women in the Qur'ān,* 104.

8. Hierarchies are often used in the study of ecology, where ecological "systems" do not exist independent of the particular frame of reference used by the observer to conduct his study. A hierarchy, defined as "a formal approach to the relationship between upper-level control over lower-level possibilities," provides a way in which the dynamic between context and content can be analyzed and assessed in a systematic and concrete fashion (T. F. H. Allen, and Thomas W. Hoekstra, *Toward a Unified Ecology* [New York: Columbia University Press, 1992], 10).

9. Abū Dāwūd Sulaymān b. Ashʿath al-Sijistānī, "Kitāb al-buyūʿ," in *Sunan Abī Dāwūd*, ed. Muḥammad Muḥyī 'l-Dīn ʿAbd al-Ḥamīd, 4 vols. (Cairo: Maṭbaʿat Muṣṭafā Muḥammad, 1935), no. 3486. See also ʿAbd al-Razzāq b. Hammām al-Ṣanʿānī, *al-Muṣannaf*, ed. Ḥabīb al-Raḥmān al-Aʿẓamī (Al-Majlis al-ʿilmī, and Beirut: Al-Maktab al-islāmī, 1970–72), vol. 9, nos. 16970, 16971, 16996; Ibn Māja (Muḥammad b. Yazīd), "Kitāb al-ashriba," in *Kitāb al-sunan*, ed. Muḥammad Fū'ād ʿAbd al-Bāqī (Cairo: Dār iḥyā' al-kutub al-ʿarabīya, 1953), no. 3383.

10. The famous metonymy/metaphor distinction put forth by Roman Jakobson does not illustrate the difference between the Ḥadīth and the Qur'ān, for the language of the Qur'ān is in no way metaphorical, but evocative. But there may be something in the notion that one of the basic differences between the two genres is that the Qur'ān does favor "selection and substitution," while the Ḥadīth prefer "combination and contexture" (for a clear summary of Jakobson's argument, see Jane Hedley, *Power in Verse: Metaphor and Metonymy in the Renaissance Lyric* [University Park and London: The Pennsylvania State University Press, 1988], 1–13).

11. For examples of this in Judaism, see Jacob Neusner, *Symbol and Theology in Early Judaism* (Minneapolis: Fortress Press, 1991), 45.

12. ʿAbd al-Razzāq provides a humorous anecdote to illustrate the point that one should not benefit from the selling of that which is prohibited: Muʿamr: al-Layth: Ṭāwūs: A man bought wine, mixed it with water, carried it to the land of India, and sold it. The sack of money was put on a boat, which also housed a monkey. The monkey took the sack, climbed up on the mast, and began to cast dirhams off the ship. He cast off all the dirhams into the sea (*al-Muṣannaf*, vol. 9, no. 16998).

13. Jacob Neusner, *Oral Tradition in Judaism: The Case of the Mishnah* (New York and London: Garland Publishing, Inc., 1987), 109.

14. "Abodah Zarah," in *The Mishnah: A New Translation*, trans. Jacob Neusner (New Haven: Yale University Press, 1988), 662–663.

15. Al-Tirmidhī (Abū ʿĪsā Muḥammad b. ʿĪsā), "Abwāb al-ashriba," in *Ṣaḥīḥ*, ed. Aḥmad Muḥammad Shākir (Cairo: Al-Maṭbaʿa al-misrīya, 1931–34), p. 65. For similar traditions that discuss the two trees, see ʿAbd al-Razzāq, *al-Muṣannaf*, vol. 9, no. 17053; Abū Dāwūd, "Kitāb al-ashriba," in *Sunan*, no. 3678; al-Dārimī (ʿAbdallāh b. ʿAbd al-Raḥmān), "Kitāb al-ashriba," in *al-Sunan*, ed. Muḥammad Aḥmad Duhmān (Cairo: Dār al-iḥyaʾ, 197–), p. 113; Ibn Ḥanbal (Aḥmad b. Muḥammad), *al-Musnad*, ed. Aḥmad Muḥammad Shākir (Cairo: Dār al-maʿārif, 1946–49), nos. 9283, 9286, 10145, 10448, 10720, 10721, 10818; Ibn Māja, "Kitāb al-ashriba," in *Kitāb al-sunan*, no. 3378; Muslim (b. al-Ḥajjāj al-Qushayrī), "Kitāb al-ashriba," in *Ṣaḥīḥ Muslim*, ed. Muḥammad Fūʾād ʿAbd al-Bāqī (Beirut: Dār al-iḥyāʾ al-turāth, 1956–1972), nos. 13, 14, 15; al-Nasāʾī (Aḥmad b. Shuʿayb), "Kitāb al-ashriba," in *Sunan*, ed. Jalāl al-Dīn al-Suyūṭī (Cairo: Al-Maṭbaʿa al-miṣrīya, 1930) p. 294; and al-Ṭayālisī (Sulaymān b. Dāwūd), *Musnad* (Beirut: Dār al-kitāb al-lubnānī, 1980), no. 2569.

16. Al-Kulaynī (Abū Jaʿfar Muḥammad), "Kitāb al-ashriba," in *Furūʿ min al-kāfī*, ed. ʿAlī Akbar al-Ghaffārī (Ṭehrān: Maktabat al-ṣadūq, 1957), p. 393, no. 1. For a similar tradition, see also p. 393, no. 2 (ʿAlī b. Muḥammad: Ṣāliḥ b. Abī Ḥammād: al-Ḥusayn b. Yazīd: ʿAlī b. Abī Ḥamza: Ibrāhīm: Abū ʿAbdallāh).

17. Al-Nasāʾī, "Kitāb al-ashriba," in *Sunan*, p. 330; al-Kulaynī, "Kitāb al-ashriba," in *al-Kāfī*, p. 394, nos. 3, 4.

18. For a discussion of how the number "two" creates balance and symmetry, see Annemarie Schimmel, *The Mystery of Numbers* (New York: Oxford University Press, 1993), 53ff.

19. The Ḥanafīs and Muʿtazilites retained the idea that *khamr* only refers to uncooked grape juice that is fermented. Given their narrow definition, they do allow for the moderate consumption of other types of alcoholic beverages (Ralph S. Hattox, *Coffee and Coffeehouses*, 52; *EI*[2], *s.v.* "mashrūbāt," by J. Saban).

20. Al-Bukhārī (Abū ʿAbdallāh Muḥammad b. Ismāʿīl b. Ibrāhīm), "Kitāb al-ashriba," in *al-Jāmiʿ al-ṣaḥīḥ* (*Ṣaḥīḥ al-Bukhārī*) (Cairo: Dār al-fikr, 1981), no. 494. For the same statements on the five things from which wine is derived (which vary slightly with regard to those items that are included in the list), see ʿAbd al-Razzāq, *al-Muṣannaf*, vol. 9, nos. 17049, 17050, 17051; Abū Dāwūd, "Kitāb al-ashriba," in *Sunan*, no. 3676; al-Bukhārī, "Kitāb al-ashriba," in *Ṣaḥīḥ*, nos. 487, 493; and "Kitāb

al-tafsīr," no. 143; Ibn Ḥanbal, *al-Musnad*, no. 5992; Ibn Māja, "Kitāb al-ashriba," in *Kitāb al-sunan*, no. 3379; al-Kulaynī, "Kitāb al-ashriba," in *al-Kāfī*, p. 392, nos. 1, 2, 3; al-Nasā'ī, "Kitāb al-ashriba," in *Sunan*, p. 295; al-Tirmidhī, "Abwāb al-ashriba," in *Ṣaḥīḥ*, p. 63.

21. Jon Vansina, *Oral Tradition as History* (Madison: University of Wisconsin Press, 1985), 14.

22. Al-Shaykh al-Ṣadūq b. Bābūya al-Qummī (Ibn Bābawayhī), *Kitāb man lā yaḥḍuruhu 'l-faqīh*, Part IV (Dār al-kutub al-islāmīya, 1962), no. 5089.

23. Ibn Māja, "Kitāb al-ashriba," in *Kitāb al-sunan*, no. 3380. See also Ibn Bābawayhī, *Kitāb man lā yaḥḍuruhu 'l-faqīh*, Part IV, no. 5089; Ibn Ḥanbal, *al-Musnad*, nos. 2899, 4787, 5390, 5391, 5716; al-Kulaynī, "Kitāb al-ashriba," in *al-Kāfī*, p. 398, no. 10, p. 429, no. 4; al-Tirmidhī, "Abwāb al-buyū'," in *Ṣaḥīḥ*, p. 29. For the only tradition that gives nine points (one may have been lost, or not copied), see Abū Dāwūd, "Kitāb al-ashriba," in *Sunan*, no. 3674.

24. For an enlightening comparison of how Judaism and Zoroastrianism take up such issues, especially in terms of the logical and legal strategies they use to resolve such problems stemming from social, dietary, ritual, and familial concerns, see Jacob Neusner, *Judaism and Zoroastrianism at the Dusk of Late Antiquity* (Atlanta: Scholars Press, 1993). In this study, Neusner examines the Talmud of Babylonia in parallel with two counterpart documents in Zoroastrianism: the Pahlavi Rivayat of Aturfarnbag, and the Rivayat that accompanies the Dadestan i Denig.

25. See Mary Douglas, *Purity and Danger*, 41–57. In this section, Douglas argues that certain biblical texts define holiness as completeness; therefore, any hybrid or ambiguous entity would be anti-holy. The examples she points to from Leviticus, such as the condemnation of the sexual mingling of humans with beasts, or the mixing of two kinds of seed in a single field, underscore this general command to "be holy."

26. Ibid., 40.

27. Al-Nisā'ī, "Kitāb al-ashriba," in *Sunan*, p. 324. See also al-Dārimī, "Kitāb al-ashriba," in *al-Sunan*, p. 113; al-Kulaynī, "Kitāb al-ashriba," in *al-Kāfī*, p. 408, nos. 5, 6; Mālik b. Anas, *Al-Muwatta of Imam Malik ibn Anas: The first formulation of Islamic law*, trans. Aisha Aburrahman Bewley (New York: Kegan Paul International, 1989), p. 356; al-Ṭayālisī, *Musnad*, no. 1916.

28. Al-Nasā'ī, "Kitāb al-ashriba," in *Sunan*, p. 331. For further condemnations of fermentations, see also pp. 324, 332.

29. Al-Nasā'ī, "Kitāb al-ashriba," in *Sunan*, p. 334.

30. Muslim, "Kitāb al-ashriba," in *Ṣaḥīḥ*, no. 11. For other examples that support this position, see Abū Dāwūd, "Kitāb al-ashriba," in *Sunan*, no. 3710; al-Dārimī, "Kitāb al-ashriba," in *al-Sunan*, p. 118.

31. Al-Kulaynī, "Kitāb al-ashriba," in *al-Kāfī*, p. 428, nos. 1, 2, 3, 4.

32. "Baba Bathra," in *The Babylonian Talmud*, eds. and trans. I. Epstein, et al. (London: Soncino Press, 1961), nos. 83B, 84B, 96A.

33. Ibid.

34. "Abodah Zarah," in *The Bablyonian Talmud,* nos. 66A, 66B.

35. Al-Nasāʾī, "Kitāb al-ashriba," in *Sunan,* pp. 323, 326. The Ḥadīth collection of ʿAbd al-Razzāq also provides several examples that suggest if one is not sure whether a drink has fermented or not, one should cut the drink with water (*al-Muṣannaf,* vol. 9, nos. 17015, 17017, 17018, 17022, 17023, 17024).

36. *Nabīdh* is a comprehensive term used for fruit drinks that often intoxicate. While *khamr* is often used to denote a wine made from grapes, *nabīdh* is the term employed for alcoholic or non-alcoholic beverages made from a variety of fruits steeped in water. The Ḥadīth are very careful to note that the type of *nabīdh* consumed by the Prophet was a fruit-drink that was non-alcoholic in nature. The Prophet's *nabīdh* was to be distinguished from the normal fermented types favored in pre-Islamic times. For more on the subject of *nabīdh,* see *EI*², *s.v.* "nabīdh," by P. Heine; and *EI*², *s.v.* "mashrūbāt."

37. *Nabīdh* was also the drink offered to pilgrims in Mecca. The religious function of *nabīdh* in this context was known as the institution of *al-siqāya.*

38. ʿAbd al-Razzāq, *al-Muṣannaf,* vol. 9, no. 17021.

39. See the treatment of mixtures and vessels, for example.

40. Al-Kulaynī, "Kitāb al-ashriba," in *al-Kāfī,* p. 409, no. 11, p. 410, no. 13.

41. Ibid., p. 416, no. 4.

42. *Encyclopaedia Judaica* (New York: Macmillan, 1971–1982), *s.v.* "wine." See also "Yebamoth," in *The Babylonian Talmud,* no. 3D (46A).

43. "ʿErubin," in *The Babylonian Talmud,* no. 54A. See also "Shabbath," nos. 76B and 77A.

44. "Taʿanith," in *The Babylonian Talmud,* nos. 17A, 26B.

45. "ʿErubin," in *The Babylonian Talmud,* no. 64B.

46. Ibid., no. 64A.

47. *Encyclopaedia Judaica, s.v.* "wine."

48. These examples represent only a small portion of the number of Ḥadīth devoted to this topic. For other examples, see al-Bukhārī, "Kitāb al-ashriba," in *Ṣaḥīḥ,* no. 506; Abū Dāwūd, "Kitāb al-ashriba," in *Sunan,* nos. 3703, 3705; Ibn Ḥanbal, *al-Musnad,* nos. 4786, 10819; Ibn Māja, "Kitāb al-ashriba," in *Kitāb al-sunan,* no. 33395; Mālik, *al-Muwatta,* p. 355, nos. 7, 8; Muslim, "Kitāb al-ashriba," in *Ṣaḥīḥ,* nos. 8, 16, 17, 18, 19, 20, 21, 23, 27, 28, 29; al-Nasāʾī, "Kitāb al-ashriba," in *Sunan,* pp. 288, 290–291, 322; al-Ṭayālisī, *Musnad,* nos. 1705, 1751, 2244; al-Tirmidhī, "Abwāb al-ashriba," in *Ṣaḥīḥ,* pp. 65–66.

49. Ibn Māja, "Kitāb al-ashriba," in *Kitāb al-sunan,* no. 3396. For like traditions, see ʿAbd al-Razzāq, *al-Muṣannaf,* vol. 9, no. 16969; Ibn Ḥanbal, *al-Musnad,* no. 9749; Muslim, "Kitāb al-ashriba," in *Ṣaḥīḥ,* no. 26; al-Nasāʾī, "Kitāb al-ashriba," in *Sunan,* p. 29.

50. Muslim, "Kitāb al-ashriba," in *Ṣaḥīḥ*, no. 22. See also ʿAbd al-Razzāq, *al-Muṣannaf*, vol. 9, no. 16973; al-Nasāʾī, "Kitāb al-ashriba," in *Sunan*, pp. 289–290, 293, 29.

51. Apparently, *zahw* was not a term familiar to the community of believers. In one *ḥadīth*, however, the Prophet is asked what this term means, and he replies that it refers to "dates (*tamr*) before ripening" (ʿAbd al-Razzāq, *al-Muṣannaf*, vol. 9, no. 16965).

52. Al-Nasāʾī, "Kitāb al-ashriba," in *Sunan*, p. 292. For similar traditions with related *asānīd*, see al-Bukhārī, "Kitāb al-ashriba," in *Ṣaḥiḥ*, no. 50; al-Dārimī, "Kitāb al-ashriba," in *al-Sunan*, p. 112; Muslim, "Kitāb al-ashriba," in *Ṣaḥīḥ*, no. 24; al-Nasāʾī, "Kitāb al-ashriba," in *Sunan*, p. 289. For similar traditions with unrelated *asānīd*, see Abū Dāwūd, Kitāb al-ashriba," in *Sunan*, no. 3704; Ibn Māja, "Kitāb al-ashriba," in *Kitāb al-sunan*, no. 3397; Muslim, "Kitāb al-ashriba," in *Ṣaḥīḥ*, nos. 25, 26; al-Nasāʾī, "Kitāb al-ashriba," in *Sunan*, p. 289.

53. In the collection of ʿAbd al-Razzāq, the combinations of ripe dates (*ruṭab*) and unripe dates (*busr*), dried dates (*tamr*) and raisins (*zabīb*), and unripe dates (*busr*) and dried dates (*tamr*), appear with great frequency. See *al-Muṣannaf*, vol. 9, nos. 16966, 16967, 16968, 16969, 16970, 16974.

54. See, for example, ʿAbd al-Razzāq, *al-Muṣannaf*, vol. 9, nos. 16969, 16970.

55. Abū Dāwūd, "Kitāb al-ashriba," in *Sunan*, no. 3707. Note that this tradition comes with an editorial disclaimer that this drink was not an intoxicant. In a second tradition that comes from the collection of Abū Dāwūd (Zīyād b. Yaḥya al-Ḥasānī: Abū Baḥr: ʿAtāb b. ʿAbd al-ʿAzīz al-Hammānī:) Ṣafīya bint ʿAṭīya comes upon ʿĀʾisha, and asks her about mixing dried dates with raisins. ʿĀʾisha said, "I used to take a handful of dried dates (*tamr*) and a handful of raisins (*zabīb*), put them into a container, and then soak them. I gave [the mixture] to the Prophet to drink" (Kitāb al-ashriba," in *Sunan*, no. 3708). A third example appears in the collection of Ibn Māja: (ʿUthmān b. Abī Shayba: Abū Muʿāwīya: Muḥammad b. ʿAbd al-Malik b. Abī ʾl-Shawārib: ʿAbd al-Wāḥid b. Zīyād: ʿAṣim: Banāna bint Yazīd al-ʿAbshamīya) ʿĀʾisha said, "We had made *nabīdh* for the Prophet of God in a waterskin. We took a handful of dried dates (*tamr*), and a handful of raisins (*zabīb*), and threw them in a skin. Then we poured water upon them, and steeped [the mixture] for a day. [The Prophet] drank [the mixture] in the evening. When we steeped [the mixture] in the evening, he drank it in the morning" ("Kitāb al-ashriba," in *Kitāb al-sunan*, no. 3398).

56. Al-Ṭayālisī, *Musnad*, no. 1481.

57. ʿAbd al-Razzāq, *al-Muṣannaf*, vol. 9, nos. 16926, 16927; Abū Dāwūd, "Kitāb al-ashriba," in *Sunan*, nos. 3690, 3693, 3694, 3695; Ibn Māja, "Kitāb al-ashriba," in *Kitāb al-sunan*, no. 3401; Muslim, "Kitāb al-ashriba," in *Ṣaḥīḥ*, nos. 33, 38, 39, 40, 41, 44, 46, 57; al-Nasāʾī, "Kitāb al-ashriba," in *Sunan*, pp. 290, 297, 304, 306–308, 319; al-Tirmidhī, "Abwāb al-ashriba," in *Ṣaḥīḥ*, p. 61.

58. Green jars (*nabīdh al-jarr*, or *al-ḥantam*) alone are prohibited in ʿAbd al-Razzāq, *al-Muṣannaf*, vol. 9, nos. 16928, 16932, 16938, 16943; Abū Dāwūd, "Kitāb al-ashriba," in *Sunan*, no. 3691; al-Bukhārī, "Kitāb al-ashriba," in *Ṣaḥīḥ*, no. 501; al-Dārimī, "Kitāb al-ashriba," in *al-Sunan*, p. 116; Ibn Ḥanbal, *al-Musnad*, nos. 4915, 11004; Muslim, "Kitāb al-ashriba," in *Ṣaḥīḥ*, nos. 43, 47, 50, 56; al-Nasāʾī, "Kitāb al-ashriba," in *Sunan*, pp. 302–304, 322—323, 333; al-Tirmidhī, "Abwāb al-ashriba," in *Ṣaḥīḥ*, p. 60. Gourds (*al-qaraʿ* or *al-dubbāʾ*) alone are prohibited in al-Nasāʾī, "Kitāb al-ashriba," in *Sunan*, pp. 304–305, 307; al-Tirmidhī, "Abwāb al-ṭab," in *Ṣaḥīḥ*, p. 199; and vessels smeared with pitch (*al-muzaffat*) in Abū Dāwūd, "Kitāb al-ashriba," in *Sunan*, no. 3709; al-Nasāʾī, "Kitāb al-ashriba," in *Sunan*, pp. 305, 308. Note that the slight shifts in vocabulary (as in the case of gourds or green jars) may represent geographical variation; the prohibition, by analogy, must extend to cover these substances as well.

59. The condemnation of gourds and vessels smeared with pitch appears in ʿAbd al-Razzāq, *al-Muṣannaf*, vol. 9, no. 16924; al-Bukhārī, "Kitāb al-ashriba," in *Ṣaḥīḥ*, nos. 498, 499, 500; al-Dārimī, "Kitāb al-ashriba," in *al-Sunan*, p. 117; Ibn Māja, "Kitāb al-ashriba," in *Kitāb al-sunan*, no. 3402; Mālik, *al-Muwatta*, p. 355, nos. 5, 6; Muslim, "Kitāb al-ashriba," in *Ṣaḥīḥ*, nos. 30, 31, 35, 36, 39, 48, 49; al-Nasāʾī, "Kitāb al-ashriba," in *Sunan*, p. 305. On the pair of green jars and gourds, see ʿAbd al-Razzāq, *al-Muṣannaf*, vol. 9, no. 16933; al-Dārimī, "Kitāb al-ashriba," in *al-Sunan*, p. 117; Ibn Ḥanbal, *al-Musnad*, nos. 4913, 5833; Ibn Māja, "Kitāb al-ashriba," in *Kitāb al-sunan*, no. 3404; Muslim, "Kitāb al-ashriba," in *Ṣaḥīḥ*, nos. 51, 52; al-Ṭayālisī, *Musnad*, no. 2743.

60. The prohibition of gourds, green jars, and vessels smeared with pitch can be found in ʿAbd al-Razzāq, *al-Muṣannaf*, vol. 9, no. 1693; Abū Dāwūd, "Kitāb al-ashriba," in *Sunan*, no. 3697; Ibn Ḥanbal, *al-Musnad*, no. 10984; al-Kulaynī, "Kitāb al-ashriba," in *al-Kāfī*, p. 418, no. 1; Muslim, "Kitāb al-ashriba," in *Ṣaḥīḥ*, nos. 37, 45, 53, 54, 55, 60; al-Nasāʾī, "Kitāb al-ashriba," in *Sunan*, pp. 306, 320; al-Ṭayālisī, *Musnad*, no. 2229. For gourds, green jars, and hollowed-out stumps (*al-naqīr*), see the following examples: al-Dārimī, "Kitāb al-ashriba," in *al-Sunan*, p. 117; Ibn Ḥanbal, *al-Musnad*, nos. 4914, 10517; Ibn Māja, "Kitāb al-ashriba," in *Kitāb al-sunan*, no. 3403; Muslim, "Kitāb al-ashriba," in *Ṣaḥīḥ*, nos. 32, 58; al-Nasāʾī, "Kitāb al-ashriba," in *Sunan*, pp. 289, 306, 309–310. For this combination—gourds, vessels smeared with pitch, and hollowed-out stumps—note the following traditions: ʿAbd al-Razzāq, *al-Muṣannaf*, vol. 9, nos. 16929, 16930; al-Kulaynī, "Kitāb al-ashriba," in *al-Kāfī*, p. 418, no. 30; Muslim, "Kitāb al-ashriba," in *Ṣaḥīḥ*, nos. 42, 59; al-Nasāʾī, "Kitāb al-ashriba," in *Sunan*, pp. 289, 297, 306, 309–310.

61. For the prohibition against a *nabīdh* that intoxicates, see Muslim, "Kitāb al-ashriba," in *Ṣaḥīḥ*, nos. 64, 65; al-Nasāʾī, *Sunan*, "Kitāb al-ashriba," p. 311.

62. Al-Nasāʾī, "Kitāb al-ashriba," in *Sunan*, p. 289. See also al-Ṭayālisī, *Musnad*, no. 2229.

63. Permitted skins tied at the mouth are mentioned in ʿAbd al-Razzāq, *al-Muṣannaf*, vol. 9, nos. 16930, 16942, 16949; Abū Dāwūd, "Kitāb al-ashriba," in

Sunan, nos. 3701, 3711, 3712; Muslim, "Kitāb al-ashriba," in *Ṣaḥīḥ*, nos. 63, 80, 84, 85; al-Nasā'ī, "Kitāb al-ashriba," in *Sunan*, pp. 309–311; al-Ṭayālisī, *Musnad*, nos. 1531, 1751, 1941, 2714, 2715. Note that one tradition specifically condemns using a skin taken from a cow ('Abd al-Razzāq, *al-Muṣannaf*, vol. 9, no. 16943).

64. For traditions that allow stone vessels to be used for making *nabīdh*, see Abū Dāwūd, "Kitāb al-ashriba," in *Sunan*, no. 3701; al-Bukhārī, "Kitāb al-ashriba," in *Ṣaḥīḥ*, nos. 495, 502; al-Dārimī, "Kitāb al-ashriba," in *al-Sunan*, p. 116; Ibn Māja, "Kitāb al-ashriba," in *Kitāb al-sunan*, no. 3400; Muslim, "Kitāb al-ashriba," in *Ṣaḥīḥ*, nos. 62, 86, 87; al-Nasā'ī, "Kitāb al-ashriba," in *Sunan*, p. 302. One tradition in the collection of 'Abd al-Razzāq permits the use of stone vessels if skins cannot be found (*al-Muṣannaf*, vol. 9, no. 16935); however, another states that stones were detested (id., no. 16943).

65. The traditions that prohibit the use of skins along with the containers mentioned above are the following: Abū Dāwūd, "Kitāb al-ashriba," in *Sunan*, nos. 3696, 3719; Ibn Ḥanbal, *al-Musnad*, nos. 9343, 10325.

66. Abū Dāwūd, "Kitāb al-ashriba," in *Sunan*, nos. 3699, 3700; al-Bukhārī, "Kitāb al-ashriba," in *Ṣaḥīḥ*, nos. 3696, 3719; Ibn Ḥanbal, *al-Musnad*, nos. 9343, 10325.

67. 'Abd al-Razzāq, *al-Muṣannaf*, vol. 9, nos. 16952, 16953.

68. Choksy, *Purity and Pollution in Zoroastrianism*, 11.

69. "Abodah Zarah," in *The Bablyonian Talmud*, nos. 32A, 33A, 33B.

70. Ibid., 29A, 29B. See also "Terumoth," in *The Babylonian Talmud*, no. 42B, where it is stated that if left uncovered for the time it takes the serpent to crawl out from a nearby place and drink, milk, wine, and water become prohibited.

71. Al-Bukhārī, "Kitāb al-ashriba," in *Ṣaḥīḥ*, no. 487. See also no. 493, and "Kitāb al-tafsīr," no. 143 in the same collection.

72. "Kitāb al-ashriba," in *Kitāb al-sunan*, no. 3377. See also 'Abd al-Razzāq, *al-Muṣannaf*, vol. 9, no. 17058.

73. Sūra 4:43 (al-Nisā').

74. Genesis 7:12.

75. Matthew 4:2; Mark 1:12; Luke 4:2.

76. "Excerpts from a Book of David," in *Medieval Handbooks of Penance*, trans. John T. McNeill and Helena M. Gamer (New York: Columbia University Press, 1938), 172.

77. Ibid., 174.

78. Ibid., 176. See also "Penitential Ascribed by Albers to Bede" (ca. A.D. 8th c.) in the same work, 231.

79. "Excerpts from a Book of David," in *Medieval Handbooks of Penance*, 176. See also "The Penitential of Cummean" (ca. A.D. 650) in the same work, 103.

80. "Excerpts from a Book of David," in *Medieval Handbooks of Penance*, 176.

81. "The Penitential of Cummean," in *Medieval Handbooks of Penance*, 102.

82. "The Penitential of Columban," in *Medieval Handbooks of Penance*, 250.

83. Al-Kulaynī, "Kitāb al-ashriba," in *al-Kāfi*, p. 402, no. 12.

84. The traditions of al-Tirmidhī and al-Ṭayālisī display the same text (*matn*) as Ibn Māja's, but have *asānīd* that resemble each other and not the one in the example above, a curious phenomenon to account for if one takes the traditional view that Ḥadīth emerged and spread from a single source. Al-Tirmidhī's version is as follows: Qutayba: Jarīr b. ʿAbd al-Ḥamīd: ʿAṭāʾ b. al-Sāʾib: ʿAbdallāh b. ʿUbayd b. ʿUmayr: his father: ʿAbdallāh b. ʿUmar: The Prophet said: God does not receive prayer for forty days from one who drinks wine. If he repents, God forgives him, but if he does it again, God will not receive prayer from him for forty days . . . if he does it again (after the third time), God will not forgive him, and cause him to drink *nahr al-khabāl*. "It was asked, O ʿAbdallāh, what is *that*?" He said: Pus from the inhabitants of Hell ("Abwāb al-ashriba," in *Ṣaḥīḥ*, p. 50). Al-Ṭayālisī's tradition contains a similar text (*matn*) and chain of transmission, but instead uses "*ṭīnat al-khabāl*" rather than "*nahr al-khabāl*" as "pus from the inhabitants from hell" (*Musnad*, no. 1901).

85. Abū Dāwūd adds a number of elements that describe what types of forbidden drinks are to be included in the forty-day punishment cycle: Muḥammad b. Rāfiʿ al-Nīsābūrī: Ibrāhīm b. ʿUmar al-Ṣanʿānī: al-Nuʿmān (b. Bashīr): Ṭāwūs: Ibn ʿAbbās: The Prophet said: Every intoxicant (*mukhammir*) is wine (*khamr*), and every intoxicant (*muskir*) is forbidden, and whoever drinks an intoxicant (even in a small amount), his prayer will not be received for forty mornings. If he repents, God forgives him. But if he repeats it a fourth time, it is incumbent upon God to make him drink *ṭīnat al-khabāl*. It was said: "What is *that*, O Prophet of God?" He said: Pus from the inhabitants of hell. Whoever serves a small amount does not know lawful from unlawful; it is incumbent upon God to make him drink *ṭīnat al-khabāl* ("Kitāb al-ashriba," in *Sunan*, no. 3680).

86. "Kitāb al-ashriba," in *Sunan*, p. 317. Al-Nasāʾī's version uses *ṭīnat al-khabāl* as well, but offers no vernacular interpretation.

87. *Musnad*, no. 6773.

88. The slight differences in vocabulary are likely due to regional variation as traditions are translated across borders of dialect.

89. *Musnad*, no. 6854. See also al-Nasāʾī, "Kitāb al-ashriba," in *Sunan*, p. 314.

90. Ibn Ḥanbal, *Musnad*, no. 4917.

91. Some Shīʿīte traditions suggest that wine causes a person to omit obligatory prayer, fornicate, rob, and defile his mother and sister. See, for example, al-Kulaynī, "Kitāb al-ashriba," in *al-Kāfi*, p. 403, nos. 7, 8. These traditions resemble the views presented in the Testament of Judah (14:1ff), where wine "disturbs the mind with filthy thoughts [leading to fornication] and heats the body to carnal union" (*The Old Testament Pseudepigrapha*, vol. 2, ed. James H. Charlesworth [New York: Doubleday, 1985]). In 3 Baruch (8:4–5) (*The Old Testament Pseudepigrapha*, vol. 1, ed. James H. Charlesworth [New York: Doubleday, 1985]), wine "beholds the lawlessness and

unrighteousness of men, namely, fornications, adulteries, thefts, extortions, idolatries, drunkenness, murders, strife, jealousies, evil-speakings, murmurings, whisperings, divinations . . . which are not well-pleasing to God."

92. Al-Kulaynī, "Kitāb al-ashriba," in *al-Kāfī*, p. 400, no. 3.

93. Ibid., p. 396, no. 3, p. 399, no. 14.

94. Ibid., p. 423, no. 7. Whether or not this tradition suggests that one is *prohibited* from praying is not clear; perhaps it simply illustrates the level of concern over the contact with such a beverage. In a tradition from the collection of Ibn Bābawayhī, it is stated that God prohibits the drinking of wine; he does not prohibit prayer in a garment stained by it (*Kitāb man lā yaḥḍuruhu ʿl-faqīh*, Part IV, no. 5090).

95. Al-Kulaynī, "Kitāb al-ashriba," in *al-Kāfī*, p. 422, no. 1.

96. See *EI*², *s.v.* "g͟hulāt," for traditions about the divine spark embedded within the Shīʿīte *imām*.

97. See Abū Dāwūd, "Kitāb al-ashriba," in *Sunan*, no. 3671, which states that ʿAlī became so drunk that he could not remember what he was supposed to say during the evening prayer service. Al-Nasāʾī also suggests that wine is linked with unbelief, and unbelief cannot be mixed with prayer ("Kitāb al-ashriba," in *Sunan*, p. 314).

98. Examples of formulae against the reciting of prayer while intoxicated can be found in al-Kulaynī, "Kitāb al-ashriba," in *al-Kāfī*, p. 401, nos. 6, 8.

99. Al-Nasāʾī, "Kitāb al-ashriba," in *Sunan*, p. 314.

100. Al-Dārimī, "Kitāb al-ashriba," in *al-Sunan*, p. 115. See also Ibn Ḥanbal, *al-Musnad*, no. 10740; al-Nasāʾī, "Kitāb al-ashriba," in *Sunan*, p. 313.

101. Shaykh al-Ṭāʾifa Abī Jaʿfar Muḥammad al-Tūsī, *Tahdhīb al-aḥkām*, Part X (Dār al-kutub al-islāmīya, 1962), no. 364(21). See also 363(20), 365(22), 366(23), 367(25), 368(25), 369(26) in the same volume. Other examples appear in Ibn Bābawayhī, *Kitāb man lā yaḥḍuruhu ʿl-faqīh*, Part IV, no. 5089; al-Kulaynī, "Kitāb al-ḥudūd," in *al-Kāfī*, p. 218, nos. 1, 2, 3, 4, 5, 6.

102. Al-Bukhārī, "Kitāb al-ḥudūd," in *Ṣaḥīḥ*, nos. 770, 764, 765, 766, 767; al-Kulaynī, "Kitāb al-ḥudūd," in *al-Kāfī*, p. 214, nos. 1, 2, 4, 5, p. 215, no. 15; al-Tūsī, *Tahdhīb al-aḥkām*, Part X, nos. 347(4), 348(5), 349(6), 350(7), 353(10), 354(11).

103. Al-Tūsī, *Tahdhīb al-aḥkām*, Part X, nos. 353(10), 354 (11), 359 (16). See also al-Kulaynī, "Kitāb al-ḥudūd," in *al-Kāfī*, p. 215, no. 8, p. 216, no. 14.

104. Al-Kulaynī, "Kitāb al-ḥudūd," in *al-Kāfī*, p. 215, no. 8, p. 216, no. 14.

105. Abū Dāwūd, "Kitāb al-ashriba," in *Sunan*, no. 3713. Similar traditions with comparable texts and chains of transmission include Ibn Māja, "Kitāb al-ashriba," in *Kitāb al-sunan*, no. 3399; Muslim, "Kitāb al-ashriba," in *Ṣaḥīḥ*, nos. 79, 81, 82; al-Nasāʾī, "Kitāb al-ashriba," in *Sunan*, pp. 320, 325, 332–333.

106. Ibn Māja, "Kitāb al-ashriba," in *Kitāb al-Sunan*, no. 3373. See also no. 3374 in the same collection. For similar traditions, see Ibn Ḥanbal, *al-Musnad*, nos. 4729, 6046, 6283; Muslim, "Kitāb al-ashriba," in *Ṣaḥiḥ*, nos. 76, 78.

107. Al-Tirmidhī, "Abwāb al-ashriba," in *Ṣaḥīḥ*, p. 48. Like traditions with similar *asānīd* appear in Abū Dāwūd, "Kitāb al-ashriba," in *Sunan*, 3679; al-Nasā'ī, "Kitāb al-ashriba," in *Sunan*, p. 318.

108. Ibn Ḥanbal, *al-Musnad*, no. 4690. See also nos. 4823, 4824 in the same collection. The following traditions support similar *asānīd* as well as texts: al-Dārimī, "Kitāb al-ashriba," in *al-Sunan*, p. 111; Mālik, *al-Muwatta*, p. 356, no. 11; Muslim, "Kitāb al-ashriba," in *Ṣaḥīḥ*, no. 77; al-Nasā'ī, "Kitāb al-ashriba," in *Sunan*, p. 317.

109. Al-Nasā'ī, "Kitāb al-ashriba," in *Sunan*, p. 318. See also Ibn Ḥanbal, *al-Musnad*, nos. 4916, 5730; Muslim, "Kitāb al-ashriba," in *Ṣaḥīḥ*, no. 73.

110. Several traditions insist, however, that one who is addicted to wine will be barred completely from the Garden. See al-Dārimī, "Kitāb al-ashriba," in *al-Sunan*, p. 112; Ibn Ḥanbal, *al-Musnad*, nos. 6537, 6882, 6892.

111. Ibn Ḥanbal, *al-Musnad*, no. 6948.

112. Al-Kulaynī, "Kitāb al-ashriba," in *al-Kāfī*, p. 400, no. 17.

113. Ibid., p. 396, no. 1, p. 397, nos. 6, 7.

114. Ibid., p. 398, no. 13.

115. Ibid., p. 397, no. 8.

116. Al-Bukhārī, "Kitāb al-ashriba," in *Ṣaḥīḥ*, no. 483.

117. Abū Dāwūd, "Kitāb al-ashriba," in *Sunan*, no. 3681. See also no. 3687 in the same collection. Traditions that follow this pattern are numerous: ʿAbd al-Razzāq, *al-Muṣannaf*, vol. 9, nos. 17006, 17007, 1700; al-Dārimī, "Kitāb al-ashriba," in *Sunan*, p. 113; Ibn Māja, "Kitāb al-ashriba," in *Sunan*, nos. 3392, 3393, 3394; al-Nasā'ī, "Kitāb al-ashriba," in *Sunan*, pp. 296, 300–301, 320–321, 324; al-Tirmidhī, "Abwāb al-ashriba," in *Ṣaḥīḥ*, pp. 58–59. Some of the traditions of al-Kulaynī display the same message and structure in "Kitāb al-ashriba," in *al-Kāfī*, p. 408, no. 6, p. 409, nos. 8, 10, 12, p. 418, no. 2, p. 430, nos. 5, 6; these examples, however, often weave this formulaic statement in a complex historical drama, where it becomes the outcome of a particular sequence of events or discussions.

118. "ʿErubin," in *The Babylonian Talmud*, no. 29B.

119. "Pesaḥim," in *The Babylonian Talmud*, nos. 109A, 109B.

120. "ʿErubin," in *The Babylonian Talmud*, no. 64A.

121. Ibid. See also 64B.

122. William A. Graham summarizes the importance and significance of the "word" in the following passage: "The content of an orally communicated, memorized, and recited text such as the Qur'ān always retains to a high degree what I am rather arbitrarily calling sensual meaning alongside, or in interaction with if not prior to, its discursive or esoteric sense. This is borne out in the immense and intense effect that recitation of the Qur'ān has on its Muslim (and not on a few non-Muslim) hearers, as well as in the symbolic or iconic character of the text, which is such that even the smallest word or phrase from the Qur'ān—"understood" or not—refers to some degree to the whole and to the authority that the whole com-

mands among Muslims" (*Beyond the Written Word: Oral aspects of scripture in the history of religion* [New York: Cambridge University Press, 1987], 113).

CHAPTER THREE: LINKS TO A SACRED PAST

1. Please note that I am not using the phrase "narrative discourse" in the restricted sense employed by narratologists in general and Gerard Gennette in particular. By "narrative discourse," I simply mean "any written expression that articulates the actions and affections of characters in a space-time continuum." Cf. G. Gennette, *Narrative Discourse: An Essay in Method,* trans. Jane E. Lewin (Ithaca: Cornell University Press, 1980), 25–32.

2. Note that Abū Hurayra is an important authoritative source within the larger tradition (see note 11, below). His presence here, however, does not contribute to the narrative outcome in any significant way.

3. Abū Dāwūd, "Kitāb al-ashriba," in *Sunan,* no. 3716.

4. Narrative discourse, with its stress on movement and succession, reflects the inherent patterns of logic that propel human thought and action. As David Carr states, "[N]arrative structure refers not only to such a play of points of view but also to the organizational features of events themselves in such terms as beginning-middle-end, suspension-resolution, departure-returning repetition, and the like. We maintain that all these structures and organizational features pertain to everyday experience and action whether or not the narrative structure, or the act of narrative structuring takes the form of explicit verbalization" (*Time, Narrative, and History* [Bloomington: Indiana University Press, 1986], 62). Narrative structure, therefore, mirrors the kind of natural movement or succession of event that is already set deep within human thought and action.

5. Gordon Newby states, "the primary credit for assimilating biblical traditions into Islam must go to Ibn ʿAbbas . . . Ibn ʿAbbas was so important for the development of the Quran commentary, particularly the type called *"Israʾiliyat,"* that subsequent generations, confronted with the necessity of assigning attribution and authority to already accepted anonymously derived *Ḥadīth* reports, chose his name as the one figure who would not be controverted" (*The Making of the Last Prophet,* 10). For more on the authority of Ibn ʿAbbās, see Nabia Abbott, *Studies in Arabic Literary Papyri,* vol. 2, *Qurʾānic Commentary and Tradition* (Chicago: University of Chicago Press, 1967), 9, 14.

6. Al-Bukhārī, "Kitāb al-ashriba," in *Ṣaḥīḥ,* no. 514.

7. Honey, like wine, is also treated as an ambiguous substance that must be contained and is listed among those substances that could potentially be turned into any intoxicant. For examples of the condemnation of honey (*bitʿ*, *ʿasal*), see al-Dārimī, "Kitāb al-ashriba," in *al-Sunan,* p. 113; Muslim, "Kitāb al-ashriba," in *Ṣaḥīḥ,* no. 70; al-Tirmidhī, "Abwāb al-ashriba," in *Sunan,* p. 63.

8. See, for example, Sūras 17:1 (al-Isrāʾ); 53 (al-Najm); 70:1–8 (al-Maʿārij).

9. Sūra 53:13–17 (al-Najm), trans. Ahmed.

10. The "night journey" (*mirʿāj*) means "ladder" in Arabic, and is linked to Jacob's vision of the heavenly ladder. As noted by Newby, the fact that Muḥammad ascended to heaven, while Jacob did not, did much to boost Muḥammad's status as the seal of the prophets (*The Making of the Last Prophet*, 18).

11. Abū Hurayra, like Ibn ʿAbbās, is also known to have had extensive knowledge of the Torah. See Abbott, *Studies in Arabic,* 9; Newby, *The Making of the Last Prophet*, 10.

12. *Musnad*, no. 10655. For similar traditions, see al-Bukhārī, "Kitāb al-ashriba," in *Ṣaḥīḥ*, no. 482; al-Dārimī, "Kitāb al-ashriba," in *al-Sunan*, p. 110; Muslim, "Kitāb al-ashriba," in *Ṣaḥīḥ*, no. 92; al-Nasāʾī, "Kitāb al-ashriba," in *Sunan*, p. 312. In Muslim's rendition, Elijah presents the two bowls, but Gabriel still makes the proclamation that God guided Muḥammad to the right decision.

13. In many other versions of Ibn Ḥanbal's and al-Bukhārī's passages, Muḥammad's journey often took place *en route* to the mosque in *Jerusalem* (as opposed to Paradise) suggesting another narrative strategy by which to divert Muḥammad away from the realm of the divine.

14. See Sūra 2:97 (al-Baqara), for example: "Whosoever is the enemy of Gabriel who revealed the word of God to you by the dispensation of God, reaffirming what had been revealed before, is a guidance and good news for those who believe" (trans. Ahmed).

15. Al-Nasāʾī, "Kitāb al-ashriba," in *Sunan*, p. 330.

16. See chapter two, p. 31.

17. Al-Nasāʾī, "Kitāb al-ashriba," in *Sunan*, p. 299. See also al-Kulaynī, "Kitāb al-ashriba," in *al-Kāfī*, p. 420, nos. 1, 3; al-Nasāʾī, "Kitāb al-ashriba," in *Sunan*, pp. 328–330, 334. *ʿAṣīr* (juice) is given the same two-thirds/one-third treatment in al-Kulaynī, "Kitāb al-ashriba," in *al-Kāfī*, p. 419, no. 1, p. 420, no. 2, p. 421, no. 11; and *al-bakhtāj* (another kind of fruit drink) in al-Nasāʾī, "Kitāb al-ashriba," in *Sunan*; p. 334; al-Kulaynī, "Kitāb al-ashriba," in *al-Kāfī*, p. 420, nos. 4, 6, p. 421, no. 7.

18. Abū Jaʿfar Muḥammad b. Jarīr al-Ṭabarī, *Taʾrīkh al-rusul wa ʿl-mulūk*, eds. M. J. de Goeje et al., 10 vols (Cairo: 1960–69).

19. Muḥammad Ibn Isḥāq, *Sīrat rasūl Allāh,* in the recension of ʿAbd al-Mālik b. Hishām's *al-Sīra al-nabawīya*, 3 vols. (Dār al-kutub al-misrīya, n.d.).

20. The *Kitāb al-mubtadaʿ* is the rescinded part of Ibn Isḥāq's original *Sīrat rasūl Allāh* that covers the history of Islam from the Creation of the world on up to the beginning of pre-Islamic Arabian history. This section contained much of the *Isrāʾīlīyāt* material, which Ibn Hishām most likely removed for polemical purposes. For an idea of what this book would have looked like, see Newby's *The Making of the Last Prophet.*

21. Al-Ṭabarī, *The History of al-Ṭabarī, vol. 2, Prophets and Patriarchs, trans. William Brinner (Albany: State University* of New York Press, 1992), 10 n. 33.

22. Ibid., 10. On Noah's exemplary position as an ideal servant of God, al-Ṭabarī writes:

> We have mentioned God's kindness and helpfulness to Noah. This was because of Noah's obedience to God and his steadfastness in the face of all the injury and unpleasantness which befell him in this world. God saved him and those of his people who believed with him and followed him. God peopled the world with his descendants and made his name a name to be praised forever, and stored up for him a life of everlasting pleasure and ease in the hereafter (id., 10).

23. Ibid.

24. Ibid., 12 n. 43.

25. Newby, *The Making of the Last Prophet,* 44.

26. Ibid., 12–13.

27. Al-Ṭabarī, vol. 2, *Prophets and Patriarchs,* 11. See also Newby, *The Making of the Last Prophet,* 48.

28. As demonstrated above, the Shīʿīte Ḥadīth contain many *Isrāʾīlīyāt* traditions that are absent from the Sunnī Ḥadīth.

29. The term "*imāma*" refers to the role of "supreme leadership" appropriated after the death of the Prophet.

30. Al-Kulaynī, "Kitāb al-ashriba," in *al-Kāfī,* p. 394, no. 3.

31. Ibid., p. 393, no. 2.

32. This particular temptation of Eve has roots in a number of Near Eastern traditions. Other traditions have also used this theme of sexual enticement in a variety of similar configurations. For example, in the *Baruch,* a work with clear traces of Jewish influences, the serpent is said to have had sexual relations with *both* Eve and Adam: "For going to Eve he deceived her and committed adultery with her, which is contrary to the law; and he went also to Adam and used him as a boy, which is also against the law. Hence arose adultery and pederasty" (A. G. Gedaliahu Stroumsa, *Another Seed: Studies in gnostic mythology* [Leiden: E. J. Brill, 1994], 41 n. 20). The seduction of Eve appears in the Nag Hammadi Texts as well, where Sammael is associated with the snake. *Pirque R. El.,* for instance, offers this: "[Sammael] riding on the serpent came to her, and she conceived" (id., 48).

33. Newby, *The Making of the Last Prophet,* 37. See also al-Ṭabarī, *The History of al-Ṭabarī, vol. 1, General Introduct*ion *and From the Creation to the Flood,* trans. Franz Rosenthal, 281. In this example, al-Ṭabarī records that as long as Adam was in his right mind, he would refuse to eat from the tree. When Eve gave him wine to drink, however, he simply lost his senses and ate from the forbidden fruits.

34. Ibid., 33.

35. Sūra 7:20-23 (al-Aʿrāf), trans. Ahmed. See also 20:120 (Ṭāhā) for the same non-causal, nonparticipatory version of the Fall.

36. Adam, like wine, also has a very ambiguous position in the Qur'ān. He did fall from Paradise, but he is also presented as one to whom the angels bowed; all except Iblis, that is. See Sūras 7:19–25 (al-Aʿrāf); 20:120–21 (Ṭāhā).

37. The following summary of the traditional argument for the gradual progression of the prohibition of wine is taken from *EI*², *s.v.* "khamr." See also al-Kulaynī, "Kitāb al-ashriba," in *al-Kāfī*, p. 406, no. 2; Hattox, *Coffee and Coffeehouses*, 47.

38. *EI*², *s.v.* "khamr."

39. Ibid.

40. Muslim, "Faḍā'īl al-ṣaḥāba," in *Ṣaḥīḥ*, no. 43. In this same chapter (no. 44), Muslim provides another dramatic scene that prompts the recitation of Sūra 4:43 (al-Nisā'):

> Musaddad: Yaḥyā: Sufyān: ʿAṭā' b. al-Sā'ib and Abū ʿl-Raḥmān b. al-Sulāmī: ʿAlī b. Abī Ṭālib said that a man from the *anṣār* called him and ʿAbd al-Raḥmān b. ʿAwf over to him, and he served them an intoxicating drink before it was prohibited. ʿAlī led them in the evening prayer, reciting "O, you believers . . ." However, he became confused with what he was saying. So it came down (Do not go near prayer when you are drunk until you know what you say).

This same tradition appears in Abū Dāwūd, "Kitāb al-ashriba," in *Sunan*, no. 3671.

41. "Kitāb al-ashriba," in *Sunan*, no. 3670. See also al-Nasā'ī, "Kitāb al-ashriba," in *Sunan*, p. 286.

42. ʿUmar b. al-Khaṭṭāb was the second caliph to rule the new community of believers. Much territory was conquered in the name of the new religious dispensation under the leadership of ʿUmar. He was revered for his piety, simplicity, and accessibility (Donner, *Narratives of Islamic Origins*, 191).

43. Al-Bukhārī, "Kitāb al-tafsīr," in *Ṣaḥīḥ*, no. 141. For similar statements, note "Kitāb al-ashriba" in the same work, no. 489; Muslim, "Kitāb al-ashriba," in *Ṣaḥīḥ*, nos. 4, 5, 9.

44. Al-Bukhārī, "Kitāb al-muẓālim," in *Ṣaḥīḥ*, no. 644. For other traditions that make the same point, see al-Bukhārī, "Kitāb al-tafsīr," in *Ṣaḥīḥ*, no. 144; Muslim, "Kitāb al-ashriba," in *Ṣaḥīḥ*, no. 3; al-Dārimī, "Kitāb al-ashriba," in *al-Sunan*, p. 110.

45. Sūra 5:93 (al-Mā'ida).

46. Al-Bukhārī, "Kitāb al-ashriba," in *Ṣaḥīḥ*, no. 505. This distaste for similar mixtures framed in the same narrative context also appears in Abū Dāwūd, "Kitāb al-ashriba," in *Sunan*, no. 3673; al-Bukhārī, "Kitāb al-ashriba," in *Ṣaḥīḥ*," nos. 486, 488, 490; Mālik, *Muwatta*, p. 356, no. 13; Muslim, "Kitāb al-ashriba," in *Ṣaḥīḥ*, nos. 6, 7, 10; al-Nasā'ī, "Kitāb al-ashriba," in *Sunan*, pp. 287–8; al-Ṭayālisī, *Musnad*, no. 533.

47. Abū Dāwūd, "Kitāb al-ashriba," in *Sunan*, no. 3669; al-Bukhārī, "Kitāb al-tafsīr," in *Ṣaḥīḥ*, no. 140; al-Nasā'ī, "Kitāb al-ashriba," in *Sunan*, p. 295.

48. "Kitāb al-ashriba," in *Sunan*, p. 332. Another example can be found in the Ḥadīth collection of Abū Dāwūd: ʿĪsā b. Muḥammad: Ḍamra: al-Saybanī [sic]: ʿAbdallāh b. al-Daylamī: his father said, "O Prophet of God, do you know who we are, and where we are from, and to whom we have come?" He said, "To God and His Messenger." We said, "O Prophet of God, we have grapes, so what do we make of them?" He said, "Steep them in the morning, and drink the beverage in the evening, and steep the beverage in the evening, and drink it in the morning. Steep them in the skin, and do not steep them in an earthen jug, for if it stays for a long period of time, it becomes vinegar" ("Kitāb al-ashriba," in *Sunan*, no. 3710). Because the introduction establishes the relationship between God and his community of believers, whatever information that is to be conveyed in the rest of the passage has been presanctioned by the divine. If you are a member of this particular community, you must abide by these rules. For other traditions that make these same points through the same narrative scene, see al-Dārimī, "Kitāb al-ashriba," in *al-Sunan*, p. 116; al-Nasā'ī, "Kitāb al-ashriba," in *Sunan*, pp. 328, 332.

49. The appearance of al-Awzāʿī in the chain of transmission indicates that this is a Syrian tradition.

50. "Kitāb al-ashriba," in *Sunan*, p. 320. See also p. 333 in the same chapter.

51. Note that the Prophet himself is not a necessary actor in either of these two passages. In other words, his personality, characteristics, or actions have nothing to do with the sayings that are given. In fact, the "Prophet" could be replaced by any other authoritative figure and the meaning in either of the passages would remain the same.

52. Al-Ṭayālisī, *Musnad*, no. 1751. See also nos. 1941, 2691.

53. Abū Dāwūd, "Kitāb al-ashriba," in *Sunan*, no. 3711. This tradition also appears in Ibn Māja, "Kitāb al-ashriba," in *Kitāb al-sunan*, no. 3398; al-Tirmidhī, "Abwāb al-ashriba," in *Ṣaḥīḥ*, p. 63.

54. Al-Ṭayālisī, *Musnad*, nos. 2714, 2715; Abū Dāwūd, "Kitāb al-ashriba," in *Sunan*, nos. 3702, 3713; Ibn Māja, "Kitāb al-ashriba," in *Kitāb al-sunan*, no. 3399; Muslim, "Kitāb al-ashriba," in *Ṣaḥīḥ*, nos. 63, 79, 80, 81, 82, 84, 85; al-Nasā'ī, "Kitāb al-ashriba," in *Sunan*, pp. 310, 332–3, 325.

55. Muslim, "Kitāb al-ashriba," in *Ṣaḥīḥ*, no. 11; Abū Dāwūd, "Kitāb al-ashriba," in *Sunan*, no. 3675; al-Dārimī, "Kitāb al-ashriba," in *al-Sunan*, p. 118.

56. Mālik, *Muwatta*, p. 356, no. 12. See also Muslim, "Kitāb al-musāqā," in *Ṣaḥīḥ*, no. 68; al-Dārimī, "Kitāb al-ashriba," in *al-Sunan*, p. 114, "Kitāb al-buyūʿ," p. 256.

57. "Kitāb al-buyūʿ," in *al-Sunan*, p. 256.

58. Al-Dārimī, "Kitāb al-ashriba," in *al-Sunan*, p. 112. See also Muslim, "Kitāb al-ashriba," in *Ṣaḥīḥ*, no. 12; al-Tirmidhī, "Abwāb al-ashriba," in *Ṣaḥīḥ*, p. 199.

Only one Sunnī tradition says that it is possible to medicate with wine; however, it is attached with a disclaimer (al-Ṭayālisī, *Musnad*, no. 1018).

59. Al-Kulaynī, "Kitāb al-ashriba," in *al-Kāfī*, p. 413, no. 2.

60. Ibid., p. 414, no. 5. See also p. 413, no. 3, p. 414, nos. 6, 8, and p. 426 no. 4 for similar passages. An especially sarcastic example appears in the same collection: Abū ʿAlī al-Ashʿarī: Muḥammad b. ʿAbd al-Jabbār: Ṣafwān b. Yaḥyā: Ibn Maskān: al-Ḥilbī said: I asked Abū ʿAbdallāh about medicine that is soaked in wine (*khamr*). He said, "No, by God, it cannot be considered. How can you be treated with it if it is in the same legal position as the fat of pigs? Surely people used *that* to treat illnesses!" (p. 414, no. 4).

61. Al-Kulaynī, "Kitāb al-ashriba," in *al-Kāfī*, p. 426, no. 3. Other examples can be located on p. 416, no. 3, p. 424, no. 1, and p. 425, no. 2.

62. Abū Dāwūd, "Kitāb al-aṭʿima," in *Sunan*, no. 3774. This tradition comes with a disclaimer attached at the end: "Abū Dāwūd says: Jaʿfar did not hear this tradition from al-Zuhrī; it is not recognized."

63. Al-Kulaynī, "Kitāb al-aṭʿima," in *al-Kāfī*, p. 268, no. 1.

64. Al-Dārimī, "Kitāb al-ashriba," in *al-Sunan*, p. 112. This tradition also appears in al-Kulaynī, "Kitāb al-aṭʿima," in *al-Kāfī*, p. 268, no. 2, but the word "sit" is substituted with the word "eat."

65. Al-Dārimī, "Kitāb al-ashriba," in *al-Sunan*, p. 115. For similar traditions, see also al-Bukhārī, "Kitāb al-ḥudūd," in *Ṣaḥīḥ*, no. 763, and "Kitāb al-ashriba," no. 484; al-Nasāʾī, "Kitāb al-ashriba," in *Sunan*, p. 313. For traditions that combine the analytic proclamations of avoiding certain types of vessels with statements summarizing the basic tenets of faith, see Abū Dāwūd, "Kitāb al-ashriba," in *Sunan*, and al-Nasāʾī, "Kitāb al-ashriba," in *Sunan*, p. 322.

66. The Qurʾān's views on hypocrisy are summarized in Sūra 63 (al-Munāfiqūn). The hypocrites are those who profess the faith, but then challenge these professions through their unrighteous actions. The text clearly states that these evil ones will be damned forever.

67. Al-Nasāʾī, "Kitāb al-ashriba," in *Sunan*, p. 319. See also ʿAbd al-Razzāq, *Muṣannaf*, no. 17040.

68. Al-Kulaynī, "Kitāb al-ashriba," in *al-Kāfī*, p. 397, no. 5. For slightly modified versions of this tradition, see the same *kitāb* in *al-Kāfī*, p. 395, no. 3, p. 396, nos. 2, 4, p. 398, no. 12, p. 421, no. 8. See also Ibn Bābawayhī, *Man lā yaḥḍuruhu ʿl-faqīh*, vol. 4, no. 5090.

69. Ibn Ḥanbal, *Musnad*, no. 6165.

70. Mark 11:15.

71. The following references taken from the *Sīra* are noted by Newby, *The Making of the Last Prophet*, 23: In the Battle of the Trench, Muḥammad serves as miracle-worker by disintegrating a monstrous boulder with his spit; he also made a handful of dates feed all the hungry people in Medina with some to spare when all

was said and done. In Ibn Ḥanbal's tradition, Muḥammad serves as prophet by elevating the word of God over and above the demands of the economy. Muḥammad's resemblance to Jesus implies an appropriation of sacred history that molds all of God's messengers into a single type of one who enounters much resistance to his faithful deliverance of the word.

72. Ibn Hishām's edition of the *Sīra*, which begins with Arabian history before the coming of the Prophet Muḥammad, stands in direct contrast to the first part of Ibn Isḥāq's *Sīra*, whose descriptions of primordial beginnings were subsequently removed and dispersed. The first part of Ibn Isḥāq's *Sīra* goes as such: I. Ḥamid: Salama b. al-Faḍl: Ibn Isḥāq: The first thing God created was light and darkness. Then he separated them and made the darkness night, black exceeding dark; and he made the light day, bright and luminous (Alfred Guillaume, *A Translation of Ibn Isḥāq's Sīrat Rasūl Allāh* (Oxford: Oxford University Press, 1955), xvii–xviii. This "Genesis" story, which is concerned with depicting the origins of the world, was later removed by Ibn Hishām, who chose instead to begin with the story of Abraham, the presumed forerunner and predecessor of Muḥammad.

73. Ibn Hishām, trans. Guillaume, 19. See also Ibn Hishām, *al-Sīra al-nabawīya* (Dār al-kutub al-misrīya, n.d.), vol. 1, pt. 1, 38.

74. Ibn Hishām, trans. Guillaume, 32; Ibn Hishām, vol. 1, Part 1, 65.

75. Ibn Hishām, trans. Guillaume, 647–648.

76. The *Sīra*'s versions are as follows:

> Ibn Isḥāq heard it from ʿAbdullāh b. Masʿūd: Burāq, the animal whose every stride carried it as far as its eye could reach on which the prophets before him used to ride was brought to the apostle and he was mounted on it. His companion (Gabriel) went with him to see the wonders between heaven and earth, until he came to Jerusalem's temple. There he found Abraham the friend of God, Moses, and Jesus assembled with a company of the prophets, and he prayed with them. Then he was brought three vessels containing milk, wine (*khamr*), and water respectively. The apostle said: "I heard a voice saying when these were offered to me: If he takes the water he will be drowned and his people also; if he takes the wine he will go astray and his people also; and if he takes the milk he will be rightly guided and his people also." So I took the vessel containing milk and drank it. Gabriel said to me, "you have been rightly guided and so will your people be, Muḥammad" (Ibn Hishām, trans. Guillaume, 182; Ibn Hishām, vol. 1, pt. 1, 397).

This same story appears again in another form:

> In his story al-Ḥaṣan said: The apostle and Gabriel went their way until they arrived at the temple at Jerusalem. There he found Abraham, Moses, and Jesus among a company of the prophets. The apostle acted as their *imām* in prayer. Then he was brought two vessels, one containing

wine (*khamr*) and the other milk. The apostle took the milk and drank it, leaving the wine. Gabriel said: "You have been rightly guided to the way of nature and so will your people be, Muḥammad. Wine is forbidden to you" (Ibn Hishām, trans. Guillaume, 182; Ibn Hishām, vol. 1, pt. 1, 398).

77. The tradition goes as follows:

> ʿAbdullah b. Abū Najīḥ, the Meccan, from his companions ʿAṭāʾ and Mujāhid or other narrators said that ʿUmar's conversion, according to what he used to say himself, happened thus: "I was far from Islam. I was a wine-bibber in the heathen period, used to love it and rejoice in it. We used to have a meeting place in al-Ḥazwara at which Quraysh used to gather near the houses of the family of ʿUmar b. ʿAbd al-ʿImrān al-Makhzūmī. I went out one night, making for my boon companions in that gathering, but when I got there, there was no one present, so I thought it would be a good thing if I went to so-and-so, the wine-seller, who was selling wine in Mecca at the time, in the hope that I might get something to drink from him, but I could not find him either, so I thought it would be a good thing if I went around the Kaʿba seven or seventy times" (Ibn Hishām, trans. Guillaume, 157; Ibn Hishām, vol. 1, pt. 1, 346).

Next ʿUmar hears the Qurʾān, weeps, and receives Islam.

78. The *Sīra* states:

> [w]hen Abū Sufyān saw that he had saved his caravan he sent word to the Quraysh, "Since you came out to save your caravan, your men, and your property, and God has delivered them, go back." Abū Jahl said, "By God, we will not go back until we have been to Badr"—Badr was the site of one of the Arab fairs where they used to hold a market every year. "We will spend 3 days there, slaughter camels, and feast, and drink wine (*khamr*), and the girls shall play for us. The Arabs will hear that we have come and gathered together, and will respect us in the future. So come on!" (Ibn Hishām, trans. Guillaume, 296; Ibn Hishām, vol. 1, pt. 1, 619).

79. ʿAbdullah b. al-Faḍl b. ʿAbbās b. Rabīʿā b. al-Ḥārith from Sulaymān b. Yasār from Jaʿfar b. ʿAmr b. Umayya al-Ḍamrī told me:

> I went out with ʿUbaydullah b. ʿAdīy b. al-Khiyār brother of the B. Naufal b. ʿAbdu Manāf in the time of Muʿāwiya b. Abū Sufyān and we made an excursion with the army. When we came back we passed by Ḥimṣ where Waḥshī had taken up his abode. When we arrived there ʿUbaydullah said to me, "Shall we go see Waḥshī and ask him how he

> killed Ḥamza?" "If you like," I said. So we went to inquire about him in Ḥimṣ. While we were doing so a man said to us, 'You will find him in the courtyard of his house. He is a man much addicted to wine (*khamr*); and if you find him sober, you will find an Arab and will get what you want from him in answer to your questions; but if you find him in his usual state, leave him alone" (Ibn Hishām, trans. Guillaume, 375; Ibn Hishām, vol. 2, pt. 2, 70).

Fortunately, they found him sober.

80. Kaʿb b. Mālik gives the following description of the day upon which the Battle of Uḥud was fought: "A day in which fighting is continuous, terrifying, burning those who kindled its blaze, long drawn out exceeding hot fighting. Fear of it keeps the baseborn away. You would think the heroes engaged in it were happily drunk and inebriated (*munazifīnā),* Their right hands exchanging cups of death with their sharp-edged swords" (Ibn Hishām, trans. Guillaume, 421; Ibn Hishām, vol. 2, pt. 2, 160).

81. The *Sīra* puts forth the following verses about Khaybar from Ḥassān b. Thābit: "At the time when Ayman's mother said to him / You are a coward and were not with the horsemen of Khaybar / Ayman was no coward, but his horse / Was sick from drinking fermented barley-water (*al-madīd al-mukhammar*). Had it not been for the state of his horse / He would have fought with them as a horseman with his right hand / What stopped him was the behaviour of his horse / And what happened to him more serious" (Ibn Hishām, trans. Guillaume, 521; Ibn Hishām, vol. 2, pt. 2, 348).

82. The *Sīra* records the following tradition from B. ʿAdīy b. Kaʿb: "ʿAdīy had a son called al-Nuʿmān who returned with the Muslims. In the caliphate of ʿUmar he was put over Maysān in the district of Basra. He composed some verses:

> "Hasn't al-Ḥasnāʾ heard that her husband in Maysān / Is drinking from glasses and jars? If I wished, the chief men of the city would sing to me/ And dancing-girls pirouette on tiptoe. If you're my friend, give me a drink in the largest cup, / Don't give me the smallest half broken! Perhaps the commander of the faithful will take it amiss that we're drinking together in a tumbledown castle." When ʿUmar heard of these verses he said: "He's right, by God, I do take it amiss! Anyone who sees him can tell him that I have deposed him." After his deposition he came to ʿUmar and pleaded that he had never acted in the way that his verses implied, but that he was a poet who wrote in their exaggerated way. ʿUmar replied that as long as he lived he would never act as his governor after having used such words (Ibn Hishām, trans. Guillaume, 529).

83. *EI*[1], *s.v.* "al-Ṭāʾif," by H. Lammens.

84. Ibn Hishām, trans. Guillaume, 590.

85. According to the *Sīra*, the name of this rival prophet was Musaylima b. Ḥabīb al-Hanafī, otherwise known as the "arch liar." Upon returning home to al-Yamāma, Musaylima apostatized, claimed to be a prophet, and lied. Then he began to utter rhymes in *saj*ʿ and speak in imitation of the style of the Qurʾān:

> "God has been gracious to the pregnant woman; He has brought forth from her a living being that can move; from her very midst." He permitted them to drink wine and fornicate, and let them dispense with prayer, yet he was acknowledging the apostle as a prophet, and Ḥanīfa agreed with him on that. But God knows what the truth was (Ibn Hishām, trans. Guillaume, 637).

86. Ibn Hishām, trans. Guillaume, 598.

87. Ibn Hishām, trans. Guillaume, 600.

88. Al-Ṭabarī, *The History of al-Ṭabarī,* vol. 1, *General Introduction and From the Creation to the Flood,* trans. F. Rosenthal, 281.

89. Al-Ṭabarī, *The History of al-Ṭabarī, vol. 3, The Children of Israel, trans. William M. Brinner.*

90. Al-Ṭabarī, *The History of al-Ṭabarī, vol. 6, Muḥammad at Mecca,* trans. W. Montgomery Watt, and M. V. McDonald.

91. Ibid., 339. Cain's descendants are also described as fornicators engaged in iniquity.

92. Ibid., 184. Noah's followers also committed wickedness, and let their pre-occupation with music divert them from focusing on God.

93. Al-Ṭabarī, *The History of al-Ṭabarī,* vol. 12, *The Battle of al-Qādisiyyah and the Conquest of Syria and Palestine,* trans. Yohanan Friedman (Albany: State University of New York Press, 1992), 197.

94. Al-Ṭabarī, *The History of al-Ṭabarī,* vol. 36, *The Revolt of the Zanj,* trans. David Waines (Albany: State University of New York Press, 1992), 48.

95. Al-Ṭabarī, *The History of al-Ṭabarī,* vol. 32, *The Reunification of the ʿAbbāsid Caliphate,* trans. C. E. Bosworth (Albany: State University of New York Press, 1987), 101–102.

96. Al-Ṭabarī, *The History of al-Ṭabarī,* vol. 12, *The Battle of al-Qādisiyyah and the Conquest of Syria and Palestine,* 151, 154.

97. Al-Ṭabarī, *The History of al-Ṭabarī,* vol. 36, *The Revolt of the Zanj,* 48.

98. For example, al-Ṭabarī records that "[t]he eunuch [al-khādim] Fatḥ used to act as al-Maʾmūn's doorkeeper when the Caliph was involved in his date-wine (*nabīdh*) drinking sessions" (*The History of al-Ṭabarī,* vol. 32, *The Reunification of the ʿAbbāsid Caliphate,* 101–102).

99. Al-Ṭabarī, *The History of al-Ṭabarī,* vol. 13, *The Conquest of Iraq, Southwestern Persia, and Egypt,* trans. Gautier H. A. Juynboll (Albany: State University of New York Press, 1989) 105.

100. Although, as noted above, the Shīʿītes reacted a bit differently to wine spilled upon one's garments, especially around the time of prayer (chapter two, p. 45).

CHAPTER FOUR: A BRIEF WORD ON THE POETIC

1. In al-Nasāʾī's collection, the Prophet states that certain vessels that were once condemned have now been deemed acceptable: Muḥammad b. Maʿdān b. ʿĪsā b. Maʿdān al-Ḥarrānī: al-Ḥasan b. Aʿyān: Zuhayr: Zubayd: Muhārib: Ibn Burda: his father: The Prophet said, "I forbade you three things. I forbade you the visiting of tombs. Now visit them, for the visiting of them provides you well. I forbade you sacrificed meats after three days. Now, eat whatever you desire from them. Third, I forbade you drinks in [certain] vessels. Now, drink whatever you want from them, but do not drink intoxicants" ("Kitāb al-asriba," in *Sunan*, p. 311). See also pp. 310–311 in the same chapter for similar examples. It is important to note, however, that these rather lenient traditions are countered by a majority that forbid all aspects of fermented drinks, including their ingredients and the type of vessel in which they are steeped.

2. Al-Nasāʾī preserves the following tradition: Isḥāq b. Ibrāhīm: Jarīr b. Shabrama: Ibrāhīm was stern with the people concerning *nabīdh*, but he permitted it ("Kitāb al-ashriba," in *Sunan*, p. 335). In the statement following this *ḥadīth*, the claim is negated: ʿUbaydallāh b. Saʿīd: Abū Usāma: Ibn al-Mubārik said, "I did not find anyone deeming an intoxicating beverage (*muskir*) legally valid (*ṣaḥīḥ*) except Ibrāhīm" (id.).

3. For example, ʿUmar II was reported to have declared that *nabīdh* was permitted. See Ibn Saʿd, as quoted by Goldziher, *Introduction to Islamic Theology and Law*, 60 n. 70.

4. According to al-Ṭabarī, many Muslims directly opposed the prohibition of wine, and continued to drink it despite condemnation and punishment:

> Al-Sarī: Shuʿayb: Sayf: al-Rabīʿ: Abū Mujālid, Abū ʿUthmān and Abū Ḥāritha: Abū ʿUbaydah wrote to ʿUmar: Several Muslims have taken to wine. We asked them about this, but they justified their act with a dictum, saying 'We have been given a choice, and we have chosen' (*The History of al-Ṭabarī*, vol. 13, *The Conquest of Iraq, South Western Persia, and Egypt,* 151–154).

5. Here "ignorance" is not used in a derogatory sense; rather it refers to a lack of knowledge about God and Islam. See *EI*², *s.v.* "dj̲āhiliyya," by Joseph Schacht.

6. According to John Wansbrough, "the fact of kinship (*qawm*) furnishes not only a form (the genealogical filiation), but also a foil, the pagan Jāhilīyya setting against which the articulation of the community can be measured" (*The Sectarian Milieu: Content and composition of Islamic salvation history* [Oxford: Oxford University Press, 1978], 33).

7. Pre-Islamic Arabs were often praised for their virtues and morals, such as their honor (*ʿirḍ*), generosity (*karam*), courage, dignity (*muruwwa*), and hospitality (*ḍayf*). Certain beliefs and practices were also privileged and preserved (although in modified forms) from the period of the Jāhilīya into the time of Islam. These include the *ḥajj*, and a variety of activities surrounding the Kaʿba. For further information on the "virtuous" life of the pre-Islamic Arabs, see *EI*², *s.v.* "al-ʿArab," by A. Grohmann; and Goldziher, Muslim Studies, vol. 1: 219ff.

8. Suzanne Pinckney Stetkevych, *The Mute Immortals Speak: Pre-Islamic Poetry and the Poetics of Ritual* (Ithaca: Cornell University Press, 1993), xii.

9. Ibid., xiii–xiv.

10. Michael Sells sums up the importance of the overall poetic structure in the following quote: "Though the qasida is based upon an archetypal pattern with universal resonances, it achieves a distinctive mythopoetic intensity in the modulation of that pattern through its own subtle and fluid conception of the sacred. . . . Within the linear and irreversible progression through the major themes of the ode, other themes, movements, and moods are evoked as subtexts, countertexts, and intertexts" (*Desert Tracings: Six Classic Arabian Odes* [Middletown, Connecticut: Wesleyan University Press, 1989], 7).

11. The study and interpretation of Jāhilīya poetry ranges from philological studies to structural analyses to postmodern readings. For classical works on the subject, see Abdulla el-Tayib, "Pre-Islamic Poetry," in *Arabic Literature to the End of the Umayyad Period,* vol. 1 of *Cambridge History of Arabic Literature,* ed. Julia Ashtiany, T. M. Johnstone, J. D. Latham, R. B. Serjeant, and G. Rex Smith (Cambridge: Cambridge University Press, 1983), 27–113; A. J. Arberry, *The Seven Odes: The First Chapter in Arabic Literature* (New York: The Macmillan Company, 1957); and Ṭaha Ḥusayn, *Fi ʿl-adab al-jāhilī* (Cairo: Dār al-maʿārif, n.d.). For contemporary works on this literature, see Kamal Abū Deeb, "Towards a Structural Analysis of Pre-Islamic Poetry," *International Journal of Middle East Studies* 6 (1975): 148–184; M. J. Kister, "The Seven Odes," *Rivisita degli Studi Orientali* 54 (1969): 27–36; Jaroslav Stetkevych, "Arabic Poetry and Assorted Poetics," in *Islamic Studies: A Tradition and Its Problems* (Malibu, CA: Undena Pub., 1980), 103–123, and "Name and Epithet: The Philology and Semiotics of Animal Nomenclature in Early Arabic Poetry," *Journal of Near Eastern Studies* 45, no. 2 (1986): 89–124; Michael Zwettler, *The Oral Tradition of Classical Arabic Poetry: Its Character and Implications* (Columbus: Ohio State University Press, 1972).

12. *EI*², "khamriyya," by J. E. Bencheikh.

13. Sells, *Desert Tracings,* 3.

14. Ibid.

15. Christopher Nouryeh articulates this implicit value judgment imposed by the category of the "Muʿallaqāt" by suggesting that the category "yields nothing but a shapeless association of ideas; nothing but a formless, unstable, isolated, nebulous condensation, whose unity and coherence, if it has such, are above all due to its

mythical status" (*Translation and Critical Study of Ten Pre-Islamic Odes: Traces in the Sand* [Lampeter, Dyfed, Wales: Edwin Mellen Press, Ltd., 1993], 29–30). For another take on the problem of the category of "Muʿallaqāt," see el-Tayib, "Pre-Islamic Poetry," 111–113.

16. S. Stetkevych, *The Mute Immortals Speak,* xii.

17. Sells, *Desert Tracings,* 7.

18. Ibid., 5.

19. S. Stetkevych, *The Mute Immortals Speak,* 4.

20. Ibid.

21. Sells, *Desert Tracings,* 6.

22. F. Harb, "Wine Poetry (Khamriyyāt)," in *ʿAbbasid Belles-Lettres,* vol. 2 of *The Cambridge History of Arabic Literature,* ed. Julia Ashtiany, T. M. Johnstone, J. D. Latham, R. B. Serjeant, and G. Rex Smith (Cambridge: Cambridge University Press, 1990), 220.

23. Maymūn b. Qays (al-Aʿshā), trans. Harb, 220.

24. Harb, p. 220.

25. ʿAntara b. Shaddād, trans. Arberry, *The Seven Odes,* 181, as quoted by Harb, 221.

26. Harb, 220.

27. ʿAlqama b. ʿAbada al-Tamīmī, trans. Harb, 221.

28. Al-Aʿshā, trans. Harb, 221.

29. ʿAlqama, trans. Harb, 221.

30. Harb, 221.

31. Ṭarafa b. al-ʿAbd al-Bakrī's dates are not known. However, what has been suggested by tradition is that he was court poet for the court of al-Ḥira. He was most closely associated with King ʿAmr b. Hind, who reigned from 554–568 (*EI*[1], *s.v.* "Ṭarafa" by. F. Krenkow).

32. Nouryeh, *Translation and Critical Study,* 71.

33. Ibid. See lines 132–142 in his translation of the Ode, 86.

34. Ibid., 72.

35. Ibid., 70.

36. Ṭarafa, trans. Nouryeh, *Translation and Critical Study,* pp. 85–86.

37. Labīd b. Rabīʿa is said to have been born in the time of the Jāhilīya, converted to Islam at the age of ninety, and died at the ripe old age of one hundred fifty or so during the reign of Muʿāwiya (*EI*[1], *s.v.* "Labīd ibn Rabīʿa," by C. Brockelmann).

38. Summary provided by S. Stetkevych, *The Mute Immortals Speak,* 9.

39. Ibid., 34.

40. Ibid.

41. Labīd, trans. S. Stetkevych, *The Mute Immortals Speak,* 32.

42. Ibid., 35. Here Stetkevych notes that the word *adkan* (red-black) and *jawna* (black) are often used to describe blood as well as wine.

43. Ibid. Stetkevych argues that the word used by Labīd—*fuḍḍa*—comes from *faḍḍa,* which is used in the context of breaking a wine seal, or deflowering a virgin.

44. Ibid. Here she cites W. Robertson Smith: "He who has drunk thy morning draught is they undoubted son" (35 n. 54, from an anecdote from al-Maydānī, cited in W. Robertson Smith, *Kinship and Marriage in Early Arabia* [Oosterhout N. B. Netherlands: Anthropological Publications, 1966], 138–139).

45. ʿAlqama thrived in the sixth century A.D., and was thought to have been a poetic rival of Imruʾ al-Qays. According to traditional accounts, ʿAlqama was involved in the struggle between the Arab kingdoms of Ghassan (Byzantium) and Lakhm (Persia) (Sells, *Desert Tracings,* 12).

46. Ibid., 11–12.

47. Ibid., 12.

48. ʿAlqama, trans. Sells (*Desert Tracings*), 14.

49. Ibid., 19.

50. Ibid., 20.

51. According to tradition, al-Aʿshā was a famous court poet (of al-Ḥīra) who was well-known for his satires and wine-songs. Living from the time of the Jāhilīya on into the time of early Islam (d. 629), al-Aʿshā was thought to have been against the new religious dispensation that condemned the drinking of wine (*EI*[1], "al-Aʿsh̲ā," by A. Haffner).

52. Al-Aʿshā, trans. Nouryeh, 215.

53. Ibid.

54. The poems that appear in the *Sīra,* for example, define the "higher good" in terms of the revelation brought forth by Muḥammad. Thus, much of the sensual poetry that appears in the *Sīra* is framed by the explicit mention of such divine truths.

55. See, for example, *EI*[2], *s.v.* "k̲h̲amriyya," and M. M. Badawi's "ʿAbbasid Poetry and its antecedents," in *ʿAbbasid Belles-Lettres,* 146–166.

56. *EI*[2], *s.v.* "k̲h̲amriyya."

57. This argument is made by Badawi, "ʿAbbāsid Poetry," 149.

58. Ibid., 151.

59. Ibid.

60. Ibid., 154. See also *EI*[2], *s.v.* "k̲h̲amriyya," especially the sections on the "Libertines of al-Kūfa" and "The Pre-Nuwāsians," which describe those poets who reveled in their descriptions of drinking bouts and varied sexual activities, and used them as a way to thwart the strictures placed upon them by the new culture.

61. *EI*[2], *s.v.* "k̲h̲amriyya." To what extent these mystics were using wine and intoxication *allegorically* is not clear. It is, after all, possible they were describing their

actual experiences with alcohol and intoxication. See also *EI*², *s.v.* "khamr." See below for further discussions on the mystical dimensions of wine-imagery.

CHAPTER FIVE: WINE AND MYSTICAL UTTERANCE

1. William James, *The Varieties of Religious Experience: A study in human nature* (Longmans, Green, 1902), 297.

2. Ibid.

3. A. J. Arberry, *The Mystical Poems of Ibn al-Fāriḍ* (Dublin: Emery Walker (Ireland), Ltd., 1956), 8.

4. Ibid., 10.

5. According to J. E. Benscheikh, Ṣūfīs like Ibn al-Fāriḍ "took possession of a well-established framework [*khamriyya*] and activated it by substituting for hedonistic motivations the decisive quest for happiness in God. From there, a whole symbolism became established. Wine becomes a divine emanation which spreads its rays from one form to another, a symbol of the supreme love which manifests itself in creation. Drunkenness is forgetfulness of all that is not He. Under the effect of this application of meanings, an inner discourse is substituted for a text apparently set in its formulae" *EI*², *s.v.* "khamriyya". Ibn Fāriḍ's *khamrīya* is in fact modelled upon the famous wine odes of Abū Nuwās (Arberry, *The Mystical Poems of Ibn al-Fāriḍ*, 12), who was a poet in the ʿAbbāsid period well-known for his works on wine and pederasty (*EI*², *s.v.* "Abū Nuwās," by Edwald Wagner).

6. R. A. Nicholson, *Studies in Islamic Mysticism* (Cambridge: Cambridge University Press, 1921), 183 n. 3.

7. Ibid., n. 2.

8. Ibn al-Fāriḍ, *Dīwān*, trans. Nicholson, *Studies in Islamic Mysticism*, 184–185.

9. Ibid., 185.

10. See, for example, Sūras 37:45–47 (al-Ṣaffāt) and 56:18–19 (al-Wāqiʿa).

11. Nicholson, *Studies in Islamic Mysticism*, 185 n. 4.

12. *Khamr* is, after all, what disturbs (*khāmara*) the mind (al-Bukhārī, "Kitāb al-ashriba," in *Ṣaḥīḥ*, no. 487). See also no. 493, and "Kitāb al-tafsīr," no. 143 in the same collection. In addition, wine is never to be used as medicine. See, for example, al-Dārimī, "Kitāb al-ashriba," in *al-Sunan*, p. 112; al-Kulaynī, "Kitāb al-ashriba," in *al-Kāfī*, p. 413, nos. 2, 3, p. 414, nos. 5, 6, 8, p. 426, no. 4; Muslim, "Kitāb al-ashriba," in *Ṣaḥīḥ*, no. 12; al-Tirmidhī, "Abwāb al-ashriba," in *Ṣaḥīḥ*, p. 199.

13. Ibn al-Fāriḍ, *Dīwān*, trans. Nicholson, *Studies in Islamic Mysticism*, 186.

14. Ibid.

15. Michael Sells, *Mystical Languages of Unsaying* (Chicago: University of Chicago Press, 1994), 2.

16. Ibid.

17. Ibid.

18. Ibid.

19. Ibn al-Fāriḍ, *Dīwān*, trans. Nicholson, *Studies in Islamic Mysticism*, 186.

20. Ibid.

21. Ibid.

22. Ibid., 187.

23. Ibid.

24. Ibid.

25. Ibid., 188.

26. Al-Kulaynī, "Kitāb al-ashriba," in *al-Kāfī*, p. 396, no. 1, p. 397, nos. 6–7, p. 400, no. 17.

27. William C. Chittick, *The Sufi Path of Love* (Albany: State University of New York Press, 1983), 1–5.

28. Nicholson, *Studies in Islamic Mysticism*, 163.

29. Rūmī, *Mathnawī*, ed. and trans. R. A. Nicholson, *The Mathnawī of Jalālu'ddīn Rūmī*, vol. 3 (London: Luzac, 1925–1940), lines 819–823, comp. Chittick, 312.

30. Rūmī, *Dīwān-i Shams-i Tabrīz*, in *Kulliyyāt-i Shams yā dīwān-i kabīr*, ed. B. Furūzānfar (Tehran: University of Tehran Press, 1957–67), line 19204, comp. Chittick, 313.

31. Rūmī, *Dīwān*, line 4277, comp. Chittick, 312.

32. Ibid., line 9062, comp. Chittick, 314.

33. Rūmī, *Mathnawī*, vol. 4, line 2685, comp. Chittick, 312.

34. Ibid., line 2691, comp. Chittick, 312.

35. Rūmī, *Dīwān*, line 4276, comp. Chittick, 312.

36. Ibn al-Fāriḍ, *Dīwān*, trans. Nicholson, *Studies in Islamic Mysticism*, 187.

37. Nicholson, *Studies in Islamic Mysticism*, 187–188 n. 4.

38. Rūmī, *Dīwān*, line 931, comp. Chittick, 313.

CONCLUSION AND FUTURE COMPARATIVE DIRECTIONS

1. Examples of "entertainment" works would be *The Tales of the Prophets of al-Kisa'i*, or *The Arabian Nights*.

2. "Book of Dress," in *Ṣaḥīḥ al-Bukhārī*, ed. and trans. Muḥammad Muhsin Khan (Chicago: Kazi Publications, 1979), no. 777.

3. "Book of Ablution," in *Ṣaḥīḥ al-Bukhārī*, ed. and trans. Muḥammad Muhsin Khan, no. 216.

4. Ibid., no. 218.

5. Ibid., no. 222.

Bibliography

Abbott, Nabia. *Studies in Arabic Literary Papyri.* Vol. 2. *Qur'ānic Commentary and Tradition.* University of Chicago Oriental Institute Publications. Chicago: University of Chicago Press, 1967.

ʿAbd al-Razzāq b. Hammām al-Ṣanʿānī. *Al-Muṣannaf.* Edited by Ḥabīb al-Raḥmān al-Aʿẓamī. 2d ed. 11 vols. Al-Majlis al-ʿilmī, and Beirut: Al-Maktab al-islāmī, 1970–72.

Abū Dāwūd Sulaymān b. al-Ashʿath al-Sijistānī. *Sunan Abī Dāwūd.* Edited by Muḥammad Muḥyī 'l-Dīn ʿAbd al-Ḥamīd. 4 vols. Cairo: Maṭbaʿat Muṣṭafā Muḥammad, 1935.

Abū Deeb, Kamal. "Towards a Structural Analysis of Pre-Islamic Poetry." *International Journal of Middle East Studies* 6 (1975): 148–184.

Allen, T. F. H., and Thomas W. Hoekstra. *Toward a Unified Ecology.* New York: Columbia University Press, 1992.

Arberry, A. J. *The Mystical Poems of Ibn al-Fāriḍ.* Dublin: Emery Walker (Ireland), Ltd., 1956.

———. *The Seven Odes: The First Chapter in Arabic Literature.* New York: The Macmillan Company, 1957.

Asmussen, Jes Peter, ed. and comp. *Manichaean Literature: Representative texts chiefly from Middle Persian and Parthian writings.* Delmar, New York: Scholars' Facsimiles and Reprints, 1975.

Auerbach, Erich. *Mimesis.* Translated by Willard Trask. Princeton: Princeton University Press, 1953.

Azami, Muhammad M. *On Schacht's "Origins of Muhammadan Jurisprudence."* New York: John Wiley and Sons, 1985.

The Babylonian Talmud. Translated and edited by I. Epstein, et al. London: Soncino Press, 1961.

Badawi, M. M. "ʿAbbāsid Poetry and its Antecedents." In *ʿAbbāsid Belles-Lettres.* Vol. 2 of *Cambridge History of Arabic Literature*, edited by Julia Ashtiany, T. M.

Johnstone, J. D. Latham, R. B. Serjeant, and G. Rex Smith, 146–166. Cambridge: Cambridge University Press, 1990.

Bencheikh, J. E. "Khamriyya." *The Encyclopaedia of Islam*. 2d ed.

Bourdieu, Pierre. *Outline of a Theory of Practice*. Cambridge: Cambridge University Press, 1977.

Brock, S. P. "Syriac views of emergent Islam." In *Studies on the First Century of Islamic Society*. Edited by G. H. A. Juynboll, 9–21. Carbondale: Southern Illinois University Press, 1982.

Brockelmann, C. "Labīd ibn Rabīʿa." *Encyclopaedia of Islam*.

Brown, Francis. *A Hebrew and English lexicon of the Old Testament with an appendix containing the Biblical Aramaic*. Boston: Houghton Mifflin, 1906.

Al-Bukhārī, Abū ʿAbdallāh Muḥammad b. Ismāʿīl b. Ibrāhīm. *Jāmiʿ al-ṣaḥīḥ* (*Ṣaḥīḥ al-Bukhārī*). 8 vols. Cairo: Dār al-fikr, 1981.

———. *Ṣaḥīḥ al-Bukhārī*. Edited and translated by Dr. Muḥammad Muhsin Khan. 9 vols. Chicago: Kazi Publications, 1979.

Burton, John. *The Collection of the Qurʾān*. Cambridge: Cambridge University Press, 1977.

Bynum, Caroline Walker. *Holy Feast and Holy Fast: The religious significance of food to medieval women*. Berkeley and Los Angeles: University of California Press, 1987.

Bynum, Caroline Walker, Steven Harrell, and Paula Richman, eds. *Gender and Religion*. Boston: Beacon Press, 1986.

Campo, Juan. *The Other Sides of Paradise: Explorations into the religious meanings of domestic space in Islam*. Columbia, SC: University of South Carolina Press, 1991.

Carr, David. *Time, Narrative, and History*. Bloomington: Indiana University Press, 1986.

Charlesworth, James H., ed. and trans. *The History of the Rechabites: Volume I: The Greek Recension*. Texts and Translations 17; Pseudepigrapha Series 10. Chico, California: Scholars Press, 1982.

———. *The Old Testament Pseudepigrapha*. 2 vols. New York: Doubleday, 1985.

Chittick, William C. *The Sufi Path of Love*. Albany: State University of New York Press, 1983.

Choksy, Jamsheed. *Purity and Pollution in Zoroastrianism: Triumph over evil*. Austin: University of Texas Press, 1989.

Combs-Schilling, M. E. *Sacred Performances: Islam, sexuality, and sacrifice*. New York: Columbia University Press, 1989.

Cook, Michael. "Early Islamic Dietary Law." *Jerusalem Studies in Arabic and Islam* 7 (1985): 217–277.

———. *Muḥammad.* Oxford: Oxford University Press, 1983.

Crone, Patricia, and Michael Cook. *Hagarism: The Making of the Islamic World.* Cambridge: Cambridge University Press, 1977.

Al-Dārimī, ʿAbdallāh b. ʿAbd al-Raḥmān. *Al-Sunan.* Edited by Muḥammad Aḥmad Duhmān. Cairo: Dār al-iḥya', 197–.

Donner, Fred. *Narratives of Islamic Origins: The Beginnings of Islamic Historical Writing.* Princeton: The Darwin Press, Inc., 1998.

Douglas, Mary, ed. *Constructive Drinking.* New York: Cambridge University Press, 1987.

———. *Natural Symbols: Explorations in Cosmology.* New York: Pantheon Books, 1970.

———. *Purity and Danger.* London: Ark Paperbacks, 1985.

Durand, Y., and J. Morenon. *L'Imaginaire du vin.* Marseille: J. Lafitte, 1983.

Durkheim, Emile. *The Elementary Forms of Religious Life.* New York: Free Press, 1995.

Eaton, Richard. *The Sufis of Bijapur: Social roles of Sufis in medieval India.* Princeton: Princeton University Press, 1978.

Eliade, Mircea. *Patterns in Comparative Religion.* New York: Meridian, 1958.

The Encyclopaedia of Islam. Edited by M. T. Houtsma, et al. 4 vols. Leiden: E. J. Brill, 1913–1934. Supplement, 1938.

The Encyclopaedia of Islam. 2d ed. Edited by H. A. R. Gibb, et al. 9 vols. (to date). Leiden: E. J. Brill, 1954–.

The Encyclopaedia of Judaica. New York: Macmillan, 1971–82.

The Encyclopedia of Religion. Edited by Mircea Eliade, et al. 16 vols. New York: Macmillan, 1987.

Fahd, T. "Maysir." *Encyclopaedia of Islam.* 2d ed.

———. "Nuṣub." *Encyclopaedia of Islam.* 2d ed.

Feeley-Harnik, Gillian. *The Lord's Table: Eucharist and Passover in early Christianity.* Philadelphia: University of Pennsylvania Press, 1981.

Foucault, Michel. *The Archaeology of Knowledge.* London: Tavistock Publications, 1972.

———. *The Order of Things: An archaeology of the human sciences.* New York: Pantheon Books, 1971.

Furūzānfar, B., ed. *Kulliyyāt-i shams yā dīwān-i kabīr.* Tehran: University of Tehran Press, 1957–67.

Gätje, Helmut. *The Qur'ān and its Exegesis.* Berkeley: University of California Press, 1976.

Gaudefroy-Demombynes, M. *Le Pelerinage a la Mekke.* Paris: Paul Guenther, 1923.

Gennette, G. *Narrative Discourse: An essay in method.* Translated by Jane E. Lewin. Ithaca, New York: Cornell University Press, 1980.

Ginzberg, Louis. *The Legends of the Jews.* Philadelphia: Jewish Publication Society of America, 1967–69.

Girard, Rene. *Violence and the Sacred.* Baltimore: The Johns Hopkins University Press, 1977.

Goldziher, Ignaz. *Muhammedanische Studien.* 2 vols. Halle: Max Niemeyer, 1889. Translated and edited by C. R. Barber, and S. M. Stern as *Muslim Studies.* 2 Vols. Chicago: Aldine, 1968, 1971.

———. *Introduction to Islamic Theology and Law.* Translated by Andras and Ruth Hamori. Edited by Bernard Lewis. Princeton: Princeton University Press, 1981.

Goodenough, E. R. *Jewish Symbols in the Greco-Roman Period.* Vol. 6, bk. 2, *Fish, Bread, and Wine.* New York: Bollingen Foundation, Inc., 1956.

Graham, William. *Beyond the Written Word: Oral aspects of scripture in the history of religion.* New York: Cambridge University Press, 1987.

———. "Islam in the Mirror of Ritual." In *Islam's Understanding of Itself.* Edited by Richard B. Hovannisian, and Spyros Vryonis, 53–71. Malibu: Undena, 1983.

Grohmann, A. "Al-ʿArab." *Encyclopaedia of Islam.* 2d ed.

Guidi, Ignazio. *L'Arabie anteislamique.* Paris: Paul Guenther, 1921.

Haffner, A. "Al-Aʿshā." *Encyclopaedia of Islam.*

Harb, F. "Wine Poetry (Khamriyyāt)." In *ʿAbbāsid Belles-Lettres.* Vol. 2 of *Cambridge History of Arabic Literature.* Edited by Julia Ashtiany, T. M. Johnstone, J. D. Latham, R. B. Serjeant, and G. Rex Smith, 219–234. Cambridge: Cambridge University Press.

Hattox, Ralph S. *Coffee and Coffeehouses.* Seattle: University of Washington Press, 1985.

Hedley, Jane. *Power in Verse: Metaphor and Metonymy in the Renaissance Lyric.* University Park and London: The Pennsylvania State University Press, 1988.

Heine, P. "Nabīdh." *Encyclopaedia of Islam.* 2d ed.

Hodgson, Marshall G. S. "Ghulāt." *Encyclopaedia of Islam.* 2d ed.

Ḥusayn, Ṭaha. *Fi 'l-abab al-jāhilī.* Cairo: Dār al-maʿārif, n.d.

Hyams, Edward. *Dionysus: A Social History of the Wine Vine.* London: Sidgwick and Jackson, 1987.

Ibn Bābawayhī (Al-Shaykh al-Ṣadūq b. Bābūya al-Qummī). *Kitāb man lā yaḥḍuruhu 'l-faqīh.* Part IV. Dār al-kutub al-islāmīya, 1962.

Ibn Ḥanbal, Aḥmad b. Muḥammad. *Al-Musnad.* Edited by Aḥmad Muḥammad Shākir. 15 vols. Cairo: Dār al-ma'ārif, 1946–49.

Ibn Hishām, 'Abd al-Mālik. *Al-Sīra al-nabawīya.* See Ibn Isḥāq, Muḥammad.

Ibn Isḥāq, Muḥammad. *Sīrat rasūl Allāh,* in the recension of 'Abd al-Mālik b. Hishām's *al-Sīra al-nabawīya.* 3 vols. Dār al-kutub al-misrīya, n.d. Translated by Alfred Guillaume as *The Life of Muhammad: A Translation of Ibn Isḥāq's Sīrat Rasūl Allāh.* Oxford: Oxford University Press, 1955.

Ibn Māja, Muḥammad b. Yazīd. *Kitāb al-Sunan.* Edited by Muḥammad Fū'ād 'Abd al-Bāqī. 5 vols. Cairo: Dār iḥyā' al-kutub al-'arabīya, 1953.

Ibn Qutayba, 'Abdallāh b. Muslim. *Kitāb al-ashriba.* Dimashq: Al-Majma' al-'ilmī al-'arabī, 1947.

James, William. *The Varieties of Religious Experience: A study in human nature.* Longmans, Green, 1902.

Jeffrey, Arthur. "Āya." *Encyclopaedia of Islam,* 2d ed.

Johnson, Hugh. *Vintage: The Story of Wine.* London: Mitchell Beazley, 1989.

Juynboll, G. H. A. *Muslim Tradition: Studies in chronology, provenance and authorship of early ḥadīth.* Cambridge: Cambridge University Press, 1983.

Kaelber, Walter O. "Asceticism." *Encyclopedia of Religion.*

Al-Kalbī, Hishām b. *Kitāb al-aṣnām.* Translated by Nabih Amin Faris as *The Book of Idols.* Princeton: Princeton University Press, 1952.

Kassis, Hanna E. *A Concordance of the Qur'ān.* Berkeley: University of California Press, 1983.

Kennedy, Philip F. "*Khamr* and *Ḥikma* in *Jāhilī* Poetry." *Journal of Arabic Literature* 20, pt. 2 (September 1989): 97–114.

Khadduri, Majid, ed. and trans. *Islamic Jurisprudence: Shafi'i's Risala.* Baltimore: The Johns Hopkins Press, 1961.

Kister, M. J. "The Massacre of the Banū Qurayza: A Re-examination of a Tradition." *Jerusalem Studies in Arabic and Islam* 8 (1986): 61–96.

———. "The Seven Odes." *Rivisita degli Studi Orientali* 54 (1969): 27–36.

The Koran. Translated by N. J. Dawood. London: Penguin Books, 1993.

Krenkow, F. "Ṭarafa." *Encyclopaedia of Islam.*

Al-Kulaynī, Abū Jaʿfar Muḥammad. *Furūʿ min al-kāfī*. Edited by ʿAlī Akbar al-Ghaffārī. 8 vols. Ṭehrān: Maktabat al-Ṣadūq, 1957.

Lammens, H. "Al-Tāʾif." *Encyclopaedia of Islam.*

Lane, Edward William. *An Arabic-English Lexicon.* 8 vols. London: Williams and Norgate, 1863–1893.

Lincoln, Bruce. "Beverages." *Encyclopedia of Religion.*

Long, Charles. "The History of Religions and the Study of Islam." In *The History of Religions: Essays on the Problem of Understanding.* Edited by J. M. Kitagawa, M. Eliade, and C. H. Long. Chicago: University of Chicago Press, 1967.

Mālik b. Anas. *Al-Muwatta of Imam Malik ibn Anas: The first formulation of Islamic law.* Translated by Aisha Aburrahman Bewley. New York: Kegan Paul International, 1989.

Marxsen, Willi. *The Beginnings of Christology: Together with the Lord's supper as a Christological problem.* Translated by Paul J. Achtemeier, and Lorenz Nieting. Philadelphia: Fortress Press, 1979.

McNeill, John T., and Helena M. Gamer, trans. *Medieval Handbooks of Penance.* New York: Columbia University Press, 1938.

Midrash Rabbah: Genesis. Edited and Translated by Rabbi Dr. H. Freeman, and Maurice Simon. Vol. 1. London: Soncino Press, 1983.

The Mishnah: A new translation. Translated by Jacob Neusner. New Haven: Yale University Press, 1988.

Muslim b. al-Ḥajjāj al-Qushayrī. *Ṣaḥīḥ Muslim.* Edited by Muḥammad Fūʾād ʿAbd al-Bāqī. 8 vols. Beirut: Dār al-iḥyāʾ al-turāth, 1956–1972.

Al-Nasāʾī, Aḥmad b. Shuʿayb. *Sunan al-Nasāʾī.* Edited by Jalāl al-Dīn al-Suyūṭī. 8 vols. Cairo: Al-Maṭbaʿa al-misrīya, 1930.

Neusner, Jacob. *The Evidence of the Mishnah.* Chicago: University of Chicago Press, 1981.

———. *Judaism and Story: The Evidence of The Fathers According to Rabbi Nathan.* Chicago: University of Chicago Press, 1992.

———. *Judaism and Zoroastrianism at the Dusk of Late Antiquity.* Atlanta: Scholars Press, 1993.

———. *The Mishnah: An Introduction.* Northvale, New Jersey: Jason Aronson Inc., 1989.

———. *Oral Tradition in Judaism: The Case of the Mishnah.* New York and London: Garland Publishing, Inc., 1987.

———. "Ritual Without Myth: The Use of Legal Materials for the Study of Religions." *Religion: Journal of Religion and Religions* 5 (Autumn 1975): 1–11.

———. "The Study of Religion as the Study of Tradition in Judaism." In *Methodological Issues in Religious Studies*. Edited by Robert D. Baird, 31–48. Chico, CA: New Horizons Press, 1975.

———. *Symbol and Theology in Early Judaism*. Minneapolis: Fortress Press, 1991.

———. *Talmudic Thinking: Language, Logic, Law*. Columbia: University of South Carolina Press, 1992.

———. "Tractate Baba Batra." In *The Talmud of Babylonia,* 93. Atlanta: Scholars Press, 1992.

Newby, Gordon D. *A History of the Jews of Arabia: From ancient times to their eclipse under Islam*. Columbia, SC: University of South Carolina Press, 1988.

———. *The Making of the Last Prophet: A reconstruction of the earliest biography of Muḥammad*. Columbia, SC: University of South Carolina Press, 1989.

———. "Tafsir Isra᾽iliyyat." *Journal of the American Academy of Religion* 47, no. 4S (1979): 685–697.

Nicholson, R. A., trans., and ed. *The Mathnawī of Jalālu᾽ddīn Rūmī*. Vol. 3. London: Luzac, 1925–40.

———. *Studies in Islamic Mysticism*. Cambridge: Cambridge University Press, 1921.

Nouryeh, Christopher. *Translation and Critical Study of Ten Pre-Islamic Odes: Traces in the Sand*. Lampeter, Dyfed, Wales: Edwin Mellen Press, Ltd., 1993.

The Oxford Annotated Bible. Edited by Herbert May and Bruce Metzger. Oxford: Oxford University Press, 1973.

Al-Qur᾽ān. Translated by Ahmed Ali. Princeton: Princeton University Press, 1984.

Quispel, Gilles. "Gnosticism." *Encyclopedia of Religion*.

Raymond, Irving Woodworth. *The Teaching of the Early Church on the Use of Wine and Strong Drink*. New York: Columbia University Press, 1927.

Al-Rāzī, Fakhr al-Dīn. *Al-Tafsīr al-kabīr (Mafātīḥ al-ghayb)*. Edited by Muḥammad Muḥyī ʻl-Dīn. 16 vols. Beirut, 1981.

Reinhart, Kevin. "Impurity/No Danger." *History of Religions* 30, no. 1 (1990): 1–24.

Robson, James. "Ḥadīth." *Encyclopaedia of Islam*. 2d ed.

Rodinson, Maxime. "Ghidhā᾽." *Encyclopaedia of Islam*. 2d ed.

Rosenthal, Franz. *Gambling in Islam*. Leiden: E. J. Brill, 1975.

———. "The Influence of the Biblical Tradition on Muslim Historiography." In *Historians of the Middle East*. Edited by B. Lewis, and P. M. Holt, 35–45. London: Oxford University Press, 1962.

Saban, J. "Mashrūbāt." *Encyclopaedia of Islam*. 2d ed.

Al-Sarakhsī, Abū Bakr Muḥammad. *Al-Mabsūṭ*. 30 vols. Cairo, 1906–12.

Schacht, Joseph. "Dj̲āhiliyya." *Encyclopaedia of Islam.* 2d ed.

———. *An Introduction to Islamic Law.* Oxford: Oxford University Press, 1964.

———. "Maysir." *The Encyclopaedia of Islam.* 2d ed.

———. *Origins of Muhammadan Jurisprudence.* Oxford: Oxford University Press, 1950.

Schimmel, Annemarie. *The Mystery of Numbers.* New York: Oxford University Press, 1993.

Schoeler, G. "Bashshār b. Burd, Abū 'l-ʿAtāhiyah and Abū Nuwās." In *ʿAbbāsid Belles-Lettres.* Vol. 2. *Cambridge History of Arabic Literature.* Edited by Julia Ashtiany, T. M. Johnstone, J. D. Latham, R. B. Serjeant, and G. Rex Smith, 275–299. Cambridge: Cambridge University Press.

Scolnic, Benjamin. *Theme and Context in Biblical Lists.* Atlanta: Scholars Press, 1995.

Sells, Michael. *Desert Tracings: Six Classic Arabian Odes.* Middletown, Connecticut: Wesleyan University Press, 1989.

———. *Mystical Languages of Unsaying.* Chicago: University of Chicago Press, 1994.

Shils, Edward. *Tradition.* Chicago: The University of Chicago Press, 1981.

Smith, Jonathan Z. *Drudgery Divine: On the comparison of early Christianities and the religions of Late Antiquity.* Chicago: University of Chicago Press, 1990.

———. *Imagining Religion: From Babylon to Jonestown.* Chicago: University of Chicago Press, 1982.

———. *To Take Place: Toward theory in ritual.* Chicago: University of Chicago Press, 1987.

Smith, W. Robertson. *Kinship and Marriage in Early Arabia.* Oosterhout N. B. Netherlands: Anthropological Publications, 1966.

Sournia, Jean-Charles. *A History of Alcoholism.* Oxford: Basil Blackwell Inc., 1990.

Speight, R. Marston. "The Function of Ḥadīth as Commentary on the Qurān, as seen in the six authoritative collections." In *Approaches to the History of the Interpretation of the Qurān.* Edited by Andrew Rippin, 63–81. Oxford: Clarendon Press, 1988.

———. "Rhetorical Argumentation in the Ḥadīth." Semeia 64 (1994): 73–92.

Stetkevych, Jaroslav. "Arabic Poetry and Assorted Poetics." In *Islamic Studies: A Tradition and Its Problems,* 103–123. Malibu, CA: Undena Pub., 1980.

———. "Name and Epithet: The Philology and Semiotics of Animal Nomenclature in Early Arabic Poetry." *Journal of Near Eastern Studies* 45, no. 2 (1986): 89–124.

Stetkevych, Suzanne Pinckney. "Intoxication and Immortality: Wine and associated imagery in al-Ma'arri's garden." In *Critical Pilgrimages: Studies in the Arabic literary tradtion.* Edited by Fedwa Malti-Douglas. *Literature East and West* (1989): 29–48.

———. *The Mute Immortals Speak: Pre-Islamic Poetry and the Poetics of Ritual.* Ithaca, New York: Cornell University Press, 1993.

Stowasser, Barbara Freyer. *Women in the Qur'ān, Traditions, and Interpretation.* New York: Oxford University Press, 1994.

Stroumsa, A. G. Gedaliahu. *Another Seed: Studies in gnostic mythology.* Leiden: E. J. Brill, 1994.

Al-Ṭabarī, Abū Ja'far Muḥammad b. Jarīr. *Ta'rīkh al-rusul wa 'l-mulūk.* Edited by M. J. de Goeje, et al. 10 vols. Cairo, 1960–69.

———. *Ta'rīkh al-rusul wa 'l-mulūk.* Translated as *The History of al-Ṭabarī.* Edited by Ehsan Yar-Shater, et al. 32 vols. Albany: State University of New York Press, 1985–.

———. *The History of al-Ṭabarī.* Vol. 2. *Prophets and Patriarchs.* Translated by William M. Brinner: Albany: State University of New York Press, 1992.

———. *The History of al-Ṭabarī.* Vol. 3. *The Children of Israel.* Translated by William M. Brinner. Albany: State University of New York Press, 1991.

———. *The History of al-Ṭabarī.* Vol. 6., *Muḥammad at Mecca.* Translated by W. Montgomery Watt, and M. V. McDonald.

———. *The History of al-Ṭabarī.* Vol. 12. *The Battle of al-Qādisiyyah and the Conquest of Syria and Palestine.* Translated by Yohanen Friedman. Albany: State University of New York Press, 1992.

———. *The History of al-Ṭabarī.* Vol. 13. *The Conquest of Iraq, South Western Persian and Egypt.* Translated by G. H. A. Juynboll. Albany: State University of New York Press, 1989.

———. *The History of al-Ṭabarī.* Vol. 32. *The Reunification of the 'Abbāsid Caliphate.* Translated by C. E. Bosworth. Albany: State University of New York Press, 1987.

———. *The History of al-Ṭabarī.* Vol. 36. *The Revolt of the Zanj.* Translated by David Waines. Albany: State University of New York Press, 1992.

The Talmud of Babylonia. Translated by Jacob Neusner. Atlanta: Scholars Press, 1992.

El-Tayib, Abdulla. "Pre-Islamic Poetry." In *Arabic Literature to the End of the Umayyad Period.* Vol. 1. *Cambridge History of Arabic Literature.* Edited by Julia Ashtiany, T. M. Johnstone, J. D. Latham, R. B. Serjeant, and G. Rex Smith, 27–113. Cambridge: Cambridge University Press, 1983.

Al-Ṭayālisī, Sulaymān b. Dāwūd. *Musnad Abī Dāwūd al-Ṭayālisī.* Beirut: Dār al-kitāb al-lubnānī, 1980.

Thackston, Jr., W. M. *Tales of the Prophets of al-Kisāʾī.* Boston: Twayne Publishers, 1978.

Al-Tirmidhī, Abū ʿĪsā Muḥammad b. ʿĪsā. *Ṣaḥīḥ al-Tirmidhī.* Edited by Aḥmad Muḥammad Shākir. 5 vols. Cairo: Al-Maṭbaʿa al-misrīya, 1931–34.

Tritton, A. S. "Ṭahara." *Encyclopaedia of Islam.*

Turner, Victor. *The Forest of Symbols.* Ithaca, New York: Cornell University Press, 1967.

———. *The Ritual Process: Structure and anti-structure.* Chicago: Aldine, 1969.

Al-Tūsī, Shaykh al-Ṭaʾifa Abī Jaʿfar Muḥammad. *Tahdhīb al-aḥkām.* Part X. Dār al-kutub al-islāmīya, 1962.

Unwin, Tim. *Wine and the Vine: An historical geography of viticulture and the wine trade.* London: Routledge and Kegan Paul, 1991.

Vajda, G. "Isrāʾīliyyāt." *Encyclopaedia of Islam.* 2d ed.

Vansina, Jan. *Oral Tradition as History.* Madison: University of Wisconsin Press, 1985.

Vööbus, Arthur, trans. and ed. *Syriac and Arabic Documents: Regarding Legislation Relative to Syrian Asceticism.* Papers of the Estonian Theological Society in Exile, no. 2. Stockholm: Dean Jakob Aunver, 1960.

Wagner, Edwald. "Abū Nuwās." *Encyclopaedia of Islam,* 2d ed.

Waldman, Marilyn Robinson. "New Approaches to Biblical Materials in the Qurʾān." *The Muslim World* 75, no. 1 (January 1985): 1–13.

———. "Nubūwa." *Encyclopedia of Religion.*

Wansbrough, John. *Qurʾānic Studies: Sources and methods of scriptural interpretation.* Oxford: Oxford University Press, 1977.

———. *The Sectarian Milieu: Content and composition of Islami salvation history.* Oxford: Oxford University Press, 1978.

Wensinck, A. J. *Concordance et indices de la tradition musulmane.* 7 vols. Leiden: E. J. Brill, 1936–69.

———. *A Handbook of Early Muhammadan Tradition.* Leiden: E. J. Brill, 1927.

———. "K͟hamr." *Encyclopaedia of Islam.* 2d ed.

———. "Nabīd͟h." *Encyclopaedia of Islam.*

———. "Nad͟jis." *Encyclopaedia of Islam.*

Zaman, Iftikhar. "The evolution of a ḥadīth: Transmission, growth, and the science of rijāl in a ḥadīth of Saʾd b. Abi Waqqas." Ph.D. diss., University of Chicago, 1991.

Zwettler, Michael. "A Mantic Manifesto: The Sūra of "The Poets" and the Qur'ānic Foundations of Prophetic Authority." In *Poetry and Prophecy*. Edited by James L. Kugel. Ithaca and London: Cornell University Press, 1990.

———. *The Oral Tradition of Classical Arabic Poetry: Its Character and Implications.* Columbus: Ohio State University Press, 1972.

General Index

abomination, xvi, 1, 6, 8, 23, 66
Abraham, 83
abstinence
  in Judaism, xii, xiii
  and oath-keeping, 82–83
Abu 'Abdallah, 31, 47, 76–78, 80, 88
Abu Dawud, 28–30
Abu Hurayra, 30, 37, 46–47, 53–54, 57, 79
Abu-Lahab, 2
Adam, 31, 55, 61–64, 85
addiction, 48–49
'A'isha, 37–39, 73
alcohol, xiii, 55, 59, 64, 69
'Ali, 60, 65, 86, 88
'Alqama (b. 'Abada), 99–100
ambiguity, xiii–xiv, 117, 119–23
  analytic discourse and, 26, 36, 41, 43, 48–49, 51–52
  definition of, xv
  mystical discourse and, 114
  narrative discourse and, 54, 65, 67, 83, 87–88
  poetic discourse and, 92, 94–95, 97–100, 102–5
  in Qur'an, 3, 16
  resolution of, xvii–xiii
anomaly, xiii, 12, 16, 22
  definition of, xv
ansar, 67–68
apocalyptic vision,
  in Hadith, 50
  in Qur'an, 13–14, 16–17, 20
asceticism
  in Christianity, xiii, 114
  definition of, xii
  in Islam, 114
  in Judaism, xii
al-A'sha, 100–2
'asir, 61
aya, 11
  See also sign

barley, 32
  drinks made from, 45, 84, 113, 118
bees, 10, 12–13, 15
blood, xi, 6–8, 10, 22, 45, 94

Cain, 85
carrion, 8, 10, 22, 28–29, 42, 47, 75
Christianity, xviii–xix, 3, 83, 86
  abstinence in, xiii, 114
  gnosis in, 11–12
  penance for wine-consumption in, 42
  wine consumption in, xi–xii, 17–18
  wine use under Islamic rule, 45, 47, 75, 78–80

Daniel, 21
dates, 31–32, 38, 40
  dried (*tamr*), 37, 39–40, 70, 79
  fadikh, 69–70
  fresh (*rutab*), 37
  ripe (*busr*), 37, 70
  ripening (*zahw*), 37, 39–40
  steeped, 73
  unripe, 79
  See also nabidh
date-palm, 10, 30–31, 62, 65, 76

Works Quoted